HOW THINGS MIGHT HAVE BEEN

How are we to distinguish between the essential and accidental properties of things such as individual people, cats, trees, and tables? Almost
everyone agrees that such individuals could have been different, in
certain respects, from the way that they actually are. But what are the
respects in which they could not have been different: which of their
properties are essential to their being the individuals that they are? And
why?

Following the revival of interest among analytic philosophers in
essentialism and *de re* modality generated by the work of Kripke and
others in the 1970s, these questions have been the subject of intense,
yet still unresolved, debate. In this book, Penelope Mackie challenges
most of the answers that have been given to these questions. Via
a critical examination of rival theories, she arrives at what she calls
'minimalist essentialism', an unorthodox theory according to which
ordinary individuals have relatively few interesting essential properties,
and intuitions that appear to support stronger versions of essentialism
are interpreted as consistent with the theory.

The topics discussed include the rivalry between the interpretation
of *de re* modality in terms of 'identity across possible worlds' and
its interpretation in terms of David Lewis's counterpart theory, some
notorious modal puzzles generated by the theory that individuals exist
with different properties in different possible words, the notion of an
individual essence, Kripke's 'necessity of origin' thesis, and the widely
held view that there are sortal properties that are essential properties of
the things to which they belong. The book also includes a discussion
of the relation between essentialism about individuals and essentialism
about natural kinds, and a critical examination of the connection
between semantics and natural kind essentialism.

Penelope Mackie is Associate Professor and   Philosophy at
the University of Nottingham.

How Things Might Have Been

Individuals, Kinds, and Essential Properties

PENELOPE MACKIE

CLARENDON PRESS • OXFORD

OXFORD
UNIVERSITY PRESS

Great Clarendon Street, Oxford OX2 6DP

Oxford University Press is a department of the University of Oxford.
It furthers the University's objective of excellence in research, scholarship,
and education by publishing worldwide in

Oxford New York

Auckland Cape Town Dar es Salaam Hong Kong Karachi
Kuala Lumpur Madrid Melbourne Mexico City Nairobi
New Delhi Shanghai Taipei Toronto

With offices in

Argentina Austria Brazil Chile Czech Republic France Greece
Guatemala Hungary Italy Japan Poland Portugal Singapore
South Korea Switzerland Thailand Turkey Ukraine Vietnam

Oxford is a registered trade mark of Oxford University Press
in the UK and in certain other countries

Published in the United States
by Oxford University Press Inc., New York

© Penelope Mackie 2006

The moral rights of the author have been asserted
Database right Oxford University Press (maker)

First published 2006
First published in paperback 2009

British Library Cataloguing in Publication Data
Data available

Library of Congress Cataloging in Publication Data
Data available

Typeset by Laserwords Private Limited, Chennai, India
Printed in Great Britain
on acid-free paper by
the MPG Books Group

ISBN 978–0–19–956240–4 (Pbk.)   978–0–19–927220–4 (Hbk.)

Preface

Things—meaning the state of the world in general—might have been different from the way they are. Things—meaning objects—might have been different, too. For example, the particular people, animals, plants, artefacts, and many other objects that actually populate this universe could have existed even if some of their properties had been different from those that they actually possess. To put the point in another way: not all of their properties are essential to their being the individuals that they are.

Or so almost all of us, myself included, are strongly inclined to suppose. But this supposition generates a puzzle. If it is part of the nature of such objects that they could have been different in certain ways, what is it that determines the ways in which they could, and the ways in which they could not, have been different?

In this book, I discuss this puzzle in the context of a set of contemporary debates about identity, necessity, and essential properties, debates initiated by the revival of interest in essentialism within analytical philosophy that was generated by the work of Saul Kripke and Hilary Putnam in the 1970s. The debates have taken place within a framework of principles which, although radical at the time of their introduction (or reintroduction), are now widely accepted. These principles include the following: that it is legitimate to distinguish between the essential and accidental properties of a thing; that the ascription of essential properties to a thing involves a species of *de re* necessity and 'metaphysical necessity' that does not coincide with analyticity or a priori truth, and that what is necessary or possible in this metaphysical sense may be characterized in terms of what is the case in possible worlds distinct from the actual world.

The issues that I discuss fall into two main categories: essentialism about individuals, and essentialism about natural kinds, although it is the former that is the main subject of this book. Essentialism about individuals may be characterized, roughly, as the view that among an individual's properties are some that it has essentially (necessarily), rather than merely accidentally (contingently). The essential properties of an individual, in the relevant sense, are those that it could not have existed without. By contrast, an individual's accidental properties are those that it possesses, but could have existed without.

To say that not all of an individual's properties are essential to it is to say that it could have been different in certain respects. To say that some of an individual's properties are essential to it is to say that there are limits to the ways in which it could have been different. That there are such limits, in the case of ordinary individuals such as people, cats, trees, and tables, may seem uncontentious. However, the attempt to find a satisfactory theoretical basis for a distinction between the essential and accidental properties of such individuals has proved remarkably difficult. Matters are complicated by the fact that the notion that the same individual could have existed with different properties (in other possible situations or 'worlds') generates puzzles that appear to support very surprising conclusions about what the essential properties of such individuals must be like.

In the first nine chapters of the book I discuss the distinction between the essential and accidental properties of individuals, and defend a version of essentialism about individuals that aims to avoid the problems that I diagnose as afflicting other accounts. In Chapters 2–5, I evaluate the view that each individual has a (substantial) 'individual essence' that distinguishes it from all other things, and consider the consequences of rejecting this 'individual essence' theory. Although I myself reject the thesis that ordinary persisting things such as people or cats or trees or tables have such individual essences, I also argue that the rejection of this thesis has certain paradoxical consequences (a commitment to what, following Graeme Forbes, I call 'bare identities') that may suggest the existence of an internal tension in our thinking about the identities of such individuals.

In Chapters 7 and 8, I cast doubt on 'sortal essentialism': a version of essentialism according to which each individual belongs essentially to some sort or kind that determines the conditions for its identity over time. In Chapter 6, I discuss the thesis that distinctive (although not necessarily unique) features of a thing's origin are essential to it, and argue that this widely accepted 'necessity of origin' thesis rests on questionable principles about individuation.

These negative arguments raise the question whether there are *any* limits to the ways in which an individual might have been different from the way that it actually is. In Chapter 9 I defend the theory that, strictly speaking, these limits or restrictions are, indeed, minimal. I try to show that the apparent objections to this 'minimalist' version of essentialism can be answered, partly by appeal to considerations suggested by David Lewis.

Kinds—as opposed to individuals that belong to kinds—enter the subject matter of this book in two distinct ways. First, it is almost universally held that, whatever other essential properties an individual may have, there is some sort or kind to which it belongs essentially: the widely accepted theory of 'sortal essentialism' represents one way in which this idea has been developed. Secondly, in addition to essentialism about individuals, the topic of essentialism about kinds themselves—or, more precisely, essentialism about natural kinds—has a place in this work as a topic in its own right. I do not try to provide a comprehensive discussion of natural kind essentialism, a subject that has generated a vast amount of literature since the revival of interest in essentialism initiated by the work of Kripke and Putnam. But in Chapters 1 and 10 I aim to clarify certain issues concerning the status of essentialism about natural kinds, both by comparing this variety of essentialism with essentialism about individuals, and by examining the relation between semantic theory and natural kind essentialism.

At various places in Chapters 2–5 I have made use of passages from my articles 'Essence, Origin, and Bare Identity', *Mind* 96 (1987): 173–201, and 'Identity and Extrinsicness: Reply to Garrett', *Mind* 98 (1989): 105–17. I thank the Mind Association, the Editor of *Mind*, and Oxford University Press for permission to do so. Section 4 of Chapter 3 incorporates, in revised form, a few passages from my article 'Forbes on Origins and Identities', in A. Bottani, M. Carrara, and P. Giaretta (eds.), *Individuals, Essence, and Identity: Themes of Analytic Metaphysics* (© 2002 Kluwer Academic Publishers), 341–52. These passages are reproduced with the kind permission of Springer Science and Business Media.

Chapter 6 includes (in Sections 1–2 and 4–7) a revised version of my 'Identity, Time, and Necessity', *Proceedings of the Aristotelian Society*, 98 (1998): 59–78; this is reproduced by courtesy of the Editor of the Aristotelian Society: © 1998.

Chapters 7 and 8 include, with some substantial revisions, material from my 'Sortal Concepts and Essential Properties', *The Philosophical Quarterly*, 44 (1994): 311–33, published by Blackwell Publishing. I thank the publishers for permission to make use of this material.

A great many people have contributed to the development of this work, and a list of their names would be too long to recite here, even if I were able to produce it. But I am grateful to all the departments, societies, and discussion groups that have allowed me to try out versions of what became the chapters of this book by inviting me to present papers, and to the members of the audiences who gave me comments on those occasions. I would especially like to thank my colleagues at the University of Birmingham between 1994 and 2004, who provided a helpful audience for my presentation of drafts of portions of this work over the years.

I am, of course, indebted to those writers with whose views I take issue in this book, notably Graeme Forbes, Baruch Brody, and David Wiggins, whose work has provided me with the stimulus to develop and defend my own opposing views. I have learnt more from their writings than my critical remarks may suggest. Like many others working on the topic of modality, I owe a great debt to the work of the late David Lewis. In particular, my strategy for attempting to defend a version of 'extreme haecceitism'—or, as I would prefer to call it, 'minimalist essentialism'—in Chapter 9 is inspired by his discussion of this issue in *On the Plurality of Worlds* (although I doubt that Lewis would entirely approve of the way in which I have developed his suggestions). More generally, while I do not endorse either of Lewis's most distinctive views about modality—his counterpart theory and his version of realism about possible worlds—the influence, direct or indirect, of his writings is evident throughout the book, not least in the frequency with which I have found myself citing them. To work on this subject would not have been half as intriguing—nor half as much fun—had it not been for his brilliant and inimitable writings.

I am grateful to two anonymous referees for Oxford University Press for detailed comments that have influenced the final version of the work, and to Simon Blackburn, Jonathan Lowe, Robert Frazier, and Peter Momtchiloff for their support for the project at various stages. Last, but not least, I thank the Arts and Humanities Research Board for a Research Leave Award that enabled me to complete the book.

P. M.

Contents

1

Preliminaries

1.1. THE NATURE OF ESSENTIALISM

In this chapter I set out, in a relatively informal way, the conceptual framework, and the chief characteristics, of the types of essentialism examined in this book.

I distinguish two main varieties of essentialism: essentialism about individuals, and essentialism about natural kinds. By essentialism about individuals—the variety of essentialism that is the principal topic of this book—I simply mean the view that individual things have essential properties, where an essential property of an object is a property that the object could not have existed without. Following standard usage, I contrast essential properties with accidental properties, an accidental property of an object being a property that it has, but could have existed without. I shall not make it part of the definition of essentialism about individuals that it requires the attribution to individuals of accidental properties as well as essential properties. It seems to me (as it has done to others) that the view, standardly attributed to Leibniz, that makes all an individual's properties essential to it should be regarded as an extreme version of essentialism, not a denial of essentialism. I shall, however, regard it as a defining feature of essentialism about individuals that it attribute to them *some* essential properties. This perhaps leaves open the possibility of a theory of modality that claims that we can make sense of the expression '*a* is essentially F', where '*a*' names an individual thing, but is not, in my sense, a variety of essentialism about individuals, because it holds that this form of statement has no true instances. However, this restriction will rule out few, if any, theories. For however parsimonious a modal theory is about the essential properties of individuals, it seems that anyone who thinks that the locution '*a* is essentially F' is acceptable will also hold that *some* properties—for example, being self-identical—are essential properties of everything.

If essentialism about individuals is the attribution to individuals of essential properties, what is essentialism about natural kinds? Although essentialism about natural kinds *may* involve the attribution, to certain entities (namely, natural kinds), of essential properties, I shall argue that it need not do so. As I shall explain (in Section 1.6 below), one might be an 'essentialist about natural kinds' without attributing to kinds (or to anything else) any essential properties, in the sense characterized above. This is one reason why I think it important to distinguish essentialism about individuals from essentialism about natural kinds.

Returning to my description of essentialism about individuals in terms of the attribution to them of essential properties: the 'could not', in my characterization of an essential property needs an explanation. 'Could not' is indeterminate in strength, unless qualified. In the literature, the concept of an essential property has been associated with a notion of 'logical possibility', broadly construed, and also with a notion of 'metaphysical possibility' (Plantinga 1974, ch. 1, sect. 1; Kripke 1980 *passim*). Logical or metaphysical possibilities are usually held to outrun possibilities of some other familiar kinds: causal possibilities, in particular. Applied to essential properties, the fact that it is causally impossible for a certain animal to survive without inhaling oxygen would not usually be considered enough to make the breathing of oxygen one of its essential properties; this would require, rather, that the supposition of the creature's anaerobic existence be unintelligible in something like the way in which a logical impossibility is unintelligible. Connected with this is the fact that essentialist necessity is generally thought of as corresponding to truth in *all* possible worlds, not to truth in some restricted class of possible worlds (such as the class of possible worlds that share their laws of nature with the actual world). In this book I shall, for the most part, simply follow the standard, if perhaps imprecise, conception of the strength of the necessity and possibility that is relevant to essentialism. This means that I shall take it for granted that there is an appropriate notion of 'broadly logical' or 'metaphysical' modality.[1]

The notions of broadly logical or metaphysical possibility that are associated with essentialism must also be contrasted with the notion of what is possible in a merely 'epistemic' sense: possible 'for all we know'. Thus, for example, even if Perkin Warbeck might, for all we know, have been the illegitimate child of Edward IV, it does not follow that he

[1] For brief discussions of varieties of necessity and possibility see Plantinga 1974, ch. 1; Hale 1997.

genuinely *could* have been the child of Edward IV in the sense that is relevant to essentialism. And some would argue that if Perkin Warbeck was not in fact Edward's child (whether or not we shall ever know this), then, as a matter of metaphysical necessity, he could not have been: that his having the parents that he actually had is one of his essential properties.

1.2. THE 'DESCRIPTION-INDEPENDENCE' OF ESSENTIAL AND ACCIDENTAL PROPERTIES

It is natural to think that it is a necessary condition for anything to be counted as a variety of essentialism that it conform to the principle that the status of an object's properties as essential or accidental to it is independent of the way in which the object is described or referred to. As Quine put it:

An object, of itself and by whatever name or none, must be seen as having some of its traits necessarily and others contingently, despite the fact that the latter traits follow just as analytically from some ways of specifying the object as the former traits do from other ways of specifying it. (Quine 1961; p. 30 in Linsky 1971)

The principle seems well captured by the slogan that essentialist possibility and necessity are 'description-independent', and I shall call it the 'Description-Independence Principle' (DIP).[2] Further, the DIP is naturally associated with the thesis that the attribution to things of essential and accidental properties involves a species of necessity and possibility that is '*de re*' as opposed to '*de dicto*': a type of necessity and possibility that concerns the things ('*res*') themselves, and not merely statements or 'dicta' about those things. However, although the association of essentialism with *de re* modality is uncontroversial, the DIP is not. David Lewis has presented an account of *de re* modality according to which *de re* modal predications do not conform to the principle (Lewis 1971; 1986a, ch. 4, sect. 5). Harold Noonan's account (1991, 1993) of modal predicates, according to which they are 'Abelardian',

---

[2] Readers may wonder why I do not use the standard term 'referentially transparent' in place of 'description-independent'. The reason is indicated later in this chapter: the translation of a 'description-independent' attribution of a modal property *into quantified modal logic* may be an adequate translation without being referentially transparent. (I was tempted to call the principle 'the *De Re* Principle', but this would appear blatantly to beg the question against accounts such as Lewis's that purport to be accounts of *de re* modality although they reject the principle.)

has the same result. Nevertheless, in my exposition in this chapter, I shall, for simplicity, assume the truth of the Description-Independence Principle, and thus assume that statements of the form '*x* is essentially F' and '*x* is accidentally G' are referentially transparent with respect to the subject place.[3,4]

If we assume the truth of the DIP, it is very natural to express essentialist statements by treating *being essentially human, being essentially greater than seven* (and perhaps also *being accidentally a bachelor*: that is, being a bachelor but possibly not a bachelor), and so on, as themselves genuine properties.[5] This makes attractive David Wiggins's proposal of a predicate-modifier account as the best formal representation of essentialist statements (Wiggins 1976; cf. Wiggins 1980, ch. 4). But remaining at an informal level, while taking seriously the idea that the modal terms in essentialist claims modify predicates, we might give the following sentences as examples of essentialist forms of expression:

(1)　　$\exists x$ (*x* is essentially-F)

(2)　　$\forall x$ (*x* is G $\to$ *x* is essentially-F)

(3)　　The G is essentially-F

(4)　　*a* is essentially-F

where '*a*' and 'the G' are a singular term and a definite description; '*x* is F' is a predicate expression; and '*x* is essentially-F' is to be a predicate

---

[3] If, e.g., it is true that *being a philosopher* is an accidental property of Plato, then, according to the DIP, 'the philosopher who wrote *The Republic* was accidentally a philosopher' must also be true. And if it is true that *being Greek* is an essential property of Plato, then, according to the DIP, 'the philosopher who is famous for presenting the Theory of Forms was essentially Greek' must also be true.

[4] According to Lewis, *de re* modal predications may fail to conform to the principle for the following reason. According to Lewis, it is possible for 'the F could not have been H' (i.e., 'the F is essentially non-H') to be true while 'the G could not have been H' is false even if the F is the G, because the expressions 'the F' and 'the G' may invoke different counterpart relations. e.g., according to Lewis, 'the statue could not have been reshaped without being destroyed' may be true and 'the piece of clay could not have been reshaped without being destroyed' false, even if the statue is identical with the piece of clay, since the first sentence is true just in case the item has no *statue-counterparts* that continue to exist when reshaped without being destroyed (which is true), and the second sentence is true just in case the item has no *piece-of-clay-counterparts* that continue to exist when reshaped without being destroyed (which is false). However, Lewis (1971) insists that the modalities are still *de re* rather than *de dicto*, since in evaluating the sentences we consider only the item that in fact satisfies the descriptions 'the statue' and 'the piece of clay' and its various counterparts in other possible worlds.

[5] I use 'property' in a broad sense, employing what has been called an 'abundant', as opposed to a 'sparse', conception of properties.

that an object satisfies if and only if it could not have existed without being F. If we take this construction to be, by definition, referentially transparent, this representation of essentialist forms of expression cannot fail to obey the DIP.

However, we can also express essentialist statements by the use of the standard necessity operator, as long as we find a way of conforming to the DIP. The strategy is a familiar one. First, in order to express general essentialist statements of forms such as (1) and (2), we need to use quantification into modal contexts. We employ a (now) standard account of the interaction of quantifiers and modal operators, distinguishing '$\Box \, \exists x$ (x is an unsuccessful contestant)', which says that there must be some unsuccessful contestants, from '$\exists x \, \Box$ (x is an unsuccessful contestant)', which is true if and only if some (actual) things are of necessity unsuccessful contestants. Evidently it is quantification *into* modal contexts that is required to express general essentialist claims. Nevertheless, '$\exists x \, \Box$ (x is an unsuccessful contestant)' will not quite do to express the view that some things are *essentially* unsuccessful contestants if we treat it as a sentence that is false if the only things that are essentially unsuccessful contestants are contingent existents (on the grounds that those things will not satisfy the predicate 'x is a contestant' with respect to possible worlds in which they do not exist). If we accept this, then the standard formulation of essentialist statements using quantification into modal contexts must be conditional: we represent (1) and (2), for example, as follows:

(1.1) $\exists x \, \Box$ (x exists $\rightarrow$ x is F)

(2.1) $\forall x$ (x is G $\rightarrow$ $\Box$ (x exists $\rightarrow$ x is F)).

As for (3), since it entails that the G exists and is F, we evidently cannot represent it simply as

(5) $\Box$ (the G exists $\rightarrow$ the G is F),

since (5) could be true even if there is in fact no such thing as the G. Nor, however, can we represent it as

(6)   The G is F & $\Box$ (the G exists $\rightarrow$ the G is F),

since $\ulcorner \Box p \urcorner$ is taken to be true if and only if p is necessarily true—true with respect to all possible worlds. The problem is that definite descriptions are not rigid designators, in Kripke's sense (1980). The truth condition, with respect to any possible world, of 'the G is F' is simply that there be some object that is, *in that world*, both uniquely G and also

F. Hence, for example, we cannot translate 'the greatest Renaissance painter is essentially Italian', in obedience to the DIP, in the style of (6)—as 'the greatest Renaissance painter is Italian, and necessarily, if the greatest Renaissance painter exists, the greatest Renaissance painter is Italian'. For this is a sentence that is false even if the greatest Renaissance painter *is* someone who is essentially Italian, as long as there is a possible world in which some non-Italian painter has the distinction of being the greatest Renaissance painter. To translate (3) in obedience to the DIP we must get the definite description outside the scope of the modal operator. One of a number of representations that will achieve this is:

(3.1)   The G is F & $\forall x$ (x = the G $\rightarrow$ $\Box$ (x exists $\rightarrow$ x is F)).

As for the representation of (4), as long as the singular term '*a*' is a rigid designator, the truth condition of

(4.1)   *a* is F & $\Box$ (*a* exists $\rightarrow$ *a* is F)

cannot fail to coincide with the condition for *a*'s being essentially F; thus (4.1) will be a satisfactory rendering of (4). (In particular, if '*a*' is a rigid designator, there seems no reason to say that we should think of its scope in the second conjunct as 'really' wider than that of the necessity operator. This would be justified if there were a 'narrow-scope' reading that delivered different truth conditions, but if '*a*' is a rigid designator there is no such reading.)[6] However, (4.1) is actually needlessly complicated, if we make the additional assumption that the use of the singular term '*a*' requires the (actual) existence of a referent. Combining this assumption with the assumption of rigid designation, we get the result that the simpler (4.2) is perfectly adequate to represent the claim that *a* is essentially-F:

(4.2) $\Box$ (*a* exists $\rightarrow$ *a* is F)

(since if '*a*' cannot be meaningful if empty, the truth of (4.2) implies both that *a* actually exists and that it is F).

---

[6] Dummett (1973: 127–8) argues that the phenomenon that Kripke describes as the fact that proper names are rigid designators can be interpreted as the fact that proper names conventionally take wide scope with respect to modal operators. But I take Dummett's view to involve the denial that proper names are *genuine* rigid designators. This appears to be implied by Dummett's claim that proper names can, albeit exceptionally, sometimes be construed as having narrow scope with respect to modal operators, and that this makes a difference to the truth conditions of the relevant sentences.

It will be noted that the (standard) characterization that I have adopted of an essential property—as a property without which a thing could not have existed—has

1.3. THE *DE RE* AND THE *DE DICTO*

Our formulations of (1)–(4) using the modal operator '□' ('necessarily') conform to the DIP. They do so although they are not themselves referentially transparent, in the usual sense. As we have seen, (4.1) may be true, and (6) false, or vice versa, even if *a* is uniquely G; in (4.1) it is only the substitution of *rigid designators* co-referential with '*a*' that is truth preserving. But this is just what we should expect, if we are conforming to the DIP, since it is not (6), but the quite different (3.1), that says that the G is essentially F. (Admittedly, by the same token we do want (3.1) to follow from (4.1) plus the identity '*a* = the G', and since we have refused to give '*a*' wider scope than '□' in the second conjunct of (4.1) we have blocked one straightforward way of giving a formal account of why this entailment holds. But I do not think that this is a significant reason for abandoning the claim (made in the previous section) that the scope of '*a*' in the second conjunct of (4.1) does not extend outside the modal operator.)

As this exposition is informal, I shall not try to provide a strict criterion for when a sentence employing modal operators counts as exemplifying modality *de re*—as a '*de re* sentence', as we can put it. But intuitively we want to count (1.1), (2.1), (3.1), (4.1), and (4.2) as *de re* in virtue of their equivalence to the essentialist sentences (1)–(4), while we want to classify (5) and (6) as not *de re*. The following criterion will serve my purposes:

A sentence containing a modal operator counts as *de re* if and only if it involves either quantification into a modal context or the presence of a rigid designator within the modal context.[8]

This inevitably raises the question what is to be meant by modality *de dicto*. Intuitively, it seems appropriate to count a modal sentence as *de dicto* if every occurrence of a modal operator in that sentence itself governs a complete (closed) sentence. Evidently, by this criterion, (4.1)

---

the consequence that (if existence is a property) a thing's existence must be one of its essential properties: perhaps a counterintuitive result. However, the consequence need not trouble us if we bear in mind that to say that existence is one of *a*'s essential properties is not to say that *a* is a necessary existent. We can distinguish '□ *a* exists', which says that *a* is a necessary existent, from '□ (*a* exists → *a* exists)' which makes the (trivial) claim that existence is one of *a*'s essential properties.

[8] Graeme Forbes (1985: 48), following Fine (1978), gives a formal criterion for the *de re*, for a language containing quantification and rigid designators.

and (4.2) count as *de dicto*. There are two ways of responding to this. One is to restrict the application of '*de dicto*' to cases that are not *de re*. The other, which I shall adopt, is to allow that a sentence containing a modal operator may be both *de re* and *de dicto*. In conformity with this usage, the reader must bear in mind that it is not in itself a barrier to a sentence's expressing modality *de dicto* that it expresses modality *de re*.

1.4. ESSENTIALISM AND NECESSARY A POSTERIORI TRUTH

Essentialism is associated with the view that there can be necessary a posteriori truths, and I shall now say something about this connection.

Following standard usage, I shall say that a sentence is 'a priori' if its truth value can be known a priori; 'a posteriori' if its truth value can be known, but cannot be known a priori; any sentences there may be whose truth value is unknowable will count as neither a priori nor a posteriori (cf. Kripke 1980: 34–5). As is usual, I leave it inexplicit *whose* epistemic powers are in question. However, bearing in mind that we could introduce relativized notions of a priori and a posteriori truth and falsehood, I shall assume, as is usual, that it is human capacities, perhaps subject to some degree of idealization (and not, for example, those of a divine mind) that are under discussion.

Nothing can be a necessary a posteriori truth unless it is a necessary truth, and p is not a necessary truth unless its necessitation, $\ulcorner \Box \, p \urcorner$, is true. In other words, necessary truth, being a property of complete sentences or statements, has to do with the notion of *de dicto* necessity as characterized at the end of the previous section.

The obvious way in which the essentialism we are considering could be a source of necessary a posteriori truths, and the one famously exploited by Kripke, involves the use of rigid designators in the context of modal operators. If our sentence (4.2) is true, its contained sentence

(7) a exists $\rightarrow$ a is F

is a necessary truth; if (7) were a posteriori it would be a necessary a posteriori truth. Kripke held that a human being's parentage is one of that human being's essential properties (Kripke 1980: 110–15). This has the consequence that, given appropriate rigid designators 'a' and 'b', the following sentence:

(8) a exists $\rightarrow$ a is a child of b

will be a necessary truth. According to Kripke, ordinary proper names are rigid designators. But obviously there need be nothing in the sense of a personal proper name that reveals to a priori inspection the named person's ancestry. From these assumptions it follows that there are sentences of the form of (8) that are necessary a posteriori truths.

Kripke's views do not commit him to taking the *transition* from knowledge of the truth of (8) to knowledge of the truth of its necessitation to involve anything but the application of a priori reasoning. On the contrary, Kripke claimed that all his examples of the necessary a posteriori have the characteristic that we can know a priori that *if* they are true, they are necessarily true (1980: 159). This makes it plausible to regard Kripke's necessary a posteriori truths as generated from a recipe whose principal ingredients are rigid designation and general essentialist principles that are themselves a priori. For example, if one holds that some instance of (8) is a necessary truth, then one is likely to hold, on a priori grounds, a general essentialist principle (a form of 'necessity of origin' principle) such as:

(NO) $\forall x \forall y\, (x$ is a child of $y \to \Box\, (x$ exists $\to x$ is a child of $y))$.

If (NO) is a priori, then no a posteriori knowledge is required to argue, via (NO), from the truth of '*a* is a child of *b*' to the truth of the necessitation of (8).[9] Similarly, on the assumption that (NO) is an a priori truth, if one knows (a posteriori) that (8) is false because *a* is the child of parents neither of whom is *b*, one can advance by a priori reasoning to the conclusion that (8) is a necessary falsehood.

The point can be expressed by saying that there is no inconsistency involved in holding both (i) that there are necessary truths and necessary falsehoods whose *truth values* can be known only a posteriori; and (ii) that the *modal status* of these sentences—the fact that they are

---

[9] Does this still hold if there can be rigid designators that are meaningful even if empty? Suppose that '*a*' is meaningful, but has no referent. (8) is then trivially true. But is it necessarily true? It would fail to be necessarily true only if, although there is *in fact* no such thing as *a*, there are possible worlds in which *a* exists and does not have *b* as a parent. So the question turns on whether there can be rigid designators that designate merely possible individuals. If there cannot be, then any empty rigid designator fails to have a referent with respect to *every* possible world, in which case if '*a*' were empty, the antecedent of (8) would be necessarily false. If this were so, one could know a priori that (8) is, if true, necessarily true, even if its truth might consist in the falsity of its antecedent rather than the truth of its consequent. On the other hand, if there *can* be rigid designators of merely possible individuals, the remarks in the text need to be qualified.

necessary rather than contingent—is susceptible of determination a priori. In particular, the proponent of necessary a posteriori truths may agree with Kant's dictum that: 'experience teaches us that a thing is so and so, but not that it cannot be otherwise'.[10]

Another often-cited essentialist principle is the principle of the necessity of identity, which we can represent as:

(NI) $\forall x \forall y \, (x = y \rightarrow \square \, (x \text{ exists} \vee y \text{ exists} \rightarrow x = y))$.

If (NI) is plausible, it is surely as an a priori principle. Yet if, as Kripke has convincingly argued, there can be a posteriori identity statements involving rigid designators, (NI), like (NO), will permit the derivation of necessary a posteriori truths.

In addition, some essentialists hold that there are certain sorts, or 'sortal categories', such that any object that belongs to one of these sorts belongs to it essentially (see Wiggins 1980, ch. 4, and Wiggins 2001, ch. 4, and the discussion in Chapters 7 and 8 below). If *frog*, for example, is a sortal category of this kind, then we have the general essentialist principle:

(NSF) $\forall x \, (x \text{ is a frog} \rightarrow \square \, (x \text{ exists} \rightarrow x \text{ is a frog}))$.

But assuming that there need be no a priori connection between the sense of a rigid designator and the sort of the thing it names, necessary a posteriori consequences may be derived from (NSF), even if (NSF) is itself a priori.

1.5. ESSENTIALISM WITHOUT THE NECESSARY A POSTERIORI?

I have not argued that essentialism carries with it an inevitable commitment to the existence of necessary a posteriori truths: indeed, I think this is false. One reason is that one could be an essentialist while refusing to adopt the mechanism of quantified modal logic: say, by couching all one's essentialist claims in terms of predicate modifiers. Returning to the formulations of Section 1.2, we can see that the claim that

(4)   *a* is essentially-F

---

[10] As is pointed out, for example, by McGinn (1975–6: 204). The quotation is from Kant's *Critique of Pure Reason*, p. 43 in Kant 1929.

is true does not by itself involve a commitment to the claim that any sentence is a necessary truth. It might be objected that if one thinks that (4) is true one is likely also to hold that it is a necessary truth that everything that is F is essentially F, and hence that

(4N) a is F & $\square$ (a exists → a is essentially-F)

is also true, where the second conjunct, and its contained conditional sentence, will be a posteriori if the first conjunct is. But this objection misses the point that to accept the legitimacy of *de re* modal sentences such as (4N) is to accept the mechanism of quantified modal logic, something that the predicate-modifier essentialist is not committed to.[11]

There are further reasons for thinking that essentialism (about individuals) is not committed to the existence of necessary a posteriori truths. For one thing, it is not plausible that necessary a posteriori truths can be generated from essentialism (about individuals) unless some singular terms are treated as rigid designators. But there seems to be no obligation, even for an essentialist, to recognize this category of singular term.[12]

Secondly, even if both rigid designators and the mechanism of quantified modal logic are admitted, it still seems possible, in principle, to avoid the derivation of necessary a posteriori truths from general essentialist principles. What might appear to be an obstacle to this is an argument that would make sentences containing rigid designators a posteriori in virtue of having a posteriori existential consequences. But, as I explain in the Appendix to this chapter, there are a number of assumptions that must be accepted if such an argument is to go through, and the acceptance of these assumptions is not mandatory. However, I shall also argue that to make use of this particular loophole is to adopt an implausible, and apparently unmotivated, version of essentialism.

---

[11] There is the further point that one might deny the principle that if *being F* is an essential property of some individuals it is an essential property of every individual that is F. Lynne Rudder Baker (2000, esp. ch. 2) denies that this principle holds even for sortal properties such as *being a person* or *being a statue*. For example, she holds that a lump of clay may be contingently a statue although it constitutes something (the thing that we usually refer to as 'the statue') that is essentially a statue. It follows from Baker's view that a may be essentially F even if it is false that everything that is F is essentially F.

[12] Dummett (1973: 110–32) allows quantification into modal contexts, but does not countenance rigid designators.

1.6. ESSENTIALISM ABOUT NATURAL KINDS: *DE RE* ESSENTIALISM AND PREDICATE ESSENTIALISM

So far, I have treated essentialism as a theory that involves the attribution of essential properties to things. But there are views, commonly described as 'essentialist', that do not appear to conform to this pattern. I refer to views that assert a necessary a posteriori connection between properties or predicates. Putnam (1973, 1975) claimed that there is a necessary but a posteriori coextensiveness between *being a sample of water* and *being composed of H_2O molecules*, but

(9) $\Box \forall x$ (x is a sample of water $\leftrightarrow$ x is composed of H_2O molecules)

does not count as a *de re* modal sentence according to the criterion that I have proposed in Section 1.3 above, and it does not, on the face of it, attribute an essential property to anything. Yet Putnam's view is usually described as a version of essentialism.

I shall reserve the title '*de re* essentialism' for essentialism in the sense (the attribution of essential properties) that has been discussed in Sections 1.1–1.5 above. Although Putnam's view does not, on the face of it, involve *de re* essentialism, one might appeal to an equivalence between (9) and

(10) $\Box$ Water $= H_2O$

and argue that (10) asserts the necessitation of an identity statement flanked by two rigid designators, and is thus *de re* by the criterion of Section 1.3; hence that (9) should count as essentialist because of its equivalence to (10).

However, this appeal is fraught with difficulties. There is the problem of what the nouns 'water' and 'H_2O' refer to (presumably to kinds, but what exactly are these?), and the related problem of what is meant by the identity in (10). Perhaps we should think of the identity as simply defined by the necessary coextensiveness of the corresponding predicates. But if necessary coextensiveness is sufficient for kind identity, it seems that Putnam's (9) will be no more essentialist than is

(11) $\Box \forall x$ (x is an oculist $\leftrightarrow$ x is an eye doctor).

For what is then to prevent us from asserting an equivalence between (11) and

(12)　$\Box$ oculist = eye doctor

with 'oculist' and 'eye doctor' treated as rigid designators of (non-natural) kinds? Putnam's 'essentialism' about natural kinds will be no more essentialist than any statement of an a priori coincidence of predicates, and this seems absurd.

We need not deny that Kripke noticed something of philosophical importance in pointing to the fact that terms such as 'water' appear to have more in common with ordinary proper names than do terms such as 'oculist' (1980: 127). But the claim that natural kind predicates are typically associated with a variety of necessary connection that is not a priori is of interest quite independently of whether, and how, the parallel between proper names and nouns for natural kinds can be defended.

We might react to these problems by deciding to withhold the title 'essentialist' from necessary a posteriori coextensiveness claims such as Putnam's (9). But this would fly in the face of established usage. Instead, I suggest that we extend 'essentialism' beyond the sense of '*de re* essentialism'. The simplest extension seems to be to allow non-*de re* modal sentences stating necessary connections between predicates to count as essentialist if, but only if, those connections are a posteriori. I shall call this 'predicate essentialism'. Of course, this proposal does not avoid all problems. For one thing, it means that

(13)　$\Box$ $\forall x$ (x is composed of H$_2$O → x contains hydrogen atoms)

(which is surely an a priori truth) will not count as essentialist, while

(14)　$\Box$ $\forall x$ (x is composed of water → x contains hydrogen atoms)

may do so; yet do both these statements not have an equal title to describe features of the 'real essence' of a kind? For another thing, although (11) will no longer count as essentialist, yet (if 'oculist' and 'eye doctor' are rigid designators) (12) will still apparently count as essentialist in virtue of being '*de re*' by the criterion of Section 1.3.

But it is difficult to see how any definition of 'essentialism' can be unproblematic if it is to apply to both individuals and natural kinds.

What appears to have happened is that the term has come to embrace both the attribution to things of essential properties and the postulation of necessary a posteriori truths. But as I have shown, *de re* essentialism need not involve the necessary a posteriori, and necessary a posteriori truth need not involve *de re* essentialism.

1.7. IDENTITY 'ACROSS POSSIBLE WORLDS'

In this book, I make frequent use of talk of possible worlds. This I find almost unavoidable: I would have great difficulty in presenting many of my arguments without the use of this idiom. But what are possible worlds? Are they to be thought of as abstract objects such as states of affairs or 'ways the world might be (or might have been)', or instead as concrete entities (as in David Lewis's theory), or perhaps just as useful fictions?[13] In this book, I do not commit myself to any particular conception of the nature of possible worlds. It is true that my appeal to possible worlds is never intended to rely on a conception of possible worlds as concrete entities of the type envisaged in Lewis's theory, and some of my conclusions are inimical to his theory. On the other hand, although I do not endorse Lewis's 'concrete realism' about possible worlds, I think that few of my arguments actually *depend* on the rejection of Lewis's version of realism, apart from some aspects of my discussion of counterpart theory in Chapter 5.

I also make frequent use of the expressions 'identity across possible worlds' and 'transworld identity' to describe the thesis that the same individual exists in different possible worlds. I am not keen on either of these phrases, neither of which seems to me appropriate to describe the idea in question.[14] Nevertheless, these terms are far too well established for it to be sensible to try to introduce an alternative, and I have followed the standard terminology throughout this book.

If, for example, we interpret the *de re* modal claim that Henry Kissinger could have been President of the United States in terms of

[13] For a recent extensive discussion of various interpretations of the notion of a possible world, see Divers 2002.

[14] The phrase 'transworld identity' seems especially inappropriate: one would expect this to mean an identity that holds 'across' (and hence within) *one* world, not an identity that holds between objects in different worlds. (As has been pointed out by others, Transworld Airlines is an intercontinental, not an interplanetary, carrier.)

possible worlds, the most natural interpretation appears to be that there is a possible world in which Kissinger exists and is President, from which it seems immediately to follow that there is a possible world that contains an object identical with Kissinger that is President. The identity between this President (in the possible world) and Kissinger (in the actual world) will therefore be what is known as an 'identity across possible worlds' or 'transworld identity'. This 'transworld identity' interpretation of *de re* modal claims has, however, an important rival, provided by David Lewis's counterpart theory. According to Lewis, the claim that Kissinger could have been President is to be interpreted, in terms of possible worlds, not as the claim that Kissinger exists, in some possible world, with the property of being President, but rather as the claim that some possible world contains an object that is a *counterpart* of Kissinger and also President, where a counterpart of Kissinger is an object that is not identical with Kissinger, but similar to Kissinger in important respects.[15] The contrast between the 'transworld identity' interpretation and the counterpart-theoretic interpretation will be a recurrent theme in my discussion of the essential properties of individuals in Chapters 2–5.

1.8. APPENDIX

At the end of Section 1.5 I said that it was theoretically possible to combine the acceptance of rigid designation and the existence of *de re* essentialist principles (involving quantification into modal contexts) with the denial that there are any necessary truths whose truth value is knowable only a posteriori.

There seem to be two versions of *de re* essentialism that could generate this combination of views. One is a theory according to which any rigid designator of an object has a sense that encapsulates, a priori, all the properties of the object that are essential to it (Version 1). The other is a theory that countenances, as essential properties of things, only properties that one can know a priori must belong to absolutely every object: for example, self-identity, or perhaps *being either a number or not a number* (Version 2).

But there is a possible obstacle to both these attempts to have all three of *de re* essentialism, quantified modal logic, and rigid designation

---

[15] See Lewis 1968; 1973, 39–43; 1986*a*, ch. 4. See also Ch. 5 below.

without the necessary a posteriori. Unless the rigid designator '*a*' can be meaningful if empty, then even

(15)   *a* exists → *a* is self-identical

and

(16)   *a* exists → *a* is either a number or not a number

will carry existential commitment. But if '*a*' designates a contingent existent, the relevant existential statements will presumably be a posteriori. Assuming, further, that any sentence that entails an a posteriori sentence is itself a posteriori, we get the consequence that (15) and (16) are not a priori after all, and hence, if necessary truths, are examples of the necessary a posteriori.

It is clear that this obstacle is not insurmountable, for one might deny one of the assumptions on which the argument depends. Gareth Evans (1979) argues that there can be rigid designators that are meaningful even if empty. One might try to claim (as Evans himself certainly did not) that *all* rigid designators have this characteristic (denial of Assumption 1). Or one might hold (the unusual position) that all rigid designators designate necessary existents whose existence is knowable a priori (denial of Assumption 2).

These proposals appear to be technically coherent. In conjunction with Version 1 and Version 2, they provide four possible ways of defending the thesis that although there are *de re* necessary sentences involving rigid designators they are one and all a priori. But it is difficult to see what the point of any of these theories could be: what attraction this heroic attempt to deny the existence of necessary a posteriori truths could have for a *de re* essentialist. Any interest that attaches to them would, it seems, be merely technical.

I have so far ignored a further strategy that might be combined with Version 1 or Version 2. Could one not deny the assumption that a posteriori status always reflects back on to a sentence from its entailments, and so maintain that even if sentences such as (15) and (16) have a posteriori existential import they are nevertheless a priori (denial of Assumption 3)?

This suggestion is of some interest in the context of a consideration of what it is for a sentence to be a priori or a posteriori. Discussions of a priori truth typically employ the principle that the fact that experience is required for *understanding* a true sentence is not sufficient to make that sentence an a posteriori truth. (Think of traditional empiricist theories of concept acquisition and a priori truth.) So why should this principle not apply to a case where a posteriori existential knowledge is required for understanding a singular term, and thus for understanding sentences that contain that term? There is an awkward question about terminology here. Nevertheless, in recent writings the practice has generally been adopted of treating a sentence that has a posteriori existential implications as itself a posteriori. I shall follow this practice here: by fiat, the denial of Assumption 3 is not to be an option. But it is clear from this that there need be no genuine dispute between those who think that there are no a posteriori truths involving rigid designators only because they use 'a priori' in a way that allows the denial of Assumption 3, and those who use 'a priori' in a way that precludes this denial.

In conclusion: if we adopt the standard interpretation of 'a priori', even Version 1 and Version 2 of *de re* essentialism do not support the rejection of the necessary a posteriori except in combination with rather bizarre assumptions about the nature of rigid designation. And Versions 1 and 2 are in any case rather curious versions of *de re* essentialism. As I have pointed out (Section 1.5), it seems possible to be a *de re* essentialist without accepting the materials for the generation of necessary truths (and falsehoods) involving rigid designators. But it will be normal, if not quite obligatory, for a *de re* essentialist who accepts these materials to countenance the existence of necessary truths whose truth value can be known only a posteriori.

2

Individual Essences and Bare Identities

In the previous chapter, I have accepted that it makes sense to say that an individual has some of its properties essentially and some accidentally. But how are we to judge, and what is it that determines, which of an individual's properties are essential, and which merely accidental? I have shown how a number of essentialist theses can be expressed as general *de re* principles such as the necessity of identity principle (NI), the necessity of origin principle (NO), and the 'sortal essentialist' principle (NSF). Many others could be formulated. I accept the coherence of these formulations, including the quantification into modal contexts that they employ. But which, if any, of these or other *de re* principles are true? What essential properties do things really have? What are the constraints on how they might have been?

I shall assume that it is innocuous to attribute to things, as essential properties, such properties as *being self-identical*, or *being either a frog or not a frog*: essential properties that belong to everything.[1] However, the claim that there are essential properties that characterize all objects indiscriminately does not represent a very exciting version of essentialism. In this chapter I begin an examination of whether we should recognize more interesting, and exacting, constraints on how individuals might have been, and if so, what these constraints are.

2.1. ESSENTIAL PROPERTIES AND INDIVIDUAL ESSENCES

I begin by considering the view that things have not only some essential properties that are not shared by all individuals, but also *individual essences*: essential properties that are unique to them alone. It may seem surprising that I start with this version of essentialism. The thesis that

---

[1] As I have mentioned earlier, I am using 'property' in a broad sense.

things have individual essences has few explicit adherents.[2] And some philosophers regard it as thoroughly misguided.[3] Or rather, this is true if the thesis of individual essences is applied to 'ordinary' individuals such as people, animals, and artefacts (as opposed to, say, abstract objects such as sets and numbers), and is interpreted as the view that these things have individual essences that are substantial, rather than trivial (in a sense that I shall explain).

I take this extreme view seriously because, although I do not believe that such individual essences exist, I think that there are interesting and powerful arguments for the conclusion that there must be such individual essences if we are to interpret *de re* modality in terms of identity across possible worlds, and that the power of these arguments has been insufficiently appreciated. I think it can be shown that to engage in *de re* modality *without* appealing to (substantial) individual essences is to pay a high price: one is forced to accept certain consequences that many will find paradoxical, and perhaps even intolerable. Moreover, the consideration of the case for individual essences raises interesting questions about individuation and identity. I should emphasize, however, that, although I think that the case for individual essences needs to be taken seriously, I also think that, ultimately, it must be rejected, for reasons that I shall explain in due course.

2.2. WHAT ARE INDIVIDUAL ESSENCES?

An individual essence of an object A would be a property, or set of properties, that is necessarily both necessary and sufficient for being A. In other words, if a property (or set of properties) φ is an individual essence of A, then A has φ essentially, and no other actual or possible object actually or possibly has φ. In the language of possible worlds, if φ is A's individual essence, then φ serves to distinguish A in all possible worlds in which A exists.

This statement gives necessary conditions for being an individual essence. Are the conditions also sufficient? I shall take it that they are. But this means that I must qualify the scope of my investigation of the claim that things have individual essences. Not every property that satisfies these criteria for being an individual essence is included within the scope of my discussion, for reasons that I shall now explain.

---

[2] Graeme Forbes is a notable exception. See the works cited below.
[3] e.g., Wiggins 1980 and 2001.

First, it seems plausible to say that there are certain properties that satisfy the criteria for being individual essences, but in a way that is trivial and uninteresting. For example, if we assume the truth of the necessity of identity principle (NI) mentioned in the previous chapter, then we must accept that if *A* is not identical with *B*, *A* will have an essential property that *B* does not, viz., *being identical with A* (where '*A*' is a rigid designator of *A*). For example, if we accept (NI), then we shall hold that Socrates has an essential property that nothing else has, viz., *being identical with Socrates*.[4] But if *being identical with Socrates* really is an essential property of Socrates, it satisfies the criteria for being an individual essence of Socrates. Hence it follows that Socrates—and, by a generalization of the example, everything else—has an individual essence. However, the thesis that I want to discuss is not the thesis that things have individual essences in this trivial sense.[5] Rather, it is a much more controversial thesis, exemplified by the claim that Socrates has an individual essence that consists not merely in the fact that he is essentially identical with Socrates, but in a set of essential properties that are (together) *non-trivially necessary and sufficient* for being Socrates. From now on, when I speak of 'individual essences' without qualification, I shall always mean individual essences in this non-trivial sense. In particular, the property of *being identical with A* is not to count as an individual essence in the intended sense, unless this property is taken to be constituted by *other* properties that non-trivially determine that its bearer is *A*.[6]

Two further qualifications are needed. First, Plantinga has pointed out that if we take any property that Socrates alone happens to have (such as the property of *being married to Xanthippe*, for example), then

---

[4] The necessity of identity principle, although very widely accepted, has been contested, notably by Allan Gibbard and David Lewis. See Gibbard 1975; Lewis 1968, 1971, and 1986a, ch. 4. I shall not argue for the principle here. For an influential defence of the principle, see Kripke 1972a and 1980.

[5] Trivial, that is, for one who accepts the necessity of identity principle (NI). However, since the necessity of identity principle is controversial (see the previous note) the claim that *being identical with Socrates* satisfies the criteria for being an individual essence of Socrates is not, in fact, a completely trivial claim.

[6] I do not know how to draw the relevant distinction between the trivial and non-trivial precisely, and I shall rely on the reader's intuitive judgements to some extent. I do not think that this will cause any serious difficulty. (One might attempt to characterize the relevant sense of 'non-trivial individual essence of *A*' in terms of essential properties that are (necessarily) sufficient for being *A* without logically entailing being *A* (cf. Forbes 2002). However, whether this is adequate may depend on one's conception of logical entailment: on some conceptions of logical entailment this characterization of the non-trivial may exclude too much.)

an appropriately 'world-indexed' version of this property (*being married to Xanthippe in the actual world*) will satisfy the criteria for being an individual essence of Socrates, at least if we accept that there are such world-indexed properties (Plantinga 1974, ch. 5, sect. 2). It may be contentious to call this world-indexed notion of an individual essence merely *trivial*. Nevertheless, such individual essences, if they exist, also belong outside the scope of my discussion. (By contrast, someone who thought that the *non*-world-indexed property of *being the sole husband of Xanthippe* is an essential property of Socrates that could not belong to anything else would be treating this property as an individual essence of Socrates in the sense that interests me, although of course the choice of this property as Socrates' individual essence would be eccentric and implausible.)

Finally, it has been suggested that Socrates can be assigned a 'haecceity': an essential property of *being Socrates* which (unlike the property of *being identical with Socrates* mentioned above) may be regarded as what 'makes' its possessor Socrates in a non-trivial sense, and yet is simple and unanalysable.[7] If there were such 'haecceities', then evidently they would satisfy the criteria for being individual essences. However, I propose to leave such alleged 'haecceities' out of consideration. I am sceptical about whether there could be such properties. But even if the notion is coherent, I think that, if the demand for something that constitutes the identity of Socrates in all possible worlds is a legitimate demand, the invocation of a haecceity of Socrates is unlikely to represent a satisfactory way of meeting it.[8]

To take stock: the notion of an individual essence that I wish to discuss is the (controversial) notion that things are distinguished by individual essences that are non-trivial (unlike the property of *being identical with Socrates*), not essentially world-indexed (unlike the property of *being married to Xanthippe in the actual world*) and do not consist in unanalysable haecceities. From now on, when I speak

---

[7] This notion of a 'haecceity' is mentioned briefly (but not endorsed) by Lowe (2002: 102–3), for example. The theory that things have 'haecceities' in this sense must be sharply distinguished from the theory referred to as 'haecceitism' later in this chapter, a theory according to which there may be differences in transworld identities that do not supervene on qualitative differences (see Appendix A below).

[8] To accept that the demand for something that constitutes the identity of Socrates in all possible worlds is legitimate, and then to proffer haecceities as a way of meeting this demand, looks like a clear case of an attempt to gain the advantages of theft over honest toil. On the other hand, if this demand (for something that constitutes the identity of Socrates in all possible worlds) is *not* accepted as a legitimate one, I fail to see what motivation there could be for the postulation of haecceities.

of individual essences, I shall always mean individual essences in this restricted sense, unless otherwise indicated. I shall also sometimes refer to them as 'substantial' or 'non-trivial' individual essences: I intend no difference between these terms. (Note that, simply for convenience of terminology, when I speak of 'non-trivial' or 'substantial' individual essences I mean to exclude both Plantinga's 'world-indexed' essences and simple unanalysable haecceities from the class of the 'non-trivial' or 'substantial'.)

One philosopher who appears to be committed to individual essences in this sense (substantial, non-trivial, individual essences) is Leibniz. According to a standard interpretation of Leibniz, he holds that *every* property of an individual is essential to it, and the Identity of Indiscernibles guarantees a non-trivial distinction between the properties of any two individuals.[9] But the consequence of this view—that of rendering false all claims to the effect that anyone or anything could have had a history in any way different from its actual history—is one that, for obvious reasons, most philosophers find unacceptable. On the other hand, if we try to preserve the spirit of the Leibnizian view, while saving the truth of the modal claims to the effect that things could have been different by reinterpreting them in the style of David Lewis's counterpart theory, the result involves no commitment to Leibnizian individual essences.[10] In so far as the new interpretation saves the truth of the proposition that (say) Socrates could have been different in some respects, it must now, if applied to the original Leibnizian thesis that all his properties are essential to him, render that thesis false.

However, the Leibnizian version of the individual essence theory is, apparently, not the only option. According to a non-Leibnizian version of the thesis that Socrates has an individual essence (in the non-trivial sense), his essence would consist in some proper subset of his properties. According to such a view, although Socrates could have existed with some different properties, there is nevertheless a set of properties that he retains in all possible situations in which he exists, and whose possession is (non-trivially) sufficient for being Socrates and no one else.

---

[9] For Leibniz's view, see, for example, sects. 8–13 of his *Discourse on Metaphysics* (1686), in Leibniz 1973; also the selections from the Correspondence with Arnauld (1686–7) in Leibniz 1973.

[10] For Lewis's counterpart theory, see Lewis 1968, 1973, and 1986a, ch. 4. See also Ch. 5 below. As Kripke (1980: 45, note 13) indicates, it is tempting to discern, in Leibniz's account of possible individuals, an anticipation of Lewis's counterpart theory as an alternative to an extreme version of essentialism.

2.3. INDIVIDUAL ESSENCES AND KNOWLEDGE OF IDENTITIES

The doctrine of (substantial) individual essences may initially strike many readers as not only implausible, but also gratuitous. Implausible, because it is obviously questionable what properties of ordinary individuals could plausibly be invoked to serve as their individual essences. Gratuitous, at least in the absence of an argument that individuals must have unique distinguishing properties that are essential to them. Some remarks of Kripke's have probably been influential in this connection:

A possible world is *given by the descriptive conditions we associate with it....* Why can't it be part of the *description* of a possible world that it contains *Nixon* and that in that world *Nixon* didn't win the election?... 'Possible worlds' are *stipulated*, not *discovered* by powerful telescopes. There is no reason why we cannot *stipulate* that, in talking about what would have happened to Nixon in a certain counterfactual situation, we are talking about what would have happened to *him*. (Kripke 1980: 44)

On the face of it, these remarks appear to support the view that in order to conceive of possibilities for Nixon we do not need to rely on a set of essential properties that distinguishes him from other individuals in all possible worlds, which is what an individual essence for Nixon would be. Even if Nixon and, say, Ronald Reagan were distinguished only by their accidental properties, we could, it seems, coherently envisage a distinction between a possible situation in which Nixon loses the election and a possible situation in which the loser of the election is Reagan. We could coherently envisage this because we could simply stipulate that the subject of the counterfactual speculation is Nixon rather than Reagan.

Nevertheless matters are not as simple as this may seem to suggest. First, in so far as the considerations that Kripke adduces are purely epistemological, they do not undermine the metaphysical thesis that there must be an underlying difference between any possible situation that contains Nixon and any that contains, say, Reagan, even if the difference need not be epistemologically accessible to the person who engages in the relevant counterfactual suppositions.[11]

---

[11] Cf. Lewis 1986a: 222. See also Kripke 1980: 46–7, and the passage from Kripke (1980: 18) quoted at the end of Sect. 2.12 below.

Secondly, even though nothing that Kripke says commits him to the view that every individual has its own unique set of essential properties, his necessity of origin thesis commits him to the view that there is an essential difference, and not merely an accidental difference, between any two human beings who are not siblings (and, perhaps, between any two siblings who, unlike identical twins, triplets, etc., do not come from exactly the same sperm and egg) (1980: 112–13). According to Kripke, we cannot say that Nixon and Reagan are distinguished from one another merely by their accidental properties. For, according to Kripke's necessity of origin thesis, since Nixon and Reagan have different parents, they have their different parents essentially. It therefore follows that when we 'stipulate' that a possible situation contains Nixon, we must, according to Kripke, be *implicitly* stipulating that the situation involves an individual who has, in that situation, one particular pair of actual individuals as parents, even if the identity of these parents need not be known to the stipulator. It is evident, then, that Kripke cannot, and surely does not, hold that, from the fact that knowing which individual one is talking about when one says 'Nixon might have lost' does not require knowledge of any essential properties of Nixon that distinguish him from Reagan, one can infer that Nixon has no such distinctive essential properties.

We may dismiss the suggestion that individual essences are required to enable us to *tell*, of an individual in some possible situation, whether that individual is identical with some actual individual. But we cannot conclude that the possibility of specifying the identity of an individual in a possible world by stipulation implies that the individual in question has no individual essence that makes it the individual that it is. Kripke's remarks about stipulation appear to be consistent with the view that to stipulate that a situation is one in which Nixon loses the election might be implicitly to stipulate that *someone with Nixon's individual essence* loses the election. And it could be—for all that has been said so far—that if Nixon had no such individual essence, the stipulation would be undermined.

2.4. THE CASE FOR INDIVIDUAL ESSENCES: INTRODUCTION

The writer who has presented the most detailed case for individual essences is Graeme Forbes.[12] Forbes argues that if we interpret

---

[12] See the references later in this chapter.

de re modality in terms of identity across possible worlds, we take on commitments that can only be satisfied by the postulation of (substantial) individual essences. As we shall see, Forbes's arguments that transworld identity requires individual essences do not appear to be vulnerable to Kripke's jibes about the 'telescope' conception of our access to other possible worlds. In addition, in an interesting twist to the discussion, Forbes argues that the demand for individual essences can be satisfied, in the case of biological individuals such as animals and plants, by appeal to features of their origins of the kind that Kripke's very own necessity of origin thesis treats as among their essential properties.

The main gist of Forbes's argument is that, unless we posit individual essences, we cannot guarantee that identities across possible worlds will be appropriately grounded in other properties. His conclusion is that if we are not to abandon a commitment to identity across possible worlds (for example, in favour of counterpart theory), we must suppose that there are individual essences.

The details of Forbes's argument are complex. Before embarking on a discussion of his argument, I shall present a simpler, but I think still compelling, argument for the conclusion that unless there are individual essences, we shall be threatened with identities across possible worlds that are not grounded in other properties, and that this result is, if not unacceptable, then at least paradoxical.

2.5. THE INDISCERNIBILITY ARGUMENT

If all objects had individual essences, then there would be no numerical difference (between individuals) without an essential difference. On the other hand, if not all individuals have individual essences, there seems to be no reason why there should not be two things that share all their essential properties, and differ only in their accidental properties.[13] Further, suppose, for the sake of argument, that human beings are among the items that do *not* have individual essences. Then there seems to be no reason why there could not be two *human beings* who share

---

[13] This is not strictly entailed by the denial of the doctrine of individual essences. For example, it is possible, in principle, that even if no human beings have individual essences, nevertheless there is an essential difference between, say, Socrates and every other *actual* human being, even if there are merely possible beings that share all their essential properties with Socrates. Cf. Sects. 2.9 and 2.10 below. But I think I can safely ignore this possibility for the present.

all their essential properties, and differ from one another only in their accidental properties. Suppose, further, just for the sake of argument, that Socrates and Plato are two such individuals.[14] Of course, there are many properties that Socrates had that Plato lacked, and vice versa. But if Socrates and Plato share all their essential properties, then all the actual differences between them must be merely accidental differences. If Socrates and Plato share all their essential properties, then any way that Socrates could have been is a way that Plato could have been, and vice versa. So any possible life (or possible history) for Socrates is a possible life (or possible history) for Plato, as long as the details of that life (or history) are specified in a way that does not logically entail that it is Socrates, rather than Plato, who leads that life. Call such a specification a specification of the life in question that is 'owner-indifferent' with respect to Socrates and Plato.[15]

Consider, then, a possible life for Socrates that is described in this 'owner-indifferent' way. The details of this alternative life do not matter, of course, but let's suppose that it is a life in which Socrates is a fisherman rather than a philosopher. Call this life 'the fisherman life'. If any way that Socrates could have been is a way that Plato could have been, then, if the fisherman life is a possible life for Socrates, it is a possible life for Plato. It appears, then, that we can describe two possible worlds, w1 and w2, in each of which there is *someone* who leads the fisherman life, but in one world (w1) the individual who leads the fisherman life is Socrates, and in the other world (w2) the individual who leads the fisherman life is Plato. *Ex hypothesi*, there need be no further difference between w1 and w2 on which this difference in the identities of the individuals who play the fisherman role depends. So let us suppose that there is no such further difference. Then the pair of worlds w1 and w2 gives us a case of what we can call a 'bare difference' in the identities of the individuals who lead the fisherman life: a difference that does not supervene on any *other* difference between the features of these worlds.

---

[14] Those who object to this supposition because they hold a version of Kripke's necessity of origin thesis should see Sect. 2.6 below.

[15] Obviously, a specification of a possible life for Socrates that is 'owner-indifferent' must exclude not only properties such as *being identical with Socrates*, but also properties such as *being older than Plato*. To avoid confusion, I should point out that a specification of a life for Socrates that is 'owner-indifferent', in the sense of being indifferent *as to whether its owner is Socrates or Plato*, need not be a purely qualitative specification. The specification could even entail the identities of *some* individuals that play a role in the life in question (Pericles, Alcibiades, Athens, etc.) as long as it does not entail either that Socrates is, or that Plato is not, the individual who leads the life.

But we can go further. Our starting assumption is that Socrates and Plato share all their essential properties; hence that any way that Socrates could have been is a way that Plato could have been, and vice versa. But one way that Socrates could have been is the way that Socrates actually is. So this must represent a way that Plato could have been. Hence we can construct a possible world containing an individual, whom we may call 'quasi-Socrates', who leads a life indistinguishable from Socrates' actual life (indistinguishable in its 'owner-indifferent' respects, of course), but in fact is Plato. Using similar reasoning, we can construct a possible world in which there is an individual, 'quasi-Plato', who leads a life indistinguishable from Plato's actual life, but in fact is Socrates. Moreover, there seems to be no reason why a possible world in which Socrates plays the Plato role and a possible world in which Plato plays the Socrates role shouldn't be the very same world. But, finally, if there is such a possible world—that is, one in which Socrates and Plato have 'switched roles'—there appears to be no reason why there should not be such a world—call it 'w(s)' ('s' for 'switching')—that differs from the actual world *only* in that in w(s) Socrates and Plato have switched roles. And all because of our starting assumption that Socrates and Plato do not differ from one another in their essential properties.

The 'role-switching' world w(s) represents a case of a 'bare' difference in identities par excellence. For there need be nothing whatsoever *in virtue of which* quasi-Socrates in w(s) is identical with Plato rather than Socrates, and nothing whatsoever *in virtue of which* quasi-Plato in w(s) is identical with Socrates rather than Plato.

The idea that we can coherently distinguish between the alleged possible worlds w1 and w2 will surely strike some people as counter-intuitive. Could there really be two possible worlds that differ *only* in that the fisherman role is played by Socrates in the one world and by Plato in the other? But even those who regard this as unproblematic may baulk at the idea that there is a possible world, such as w(s), that duplicates all the features *of the actual world* except for the facts about the identities of the individuals who play the roles of Socrates and Plato. This is hard to accept partly for the following reason. We are imagining that w(s) is *exactly* like the actual world except for the switch of roles between Socrates and Plato. But, *inter alia*, this appears to imply that everything that happened up to the coming into being of Socrates in the actual world—that is, the course of events that actually resulted in the existence of Socrates—was not sufficient for it to be *Socrates* who then came into existence, rather than someone else. *Ex hypothesi*, w(s) contains exactly that course of events, yet in w(s) it is Plato, not Socrates, who is the individual produced by Socrates' actual parents, at precisely the time and place, and in exactly the same circumstances, in which Socrates actually came into existence. But this seems close to incredible. For what *more* could be required for it to be *Socrates* who came into existence out of that course of events?[16] This version of the indiscernibility argument appears to imply that the fact that it was Socrates who emerged from this course of events is a fantastic accident, since it could just as well have been someone else who did so. I think the argument that there could be a 'role-switching' world such as w(s) deserves to be called a paradox. I shall call it the Paradox of Indiscernibility.[17]

2.6. CLARIFICATIONS

Of course, the particular versions of the 'indiscernibility' argument that I have just given could be blocked without invoking anything as demanding as individual essences for Socrates and Plato. As long as there is *some* appropriate essential difference between Socrates and Plato—as long as one of them has some essential property that the other essentially lacks[18]—then, even if neither of them has an individual essence, it will be impossible for each of them to occupy *exactly* the same 'fisherman role' in a possible world, and impossible for them to switch roles as envisaged in w(s). Moreover, those who accept Kripke's necessity of origin thesis will believe that there is such an essential difference between Socrates and Plato, since they hold, for example, that Socrates essentially has, and Plato essentially lacks, the property of having Socrates' actual parents. Hence, adherents of the necessity of origin thesis, even if they

---

[16] Cf. Prior 1960: 70–2 in the version reprinted in Prior 1968.

[17] Readers may be reminded of Chisholm's paradox concerning Noah and Adam (Chisholm 1967). But my Paradox of Indiscernibility is significantly different from Chisholm's. Chisholm arrives at his 'role-switching' duplicate of the actual world by a series of steps, suggesting that his argument may have the form of a *sorites*. And there is no such series of gradations in my argument. I discuss Chisholm's Paradox briefly in the next chapter of this book. My Paradox of Indiscernibility is, I think, closer to an argument used by Adams (1979), on which see Appendix B to this chapter.

[18] Note that it would not be enough, to avoid the indiscernibility argument, for there to be some essential property F of Socrates that is not an essential property of Plato. This difference in essential properties would not preclude there being a possible world in which Plato is F, and hence would not preclude there being a possible life for Socrates that is also a possible life for Plato. As indicated in the text, what is required is an essential property of Socrates that Plato *essentially* lacks, or vice versa.

do not believe in individual essences, will hold that there must be a difference between the Socratic and the Platonic fishermen of w1 and w2, however otherwise alike they may be, consisting in the fact that the fisherman of w1 has Socrates' actual parents, whereas the fisherman of w2 has Plato's. Moreover, according to the proponent of the necessity of origin, however many properties we may coherently envisage Socrates and Plato as exchanging, one thing that they cannot exchange with one another in any possible world is their ancestry; if so, the 'role-switching' world w(s) envisaged in the last section is an impossibility.

However, the argument that I exemplified using Socrates and Plato is, of course, completely general, and the choice of Socrates and Plato purely illustrative. As long as human beings do not have individual essences, there may be *some* pairs of human individuals (let these be, in order to placate adherents of the necessity of (parental) origin, pairs of siblings, or pairs of identical twins) that are not distinguished from one another by their essential properties.[19] But if A and B share all their essential properties, then any way that A could have been is a way that B could have been, and vice versa. And if any way that A could have been is a way that B could have been, then there is no obstacle to the construction of two possible worlds that are indiscernible from one another except for the identities of A and B. Worse, there is no apparent obstacle to the construction of a possible world that differs from the actual world only in that in this possible world A and B have 'exchanged roles'.[20]

The hypothesis that actual individuals have doppelgängers in other possible worlds that differ from them only in their identities is discussed by Graeme Forbes in the following passage:

Consider the supposition that things could have been exactly as they are except that the steel tower in Paris opposite the Palais de Chaillot is different from the one actually there. To make sense of this supposition, it is not permitted to imagine that the tower is made of different metal from the metal which actually constitutes it, or that it has a different design, or designer, or history. The *only* respect in which the imagined situation is to differ from the actual world is in the identity of the tower. The extent to which such a difference seems

---

[19] Subject to the caveat in note 13 above.

[20] Also, of course, even if it were the case that all *human beings* are distinguished from one another by individual essences, as long as there are some individuals that are not distinguished from one another by individual essences, there would still be the possibility of pairs of 'indiscernible' worlds that differ only in the identities of some of the individuals that they contain.

unintelligible is some measure of the plausibility of the view that transworld differences must be grounded: in Dummett's terminology, the example shows the strangeness of the idea that there can be 'bare' differences in transworld identity; rather, there must be something in which such differences consist. (Forbes 1985: 128)

There is obviously some plausibility in Forbes's suggestion that it is unintelligible to postulate a situation in which the Eiffel Tower is duplicated in this peculiar way. If it is true that the belief in identity across possible worlds, when combined with the denial of individual essences, involves a commitment to the possibility of such cases of duplication, then this fact provides a prima facie case for the postulation of individual essences.

2.7. FORBES ON INDIVIDUAL ESSENCES

I hope that the indiscernibility arguments of the previous sections have persuaded the reader that the hypothesis that transworld identities must be underwritten by individual essences, whether or not it is ultimately defensible, is not a gratuitous one. Unless we suppose that there are individual essences, there is a serious question whether we can avoid the construction of possible worlds that differ from one another only in the identities of some of the individuals that they contain, and even the construction of possible worlds that differ from the actual world only in the identities of some of the individuals that they contain. Yet can we really admit that there are such possible worlds? It appears that the logic of identity, in combination with some intuitive judgements about possibility, leads to paradox without the postulation of individual essences.

Nevertheless, my indiscernibility argument concerning Socrates and Plato was in some respects sketchy. Because of this, readers may be suspicious about whether it really does warrant this conclusion. However, as I shall now show, we can give a more rigorous, although lengthier, argument that transworld identity without individual essences leads to 'bare identities'. The argument is based principally on materials presented by Graeme Forbes.

In a number of writings, Forbes has argued that if we interpret *de re* modality in terms of identity across possible worlds, then we put severe constraints on the range of possibilities that we are allowed to countenance, constraints that are so severe that it seems that nothing short of the ascription of individual essences could satisfy them.[21] He employs two principles about identity across possible worlds. The first principle receives various formulations, but may be summed up as follows: the identity (or distinctness) of A and B must be grounded in facts other than the identity (or distinctness) of A and B itself. Alternative expressions of this are that identity and distinctness cannot be 'bare', but must hold in virtue of other facts (e.g., Forbes 1985: 127–8).[22] I shall call this 'the No Bare Identities Principle'.[23] The second principle involves a restriction on the kinds of fact that can legitimately be taken to ground an identity (or distinctness): at least as a first approximation, we can say that these facts must be 'intrinsic' rather than 'extrinsic' (cf. Forbes 1985, ch. 6, sect. 4). Although the precise formulation of this principle (which will shortly be exhibited in operation) is a vexed issue, the main point is that this principle is intended to have the effect of disallowing the suggestion that A may be identical with B in virtue of the absence from the scene of any object that would compete with A for identity with B.[24] (A version of this principle is sometimes invoked in discussions of 'best-candidate' theories of identity over time.) I shall call it 'the No Extrinsic Determination Principle'.

I shall now show how these two principles, if accepted, do support a doctrine of individual essences. My first argument (which I call 'the reduplication argument') derives its basic structure from an argument that Forbes employs, but I have exploited these materials for my own purposes.[25] My second argument ('the multiple occupancy argument') represents a supplementation to Forbes's own discussion, but one that

[21] e.g., Forbes 1985, 1986, 2002; cf. Forbes 1980. It is important to note that Forbes's argument for individual essences involves this conditional. As Forbes emphasizes, since his principles concern *identity*, it appears that the argument can be evaded by interpreting *de re* modality in terms of counterpart theory rather than identity across possible worlds. See also Sect. 2.11 below.

[22] This formulation may be slightly misleading, since Forbes allows that the facts in virtue of which one identity or distinctness obtains may include facts about the identity or distinctness of other items. In fact, this plays an important role in his argument for the necessity of origin, as will be seen in the next chapter.

[23] Of course, to avoid triviality the No Bare Identities principle must be interpreted as implying that the identity of A and B cannot consist merely in the possession by A and B of the property of *identity with A*; nor can the distinctness of A and B consist merely in the possession by A and B of incompatible properties of *being A* and *being B*.

[24] For a discussion of some problems concerning the notion of 'extrinsicness' employed in the principle, see Forbes 2002.

[25] Forbes's own main arguments for individual essences in his 1985 are contained in ch. 5, sect. 5 (on sets) and ch. 6, sects. 1–5 (organisms). I discuss Forbes's own version of what I call 'the reduplication argument' in the next chapter.

appears to be required to complete the transition from Forbes's principles to the conclusion that there are individual essences.

2.8. THE REDUPLICATION ARGUMENT AND THE MULTIPLE OCCUPANCY ARGUMENT

Suppose that we take for consideration a claim that some individual C, in a possible world, w1, is Bishop Berkeley, and also a claim that some individual, D, in a different possible world, w2, is also Berkeley. Given Berkeley's actual properties, Forbes's principles about transworld identity require that if C is Berkeley, this is in virtue of the properties that C has in w1 (excluding, of course, identity with Berkeley itself) and similarly that if D is Berkeley, this is in virtue of the properties that D has in w2. But how can Forbes's principles lead to the conclusion that the properties in virtue of which C is Berkeley have to be the *same* ones as the properties in virtue of which D is identical with that philosopher, which is the result that the doctrine of individual essences would give us? For example, why can't we secure accord with Forbes's principles by, as Ayer has put it, 'anchoring' C's career in w1 to certain items in Berkeley's actual biography, and anchoring D's career to certain quite different items in that same biography? (cf. Ayer (1973: 197–8)). It is true that this procedure might commit us to the assignment to Berkeley, as one of his essential properties, the disjunction of all distinct sufficient conditions for being Berkeley. But such a 'disjunctive essential property' does not represent the type of individual essence that Forbes has in mind. So the question is: how can we get, from the claim that every identity with Berkeley must be grounded in some set of properties, to the conclusion that there is some set of properties that must ground every identity with Berkeley?

The route is as follows. Suppose that C in w1 is Berkeley; Forbes's first principle requires that there be features that C has in w1 (not including identity with Berkeley itself) in virtue of which C is Berkeley. Call the relevant set of features 'F1'. But, and this is crucial, if it really is just in virtue of having F1 that C is Berkeley, then *any* object with F1 must also be Berkeley: that is, F1 must represent a strictly sufficient condition for being Berkeley. Suppose now that there is another sufficient condition for being Berkeley, namely F2; let us assume that D in w2 is Berkeley in virtue of having F2. If F1 and F2 are to be genuinely sufficient, there must be something about them that serves to guarantee that there is no possible world in which there are two objects, one of which has F1 and the other of which has F2. One way of achieving this would be to include in each of F1 and F2 the absence of a competitor for identity with Berkeley.[26] But this would offend against Forbes's second principle, that identity must be determined only by 'intrinsic' features. Yet if this stratagem is ruled out, the only way to guarantee that there will be no possibility of reduplication seems to be to assign to Berkeley, as essential to his identity, some property that is such that it cannot be shared by two objects in any one possible world. If Berkeley has some such *unshareable essential property* U, then U must be a component of any sufficient condition for being Berkeley—so it must be a component of F1 and a component of F2.[27] Thus we secure the desired result that there can be no offending 'reduplication' world in which F1 and F2 are instantiated by two different objects.[28]

Unshareable essential properties in this sense (UEPs) need not amount to individual essences, although every individual essence is, of course, a UEP. Suppose (purely for the sake of an example), that Berkeley has the property of *being the author of Three Dialogues Between Hylas and Philonous* essentially, and Hume has the property of *being the author of A Treatise of Human Nature* essentially.[29] Evidently, since each of these is an unshareable property, it follows that each of Berkeley and Hume has a UEP. But nothing that has so far been said precludes the existence of a possible world in which Berkeley's UEP is possessed by Hume: a possible world (from which Berkeley is absent) in which the author of the *Three Dialogues* is not Berkeley but Hume.

[26] Equivalently: F1 will include a proviso that there is no distinct object that satisfies another sufficient condition for being Berkeley, so will F2, and so will every sufficient condition for being Berkeley.

[27] What I am calling 'unshareable properties' have also been referred to as 'exclusive properties' (Robertson 1998; Forbes 2002).

[28] The strategy of writing into each of the Fs the absence of a competitor is, of course, a way of generating what is, in a sense, an unshareable essential property of Berkeley: the property of being the only object that satisfies some sufficient condition for being Berkeley. But this would be an unshareable essential property in a degenerate sense. Similarly, the disjunctive property consisting in all distinct sufficient conditions for being Berkeley, with this proviso included, would also be an unshareable essential property, but again in a trivialized sense. In general, when I speak of unshareable essential properties, I shall intend to exclude such degenerate and trivial cases.

[29] Since these properties have been chosen purely for the sake of an example, the implausibility of the claim that these are *essential* properties of Berkeley and Hume does not matter. Nor does the fact that these properties might be held to violate Forbes's 'No Extrinsic Determination' principle, since 'being the (sole) author of x' implies the non-existence of another author of x.

However, a second argument from Forbes's two principles will tend to close this gap.[30] If F1, F2, ... Fn, ... is the suggested list (possibly open-ended) of non-trivial sufficient conditions for being Berkeley, and G1, G2, ... Gn, ... is the corresponding list that belongs to Hume, something about the Fs and the Gs must serve to guarantee that there can be no single object in a possible world that has both one of the Fs and one of the Gs. We could achieve this in an ad hoc way if we were allowed to include, in the Fs or the Gs, or both, a clause explicitly ruling out competition. (For example, we might simply make it an explicit component of each of the 'Berkeley-making' properties (the Fs) that its possessor lacks every one of the 'Hume-making' properties (the Gs).) But if this is not permitted (as conflicting with Forbes's second principle), the obvious move must be to take some property I1 that Berkeley has and some (different) property I2 that Hume has, such that I1 and I2 cannot be instantiated by a single object in any possible world, and make these essential to being Berkeley and being Hume respectively.

We have now given an argument for assigning to Berkeley and Hume what I shall call 'incompatible essential properties' (IEPs).[31] I call the argument for unshareable essential properties 'the reduplication argument' (since the danger to be avoided is the reduplication of Berkeley); the argument for incompatible essential properties I call 'the multiple occupancy argument', since the danger to be avoided is that Hume and Berkeley will attempt to 'lodge themselves' in the same object in some possible world.[32]

---

[30]   This second argument appears to add to the case that Forbes himself presents for the conclusion that individual essences are needed to avoid bare (or at least 'inappropriately grounded') identities. However, it seems clear that an argument of this second type (the 'multiple occupancy argument') is required to supplement the reduplication argument if Forbes's principles are to yield the conclusion that things have individual essences, as opposed to mere unshareable essential properties that do not amount to individual essences.

[31]   In Mackie 1987 I called such properties '(mutually) exclusive essential properties' (EEPs).

[32]   The 'multiple occupancy argument' is obviously structurally very similar to the 'indiscernibility argument' presented in Sect. 2.5 above. I distinguish the arguments on the grounds that the multiple occupancy argument, as I present it here, relies on a *premise* that there must be non-trivial sufficient conditions for an individual's identity across possible worlds: hence the danger that instead of indiscernible worlds we shall have 'multiple occupancy'. By contrast, the 'indiscernibility' argument of Sect. 2.5 did not use as a *premise* the principle that there must be non-trivial sufficient conditions for identity. Instead, the conclusion of the argument was to the effect that there can be no

Many of the properties possessed by Berkeley and Hume are incompatible in the above sense: for example, Berkeley and Hume were born in different years; they died in different years; the dates at which they first read Locke's *Essay* are different; they were at different locations in the year 1750, and so on. It is obviously a further question whether any of these 'incompatible properties' can plausibly be regarded as among the *essential* properties of Berkeley and Hume. But suppose that, for the sake of argument, we waive these considerations of plausibility, and assume that, for each of Berkeley and Hume, the exact date of his birth is one of his essential properties. Evidently, the assignment of these IEPs to Berkeley and Hume would solve this particular example of the multiple occupancy problem. However, the multiple occupancy argument can obviously be generalized to apply to *all* pairs of actual individuals. To provide a general solution to the multiple occupancy problem, it appears that we shall have to find a range of properties such that: (a) each actual individual has one from the range; (b) no two individuals actually have the same one; and (c) the properties are necessarily mutually exclusive. Any properties that conform to this specification are likely to be also unshareable. But incompatible properties, although they must be actually unshared, would not *have* to be unshareable (in the sense of 'incapable of belonging to two objects in a single possible world'). To show this, consider the following (fanciful) scenario. Suppose that it just happens to be the case that every person is born on a different day from every other person. If so, then the property of *being a person born on 1 January 1900* (for example) would be unshared, although it would not be unshareable, since there are possible worlds in which two people are born on that date. Moreover, if each actual person had his or her actual date of birth essentially, then—in the fanciful scenario in which no two people actually share a birth date—each actual person would have an essential property that is incompatible with the essential properties of every other actual person. Finally, if we add to our fanciful scenario the additional (and less far-fetched) assumption that every person is essentially a person, and nothing that is not a person could have been a person, then every actual person would have an essential property that is incompatible with the essential properties of every other

such sufficient conditions for individuals that share all their essential properties. Note that my 'multiple occupancy' argument has nothing to do with the 'multiple occupancy thesis' advocated by some theorists in response to puzzles about identity over time (on which see Robinson 1985; also, e.g., Noonan 1989).

actual individual, whether or not that other individual is a person. Yet these incompatible essential properties, such as *being a person born on 1 January 1900*, would not be *unshareable* essential properties.

2.9. DISTINCTIVE ESSENTIAL PROPERTIES

The reduplication argument leads to the conclusion that, if transworld identities for individuals must be grounded in intrinsic properties that are sufficient for those identities, then those individuals must have UEPs. The multiple occupancy argument leads to the conclusion that, if transworld identities for individuals must be grounded in intrinsic properties that are sufficient for those identities, then those individuals must have IEPs. We have yet to show that these arguments lead to the conclusion that if transworld identities for individuals must be grounded in intrinsic properties that are sufficient for those identities, then those individuals must have *individual essences*. To establish this conclusion is the task of this section and the next.

Suppose, for the sake of argument, that every actual individual has an IEP, together with some UEP. Does it follow that of each of them has an individual essence? For example, could there be some individual in a possible world that is the author of the *Three Dialogues* (assuming this to be Berkeley's UEP) *and* a person born on 12 March 1685 (assuming this to be Berkeley's IEP, in accordance with the fanciful scenario envisaged in the previous section) and yet is not Berkeley? Clearly, this hypothetical individual could at best be a merely possible being. Its date of birth disqualifies it from being Hume, and from being any other actual person distinct from Berkeley (given our fanciful assumption that all actual persons are essentially distinguished from one another by their different dates of birth). And its being a person disqualifies it from being any actual individual that is not a person (given our assumption that every actual non-person is essentially a non-person). Yet even if it were a merely possible individual, it would be a counterexample to the claim that Berkeley's combined UEP and IEP is Berkeley's individual essence. Let us call the assignment to all actual individuals of combined UEPs and IEPs the assignment to them of *distinctive essential properties* (DEPs). The problem is that although no other *actual* individual could possibly have Berkeley's distinctive essential property, his distinctive essential property need not be an individual essence in the strict sense of a (necessarily) necessary *and sufficient* condition for his identity.

One reason why a DEP would not be expected to be an individual essence is that a DEP, as I have defined it, need not include *all* the essential properties of the individual in question. But, obviously, no individual in any possible world can be Berkeley unless that individual has all Berkeley's essential properties.[33] However, a more interesting point is that even if we supplement Berkeley's DEP with any other *shareable* essential properties that Berkeley has (call this a DEP +), this is not guaranteed to represent a genuinely sufficient condition for being Berkeley. For it seems that there could be, in some possible world, a (merely possible) individual that has all Berkeley's shareable essential properties and also has Berkeley's IEP and UEP, and yet is not Berkeley. But about this worry we can make two points.

The first point is that even if the two principles were to lead to nothing more than a demand for non-trivial *distinctive* essential properties, this would be a significant and striking result. If it is hard to accept that we are obliged to credit things with (non-trivial) individual essences, there is little comfort to be gained by supposing that we have, instead, the obligation to supply non-trivial essential properties that distinguish each actual individual from every other actual individual.

Secondly, however, we have not yet examined the results of a completely general application of Forbes's two principles. In the next section I shall argue that, if we suppose those principles extended, so as to apply to the transworld identities of all merely possible individuals, as well as actual ones, there is no way of achieving a result that both coheres with the logic of identity and does not result in the assignment of individual essences in the strict sense.

2.10. FROM DISTINCTIVE ESSENTIAL PROPERTIES TO INDIVIDUAL ESSENCES

To avoid a 'multiple occupancy problem' involving two actual individuals, we had to suppose that for every pair of *actual* objects x and y, x and y are distinguished from one another by incompatible essential properties (IEPs). Otherwise, there would be no barrier to the construction

---

[33] e.g., suppose, just for the sake of argument, that Berkeley is essentially male, but that there could have been a woman who was the sole author of the *Three Dialogues*, as well as being born on 12 March 1685. Obviously, this (merely) possible woman, although she has (what we are assuming to be) Berkeley's DEP, cannot be identical with Berkeley, since she lacks one of Berkeley's essential properties.

of a possible world that contains a single individual that satisfies the proposed sufficient conditions for identity with each of x and y. In effect, what the multiple occupancy problem shows is that if (in order to avoid bare identities) we suppose that for every actual individual there are genuinely sufficient conditions for being that individual (and that these sufficient conditions are restricted to 'intrinsic' properties), we cannot suppose that there are *any* two actual individuals that differ from one another merely in their accidental properties.

However, as I have shown in the previous section, this does not by itself rule out a possible world in which there is an individual that has all Berkeley's essential properties (including his DEP) and yet is not Berkeley. The crucial point is that so far we have assigned pairs of mutually incompatible essential properties only to pairs of *actual* individuals.

Evidently, however, if we suppose that for every pair of individuals x and y, *whether x and y are actual or merely possible*, x and y have incompatible essential properties, then *everything* has some incompatible essential property that is also its individual essence.[34] The proof is as follows. Suppose, for the sake of a *reductio*, that none of x's incompatible essential properties is an individual essence of x. Then there is some possible world wn in which there is an object, y, that shares all the essential properties of x (including all x's IEPs), and yet is not x. If all objects, actual and possible, are distinguished from one another by incompatible essential properties, however, there can be no such world as wn. For if y is a distinct individual from x, and all objects are distinguished from one another by incompatible essential properties, then y must have some essential property that is incompatible with some essential property of x, contradicting the assumption that there is a possible world in which y has all x's essential properties. QED.

An interesting feature of the argument just given is that, once we apply the requirement of *incompatible* essential properties to all individuals, actual and possible, the attribution of UEPs *in addition to IEPs* is no longer needed in order to avoid the reduplication problem. In other words, if all actual *and possible* individuals are distinguished from one another by IEPs, each of them must have an IEP that is also a UEP. Here is the proof. Suppose, for the sake of a *reductio*, that A has an IEP, Ia, that distinguishes it from all other actual and possible individuals,

---

[34] I'll count a conjunction of essential properties as an essential property, and I'll count any consistent conjunction of essential properties as itself an 'incompatible essential property' if at least one of its conjuncts is such a property.

but has no UEP distinct from Ia. Could there be some possible world in which there are two distinct individuals, both of which have Ia (thus implying that Ia is not an UEP, and generating an example of a reduplication problem concerning *A*)? Not if Ia belongs to a range of IEPs such that every actual or possible individual has a distinct property from that range. Let the two individuals both of whom are supposed to have Ia in some single possible world be *B* and *C*. Then at least one of *B* and *C* must have an IEP that is incompatible with Ia. But if *x* has an IEP that is incompatible with Ia, then *x* does not have Ia. So at least one of *B* and *C* does not have Ia after all. QED.

2.11. CONSEQUENCES

I take the reduplication and multiple occupancy arguments to have established that if we construe *de re* modality in terms of identity across possible worlds, *and* we also accept Forbes's two principles about identity, we are committed to the existence of (non-trivial) individual essences. Hence we seem to have just four options to choose from, in the case of any category of individuals:

(1)   abandon the interpretation of *de re* modality in terms of identity across possible worlds;

(2)   commit ourselves to finding non-trivial individual essences (and, a fortiori, non-trivial distinctive essential properties);

(3)   reject the principle that there can be no bare transworld identities and non-identities;

(4)   reject the principle that transworld identity cannot be 'extrinsically determined'.

The principal interest of the arguments, I think, consists in the fact that *each* of these options appears to have objectionable features. Hence the argument for individual essences can, I think, be regarded as generating a genuine paradox about *de re* modality.

The first option requires either the complete abandonment of *de re* modality, or a reconstrual of *de re* modality in terms of counterpart theory: a theory that, although it has distinguished defenders, has features that many find objectionable. The second option requires a commitment to non-trivial individual essences that, I think, cannot plausibly be met, in spite of Forbes's heroic attempts to support this solution (to be discussed in the next chapter). As we have seen, the third option—the acceptance of bare identities—requires us to accept the paradoxical thesis that there may be possible worlds that differ only in the identities of the individuals that they contain. Finally, the fourth option is, I shall argue, unworkable: when applied to identity across possible worlds, the idea that identity is 'extrinsically determined' (in a sense that is relevant to the reduplication and multiple occupancy puzzles) turns out either to be incoherent or to involve a commitment to bare identities after all.

2.12. A SCEPTICAL REACTION

In the chapters that follow, I shall discuss, and reject, the three options that attempt to respond to the puzzles about identity across possible worlds *without* either abandoning *de re* modality entirely or accepting bare identities: the appeal to individual essences (Chapter 3), the appeal to 'extrinsically determined' identity (Chapter 4), and the adoption of counterpart theory (Chapter 5).

However, I must guard against a certain dismissive reaction to the arguments presented in Sections 2.7–2.11 of this chapter: a reaction that, if justified, would tend to undermine the point of my inquiry into the various responses to the puzzles. When Forbes presents his two principles about transworld identity, one's immediate reaction may be that neither of the principles is plausible. Moreover, Forbes's appeal, in support of his principles, to a parallel between identity over time and identity across possible worlds (1985, ch. 6, sect. 5) will be found unconvincing by many, including those who think that there are differences between the metaphysics of time and of possibility that make the appeal to such a parallel precarious. However, I think that it would be wrong to dismiss the arguments on these grounds. If we construe *de re* modality in terms of identity across possible worlds, we are committed to the view that individuals identical with actual individuals exist in other possible worlds, *however* we construe this claim, and however deflationary its interpretation. But the arguments from Forbes's principles show that if we really do believe that Socrates (for example) exists in other possible worlds, then we must confront the question whether his existence in other possible worlds involves the existence of an individual who possesses, in each of those worlds, properties that are non-trivially sufficient for being Socrates. It is, of course, open to us to answer this question in the negative. But I want to insist that merely because the question *can* be answered in the negative does not mean that there is no 'problem of transworld identity'. The 'problem of transworld identity' reappears as the problem that, if there are no properties that are non-trivially sufficient for being Socrates in another possible world, then we must recognize pairs of possible worlds that differ from one another only in the identities of the individuals that they contain.[35]

To supplement the considerations already given for the claim that a commitment to bare identities is in need of a defence, it is worth noting that, to the question whether there are distinct possible worlds that differ from one another only non-qualitatively, Kripke does not give an affirmative reply, but expresses agnosticism:

With respect to possible states of the entire world, I do not mean to assert categorically that. . . there are qualitatively identical but distinct (counterfactual) states. What I do assert is that *if* there is a philosophical argument excluding qualitatively identical but distinct worlds, it cannot be based simply on the supposition that worlds must be stipulated purely qualitatively. What I defend is the *propriety* of giving possible worlds in terms of certain particulars as well as qualitatively, whether or not there are in fact qualitatively identical but distinct worlds. (Kripke 1980: 18, note 17)

Following David Lewis (1986*a*: 227), I take it that what Kripke is considering is the existence of qualitatively indiscernible worlds that differ only in the identities of some of the individuals that they contain, rather than worlds that differ in no respect at all. For example, I take it that the issue is whether there could be worlds that differ only in that in one of them Nixon, say, has a certain history whereas in the other it is, say, Reagan who has that history.

2.13. APPENDIX A: BARE IDENTITIES AND HAECCEITISTIC DIFFERENCES

The bare identities thesis discussed by Forbes may be regarded as the denial of a certain supervenience thesis. The supervenience thesis is to the effect that, for any transworld identity, there must be something (other than that identity) in virtue of which the identity holds. Alternatively, the supervenience thesis may be stated as follows: if x in w1 is identical

---

[35] Van Inwagen (1985) insists that there is no 'problem of transworld identity', and that Plantinga has exposed as baseless the reasons that have been given for supposing that there is one. But van Inwagen does not discuss arguments such as those presented in this chapter.

with y in w2, where w1 and w2 are distinct possible worlds (one of which may be the actual world), then there must be something other than that identity in virtue of which the identity holds. Moreover (apparently in contrast with the case of identity over time) it appears that the facts that are available to ground the identity between x and y across the worlds must be restricted to facts about the properties that x has in w1 and the properties that y has in w2, rather than including any irreducible causal or spatio-temporal relations between x in w1 and y in w2.[36] It therefore follows that, if the supervenience thesis is true, then, if x in w1 is identical with y in w2 in virtue of these properties (and resulting similarities and dissimilarities), *any* object z, in any possible world w3, that has in w3 exactly the same properties as y has in w2 is identical with x. The denial of this supervenience thesis, then, involves the acceptance of the claim that there can be two possible worlds, w2 and w3, that differ only in that one of them contains an individual identical with x in w1, and the other contains an exactly similar individual that is not identical with x in w1.

Is this thesis of bare identities the same as the thesis that there can be a difference in transworld identities that does not supervene on any qualitative difference? The thesis that there *can* be such non-qualitative differences—that there can be a difference in 'thisness' across possible worlds that is not underpinned by a difference in 'suchness'—is sometimes referred to as 'haecceitism'.[37]

---

[36] This obviously follows if distinct possible worlds are causally and spatially isolated from one another, as on David Lewis's conception of possible worlds. It is less obvious that this restriction must hold on a conception of possible worlds as abstract objects, such as possible states of affairs, but I shall assume, for simplicity, that this is so. An obvious question arises about those theories according to which identity across possible worlds is, in a sense, reduced to identity over time (such as the theory presented in Brody 1980, for example). For according to such a theory, it seems that the identity of Socrates in any possible world with the actual Socrates may, in a sense, consist in the holding of the same causal and spatial relations over time as constitute the identity of Socrates over time in the actual world. However, on further reflection it appears that this is not so: not, at least, unless the other possible world and the actual world are being thought of as *literally* including the same course of events up to a certain time. If they are not, then the 'branching' conception involved in the idea of reducing identity over time to identity across possible worlds requires transworld identities (holding between individuals in the portion before the 'branch point') that will themselves need to be grounded. Cf. Appendix B to this chapter; also Lewis's distinction between 'branching' and 'divergence' of worlds (1986*a*: 206 ff.).

[37] See Adams 1979 and Lewis 1986*a*, ch. 4. For the terminology of 'thisness' and 'suchness', see Adams 1979. (Lewis's characterization of 'haecceitism' is not couched in terms of identity across possible worlds. Nevertheless, my notion of haecceitism and

The question whether the bare identities thesis is equivalent to haecceitism (in this sense of 'haecceitism') is not straightforward. However, on the face of it, as I explain below, it appears that one might *accept* haecceitism: the view that there can be differences in transworld identity that do not supervene on qualitative differences, while *denying* that there can be bare identities (thus holding that for every difference in transworld identities, there is *some* further difference, albeit not necessarily a qualitative difference, upon which it supervenes). In contrast, it appears that anyone who accepts the thesis of bare identities must also accept haecceitism.

To clarify this issue, we need to consider what the *denial* of the bare identities thesis allows us to include in the supervenience base for facts about a given difference in transworld identities: in particular, whether we are always permitted to include facts about the identities of *other* individuals. It may appear that, if the 'No Bare Identities' supervenience thesis applies quite generally, it must apply to the identities of these other individuals, and to any identities on which the identities of these other individuals supervene, and so on. The consequence appears to be that, unless an infinite regress is postulated, the denial of the bare identities thesis implies that every transworld identity must supervene, ultimately, on facts that do not include identity facts, and hence that (unless an infinite regress is postulated) the denial of bare identities implies the denial of haecceitism, contrary to the suggestion of the previous paragraph.

Nevertheless, there are two reasons for suggesting that haecceitism does not, strictly speaking, entail the thesis of bare identities, although the latter entails the former. First, perhaps one could coherently accept haecceitism, while holding that there may indeed be an infinite regress in which identity facts across possible worlds always depend, in part, on further identity facts. Secondly, things are complicated by the fact that someone may assert, as does Graeme Forbes, that the identities on

Lewis's are, I think, very substantially the same.) As I have mentioned earlier, despite its name, 'haecceitism' in this sense is *not* the same as (and does not entail) a commitment to 'haecceities' in the sense described in Sect. 2.2 above. To believe that an object has a 'haecceity' in the sense described in Sect. 2.2 is to believe that it has some unanalysable non-qualitative property that *underpins or constitutes* its being the object that it is. But the claim that there can be differences in identities that are not underpinned by qualitative differences does not require the belief that there are such non-qualitative identity-constituting properties. For example, I might believe in 'haecceitistic' differences in identities that are not constituted by anything else at all, not even by differences in non-qualitative 'haecceities'. (On this point, see also Lewis 1986*a*: 225.)

which transworld identities may supervene can include identities that may be, in a sense, taken for granted, without offending against the bare identities principle. Forbes appeals to a conception of possible worlds as 'branching', in the sense of actually *sharing* a common initial segment (Forbes 1985, ch. 6, sect. 6). If two possible worlds literally share such a segment, they will, obviously, share any individuals that exist in that common segment. Thus, Forbes argues, if w1 and w2 are two such worlds with an overlapping common segment, it may be that a difference between the identities of two individuals in the later portions of w1 and w2 depends on their relations to distinct individuals that exist in the common segment. But the question 'what does the distinctness of those shared individuals consist in?' need not be construed as a question about transworld identity, and hence does not fall within the scope of Forbes's 'No Bare Identities' principle (which is a principle about transworld identity). Furthermore, unless Forbes is committed to an 'intra-world' version of the Identity of Indiscernibles, he need not even appeal to a qualitative difference between the individuals in the shared segment to justify the claim that these individuals are numerically distinct.

Because of the 'shared segment' possibility and the 'infinite regress' possibility, I shall not take the denial of the thesis of bare identities to imply that *every* transworld identity must hold (ultimately) in virtue of facts that do not themselves include identity facts. This means that the 'bare identities' thesis is not quite the same as, and is not, strictly speaking, entailed by, a commitment to 'haecceitism' as characterized above.

To sum up. One supervenience thesis is that when all the qualitative facts about a possible world are settled, the identity facts about that world are also settled. In other words, this supervenience thesis says that the supervenience base for a given identity cannot *ultimately* appeal to identity facts about other individuals, but must ultimately appeal to qualitative differences. We may take haecceitism to be the denial of this supervenience thesis. Another supervenience thesis says that any transworld identity must supervene on facts other than that identity, although these facts may always include facts about the identities of other individuals. According to the denial of this supervenience thesis, there can be two possible worlds that differ only in the identities of two individuals *A* and *B*, even if there are neither qualitative facts *nor* identity facts about other individuals that ground this non-identity. We may take the thesis of 'bare identities' to be the denial of this second supervenience thesis. If the argument of this section is correct, although the supervenience theses are closely related, and the 'anti-haecceitist' supervenience thesis entails the 'anti-bare-identities' supervenience thesis, one might in principle accept the second supervenience thesis while rejecting the first, and hence be a haecceitist who rejects bare identities.

2.14. APPENDIX B: ADAMS'S INDISCERNIBILITY ARGUMENT

The structure of the reasoning I have employed in my 'indiscernibility argument' concerning Socrates and Plato is very similar to that famously used by Adams in his (1979). However, in Adams's hands, the argument has a further twist. For Adams strengthens the case for there being two individuals that do not differ in their essential properties by taking two individuals (his two globes) that are already qualitatively indiscernible. Given their qualitative indiscernibility, they are, of course, not distinguished from one another even by their qualitative accidental properties; a fortiori, they could not be distinguished from one another by qualitative essential properties. This is not to say that there is no *non*-qualitative distinction between them. Since they are two, they must be at different spatial locations. But I take it that we are to assume that these spatial locations cannot be distinguished from one another in qualitative terms. And presumably this means that even if we were to say that it is being at *that* particular spatial location that is essential to one of the globes' being the globe that it is and not the other, we would still be left with a 'haecceitistic' difference between two possible worlds—a difference in 'thisness' that is not founded in a difference in 'suchness', to use Adams's terms—even if this is a difference in the identities of the spatial locations of the globes rather than a 'bare' difference in the identities of the globes themselves. (There is, of course, the additional point that it seems implausible to say that the spatial location of either globe is essential to it, and hence implausible to suggest that this non-qualitative difference could represent an essential difference.)

If Adams's argument is accepted, it seems that we have a clear case of a haecceitistic difference.[38] Given the characterization of the globes, there

---

[38] We also appear to have a clear case of 'bare identities': if not a 'bare difference' between the identities of the globes themselves, then a 'bare difference' between their spatial locations. On the distinction between 'bare identities' and 'haecceitistic differences', see the previous section.

appears to be *nothing* that could serve as their distinctive qualitative essences. Nevertheless, it may be questioned whether Adams's argument gives us a *general* reason for supposing that things do not have (non-trivial) individual essences. First, Adams's argument does not, of course, show that there are no cases where identities are preserved by such individual essences. And there are some fairly uncontroversial cases where unique essences are plausible: for example, the number five. So it might be open to someone to claim that the denial of individual essences is not plausible for, say, human beings, or plants or animals, even if it is plausible for Adams's globes.[39]

Secondly, Graeme Forbes has argued that Adams's argument can be reconciled with the denial of bare identities by supposing that we can make sense of Adams's two possibilities only by seeing them as possible extensions of a world in which the globes are *already* distinguished, albeit not qualitatively (Forbes 1985: 148–52). As indicated in the previous section, Forbes holds that if a possible world is actually an *extension* of the actual world, the demand for a grounding for identities can sometimes be met without an appeal to uniquely distinguishing essential properties. Although there are difficulties with Forbes's response (see Mills 1991), it is sufficiently plausible to make one wonder whether Adams's argument, just by itself, can be generalized to support a more comprehensive advocacy of 'bare' identities.

---

[39] However, it seems plausible that Adams's indiscernibility argument can be generalized to apply to any kind of individual such that it is possible for an individual of that kind to have a qualitative duplicate; arguably, this includes such individuals as humans, plants, and animals.

3

Origin Properties and Individual Essences

In response to the identity puzzles discussed in the previous chapter, Graeme Forbes has argued that many 'ordinary' individuals, including animals and plants, may plausibly be assigned individual essences. If Forbes were right about this, the view would be an attractive one. It would allow us to construe *de re* modal claims about such individuals in terms of identity across possible worlds, while allowing that their identities are always grounded in other properties, thus avoiding any commitment to paradoxical 'bare' differences in identities across possible worlds. In this chapter, I shall argue that Forbes's proposal is unsuccessful. More generally, the problems that undermine Forbes's proposal are sufficient to show that no variant of his proposal is likely to succeed. I conclude that the claim that ordinary persisting things have non-trivial individual essences, properties that are non-trivially sufficient for their being the entities that they are in all possible worlds, is untenable.

3.1. REDUPLICATION AND MULTIPLE OCCUPANCY: THE CASE OF THE OAK TREE

As an introduction to Forbes's proposal, I shall present an outline of his own version of the 'reduplication argument' of the previous chapter. (I have changed a few details, and added others, but the crucial points are unaffected.)[1] We begin with the supposition that there was, in the actual world, an acorn a1, planted in a particular spot, p1, at some time (let us say, in 1900), and that a1 grew into an oak tree, O1, which is still

---

[1] See Forbes 1985: 138–45. See also Forbes 1980, 1986, 2002. The correspondence between my labelling of these worlds and Forbes's own labelling in his (1985) is as follows: w1: Forbes's w*; w2: Forbes's w; w3: Forbes's v; w4: Forbes's u.

growing there in 2004. (We are to assume that the oak is not identical with the acorn from which it grew.) Suppose now that someone thinks that in addition to the actual world (w1) there are two possible worlds, in the first of which, w2, the oak tree O1 grows from a different acorn, a2, but in the same place, p1, and in the second of which, w3, that same oak O1 grows from the same acorn a1 but in a different place, p2 (see Figure 3.1). Suppose also that nothing about the characteristics that O1 has in w2 and w3 prevents the construction of a possible world w4 in which there are two oak trees, O2 and O3, where O2 has a history that is in an intuitive sense just like the history that O1 has in w2, and O3 has a history that is in the same sense a replica of the history that O1 has in w3. (By an appropriate choice of w2 and w3, the respects in which the 'replica' trees in w4 simulate their originals may include their growing from numerically same acorns (a2 and a1) as their originals in w2 and w3, and being composed of the very same matter at all times as those originals.)

The problem posed by the construction of the possible world w4 is this. We cannot say that both O2 and O3 are identical with the actual tree O1. It follows that we must suppose that there are some features relevant to identity that have not been transferred from w2 and w3 to the 'reduplication world' w4. However, we can suppose this only if we deny one or other of Forbes's two principles about transworld identity

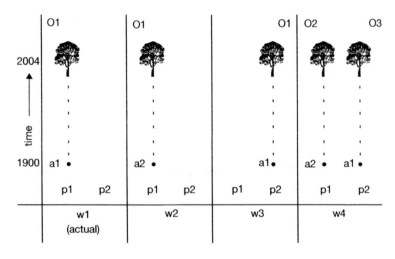

Figure 3.1

and distinctness described in Section 2.7 above: the 'No Bare Identities Principle' and the 'No Extrinsic Determination Principle'. If we think that transworld identity and distinctness can be 'bare', we can say that the feature relevant to identity that has not been reduplicated in w4 is simply identity itself. We could say that O2 is a different tree from O1 in w2, or that O3 is a different tree from O1 in w3, although in each case there is no *further* difference upon which the difference in identities could be supposed to depend. (In fact, it would be natural for the bare identity theorist to suggest that there are three sorts of possible world that have the features attributed to the reduplication world w4, which differ only in that in some O1 occupies p1, in others O1 occupies p2, and in yet others O1 does not occupy either place.)

Alternatively, we could retain Forbes's first principle, but argue that there is a further relevant difference between each of O2 and O3 and its replica in w2 or w3 on which a difference of identity could supervene: O2 has a property that O1 in w2 lacks, namely *being in the presence of another oak tree growing some distance away at p2*; similarly, there is a difference between the history of O3 in w4 and the history that O1 has in w3, in virtue of the presence of an extra oak tree in w4. But this proposal involves a violation of Forbes's second principle about transworld identity. The properties that are being appealed to are not intrinsic features of these trees; hence, according to Forbes's second principle, they cannot legitimately be invoked as relevant to the identity question. We can also note that the appeal to these properties as relevant would seem to be motivated solely by the thought that in w4 there is *competition* for identity with O1.

What happens if we make neither of these responses to the reduplication problem? The upshot is, evidently, that to accept Forbes's two principles, yet claim that there are possible worlds w2 and w3 of the kind that we have described, is to be guilty of outright contradiction: one must concede that the (intrinsic) characteristics that the trees have in w2 and w3 are sufficient to make them the actual tree, and yet also not sufficient, because of the possibility of reduplication.

The moral that Forbes draws from the argument is that we must count certain properties of the oak tree's actual origin as essential to its identity, and his preferred candidate for this origin property is that of *originating from the acorn a1 and no other* (1985: 138–40 and 144). On this view there is no such world as w2, and its elimination disposes of this particular example of the reduplication problem. But it is obvious that no conclusion specifically about origin can possibly be the *immediate* implication of the argument that Forbes gives. All that one needs to do, to avoid the possibility of reduplication, while accepting Forbes's principles about identity, is to assign to the tree *some* essential property that is 'unshareable' in the sense explained in Section 2.8. Nothing in the logic of the argument requires that this property have anything to do with the beginning of the tree's existence.[2] Such an unshareable property might, for example, concern the exact location of the tree at some precise moment in 1950, long after its original planting. Evidently, such a proposal would conflict with the intuition that it is not an essential property of an individual such as a tree that it *continue* in existence for any significant length of time. So it is quite true that, if we undertake to assign unshareable essential properties to things such as trees, we shall, *given other assumptions about possibility and identity*, be driven to make use of features of the way those things originated. However, obvious though this may be, this step in Forbes's argument for the necessity of origin should be made explicit.

The reduplication argument is thus, at most, an indirect argument for the necessity of origin. What is more, it only serves, even indirectly, to support that thesis if features of a thing's origin can play a non-redundant role in the assignment to it of an unshareable essential property. Suppose that it is possible for twin oak trees to grow from the single acorn a1. Then we cannot guarantee that there will be no reduplication world simply by legislating that every sufficient condition for being the oak tree O1 must include the property of originating from the acorn a1. If we are to pursue Forbes's strategy we shall (given the possibility of twins) have to find some intrinsic property of the oak tree's actual origin that distinguishes it from one or other—or, perhaps more plausibly, from both—of the possible twins that its acorn might have produced.

Finally, we can note that the materials used to generate Forbes's reduplication problem can be adapted for the construction of a 'multiple occupancy' problem involving oak trees, as depicted in Figure 3.2.[3] Suppose that w4 were actual; suppose also that someone suggests that there is a possible world (call it 'w5'), in which O2 has a history that is intrinsically just like the history of the tree in our original world w1. If this person also suggests that it is possible for O3 to have had a history like this (as represented by w6), then we should have (in w5 and w6)

---

[2] A point acknowledged in Forbes 2002. Cf. Mackie 1987: 186; Yablo 1988; Robertson 1998: 741, and Mackie 1998: 64–5.

[3] For the 'multiple occupancy problem', see Sect. 2.8 above.

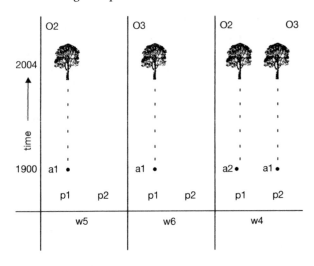

Figure 3.2

what purport to be two possible worlds that differ only in that they contain different trees.

One who believes that there can be bare identities need have no qualms about this. The holder of Forbes's view, however, will say that there is no such world as w5: the fact that O2 and O3 come from different acorns in w4 provides them with what I have called (in the previous chapter) 'incompatible essential properties'. Finally, someone who wants to employ an 'extrinsic determination' solution to this problem will presumably say that if we consider any possible oak tree with the kind of history envisaged for the trees in w5 and w6, then either O2 will be a better candidate for identification with that tree than O3 is, or O3 will be a better candidate than O2 is, or they will be equally good candidates, in which case neither will 'win'. Hence the proponent of the 'extrinsic determination' solution will deny the possibility of at least one, if not both, of the alleged worlds w5 and w6.

3.2. INDIVIDUAL ESSENCES FOR BIOLOGICAL THINGS AND ARTEFACTS

Generalizing from the reduplication argument concerning the oak tree, Forbes makes the proposal that biological things can, in general, be assigned individual essences (and hence what I referred to, in Section 2.9, as 'distinctive essential properties') in terms of the identities of their biological antecedents, and the sort to which they belong.[4] Forbes introduces the expression '*x* is a propagule of *y*' to represent the relation that holds between one biological entity and another when the first is one of the entities that (immediately) generated, or developed into, the second (1985: 133). (I say 'immediately', because Forbes treats the relation as intransitive.) He gives, as examples, that the acorn is the propagule of the oak tree; the sperm and egg are the propagules of the zygote; the zygote is the propagule of the human being that develops from it. Using this terminology, Forbes's view can now be stated as the thesis that every biological thing that has propagules has its own individual essence, consisting in (1) coming from exactly the propagules from which it actually came and (2) being of some particular sort (an oak tree, for example, or, perhaps, a tree).[5]

On the face of it, it is an advantage of Forbes's proposal that it appears to cohere with intuitions that many people already have (or can be prompted to have) about the necessity of origin for biological things. In fact, Forbes suggests that Kripke's thesis of the necessity of origin for biological organisms (which many people find intuitively appealing) may be seen as a consequence of the stronger thesis that there are unique features of the origin of a thing that contribute to its *individual essence*.[6]

---

[4] Forbes 1985, ch. 6; also Forbes 1980, 1986, 1994, 1997, 2002.

[5] e.g., Forbes 1985: 145–6. An apparent difficulty for Forbes's proposal is that the property of *coming from a certain propagule* appears to be a relational property, and hence not an intrinsic property, in at least one sense of 'intrinsic property'. This raises the question whether Forbes's proposal for the individual essences for biological things is consistent with his own second principle about transworld identity: his 'No Extrinsic Determination Principle'. However, I shall not explore the question (discussed, e.g., in Forbes 1986 and Forbes 2002) whether there is an appropriate sense of 'intrinsic property' according to which such relational properties can count as intrinsic. Even if Forbes can dismiss this problem, I shall argue that his theory confronts problems that are much more serious.

[6] Kripke's necessity of origin thesis, as he states it in his (1980), does not by itself involve the commitment to the view that *unique* features (let alone *necessarily* unique features) of an organism's origin are essential to its identity. For example, although he claims that the Queen could not have come from a sperm and egg other than those that produced her, he does not claim that his argument depends on her being the *only* individual that actually developed from that sperm and egg. However, the 'sufficiency argument' suggested by Kripke in support of a necessity of origin thesis (in 1980: 114, note 56) does appear to require that some of the essential features of a thing's origin also be unique (and indeed necessarily unique) features. For further discussion, see Ch. 6 below.

However, if Forbes's proposal is to fill the bill, it had better be the case that each biological entity really does have its very own set of 'propagules' that distinguishes it from every other entity of the same sort. The question immediately arises as to what to say about identical (monovular) twins that are generated from the same zygote, the cell formed by the fusion of the sperm and egg. Each twin will have to have some propagule that the other does not share: these will have to be the two daughter cells into which the zygote splits in the process of producing twins.[7]

We may seem to have solved this problem. But in fact, the example involves a biological phenomenon—the *division* of one thing into two or more things—that creates a difficulty for Forbes's project. If the identities of biological things such as trees or animals cannot be bare, then neither can the identities of their propagules. But at some point we shall come to propagules that are generated by the division of one thing into two or more things, as in the case of the division of a single cell into two cells. (Spermatozoa are produced by cell division, for example.) And it will simply not be true that there were two things *before* the division, and that one cell came from one of these, and one from the other. So if Forbes is to say that each propagule has its own individual essence, his account must become more complex, the most obvious move being to count the particular *matter* from which each of the daughter cells in our example came as essential to that cell's identity (cf. Forbes 1997: 521–2). But even someone attracted to Forbes's initial proposal (that the identity of an individual such as an animal depends essentially on the identity of the cells—such as the sperm and egg—from which it came) may be reluctant to accept that the identity of those cells (and hence of the resulting individual) depends essentially on the identity of the matter of which those cells were originally composed.[8]

This is not the only difficulty that besets the attempt to find plausible candidates for the individual essences of biological things in terms of features of their origins, as we shall see in the following sections. And there is a further question about Forbes's project. Are we to apply Forbes's theory of individual essences to persisting things other than biological

[7] See, e.g., Forbes 2002: 338, note 11.

[8] e.g., Colin McGinn has explicitly combined a necessity of origin thesis for biological entities that implies that a human being essentially comes from the particular sperm and egg that produced it with the claim that biological entities are not essentially composed of their original matter (McGinn 1976: 133, note 5).

individuals: in particular, to artefacts? There seem to be two powerful reasons why, if Forbes's proposal is genuinely acceptable for biological individuals, it should also apply to artefacts. First, Forbes's proposal is based principally on the allegedly unsatisfactory consequences that result from a failure to attribute individual essences to biological things (in particular, the consequential need to accept either bare identity or extrinsically determined identity). But if it turns out that artefacts can get away with lacking individual essences, why should the same not be true of biological things? Secondly, as I have shown, part of the case for Forbes's theory of individual essences for biological things rests on its apparent ability to explain the intuitive plausibility of Kripke's necessity of origin thesis. But a necessity of origin thesis has been found plausible for artefacts too: many have agreed with Kripke that it seems essential to a particular table that it be originally composed of the particular matter from which it was in fact originally composed, for example (cf. Kripke 1980: 113–15). Yet if the intuitive plausibility of a necessity of origin thesis for artefacts is to be explained without supposing that artefacts have *individual essences* that include distinctive features of their origins, this threatens to undermine part of the support for Forbes's proposal to attribute individual essences to biological things.

Forbes's own position on the application of the 'individual essence' thesis to artefacts is not entirely clear. In his earlier work (1985), he suggests that, because of the severe difficulty of finding suitable candidates for the individual essences of artefacts, we should adopt counterpart theory for the interpretation of *de re* modal claims concerning artefacts (thus avoiding the need to attribute individual essences to them). However, in a recent contribution to the debate (2002), he suggests that there is a general necessity of origin principle that applies to what he calls 'composite objects', including both biological things and artefacts, and that this principle can be supported by the type of argument (the need to provide grounding for identities) that was discussed above. But this 'grounding argument' is an argument for nothing less than *individual essences.*[9]

Since the proposal that both biological things and artefacts have individual essences that involve their origin properties is of interest in its own right, in what follows I shall examine this stronger thesis. As we shall see, although the problems encountered by this thesis when applied to the case of artefacts may be more severe, the difficulties in the case of biological things are not negligible. Indeed, one of these difficulties (the

---

[9] As emphasized in Mackie 2002, responding to Forbes 2002.

'recycling problem') has apparently led Forbes himself to depart, in his recent work, from his official doctrine of individual essences.[10]

3.3. WEAKLY UNSHAREABLE PROPERTIES, STRONGLY UNSHAREABLE PROPERTIES, AND THE LOGIC OF INDIVIDUAL ESSENCES

If there is a property (or set of properties, but I'll assume from now on that a set of properties can be treated as a single conjunctive property) that constitutes a non-trivial individual essence of an individual A, it must, by definition, be a property the possession of which is both necessary and sufficient for identity with A in any possible world. To perform this role, a property that is a non-trivial individual essence must have (*inter alia*) the following characteristics. First, it must be a property that is unshareable in the sense (explained in the previous chapter) that it cannot be possessed by two distinct individuals within a single possible world. (I shall refer to this as the 'weak' sense of 'unshareability'.) Secondly, it must be a property that is unshareable in the stronger sense that it cannot be possessed by two distinct individuals at all, either within the same world or in different worlds. For example, if E1 is A's individual essence, then no object distinct from A can possess E1 (even as an accidental property) in any possible world. Moreover, it follows from this second requirement (strong unshareability) that any two properties that are individual essences of distinct individuals must be properties that are incompatible, in the sense that no object can have both properties within a single possible world. It follows, of course, that if two properties E1 and E2 are both incompatible and essential to each of two distinct individuals, then they must also be incompatible in the further sense that if x has E1 in one possible world, x cannot have E2 in any possible world (cf. Section 2.10 above).

In addition, it follows, evidently, from the principle that every individual has an individual essence, that there cannot be two individuals that differ only in their accidental properties. There must always be, in addition to any merely accidental differences between them, an essential difference as well.[11]

---

[10] This is argued in Mackie 2002. See also Sect. 3.4 below.

[11] This is a consequence of the thesis that *everything* has an individual essence. The consequences of the thesis that all things of certain kinds: for example, all biological things, have individual essences are less extreme, but still very demanding.

These logical requirements on a property that is fit to serve as an individual essence are extremely demanding. I do not believe that, in the case of persisting individuals such as persons, animals, plants, or artefacts, there are any properties that satisfy these logical desiderata and are also plausible candidates for being (non-trivial) essential properties.[12] Indeed, I do not think there are any plausible candidates for properties that even pass the test of being both unshareable in the weak sense (unshareable within a world) and also (non-trivially) essential to individuals such as these. Not, of course, that there is any technical difficulty in finding, for every such individual, some property that it possesses that is unshareable in the weak sense. Every object, or at any rate, every object that traces a unique path through space and time, has many such properties. The difficulty is in finding candidates for unshareable properties that can also plausibly be regarded as *essential* to the things that have them. To elaborate: every ordinary persisting thing (for example, every animal, plant, or artefact) has, as a matter of fact, many features that uniquely distinguish it from every other (actual) individual. (Assume that even if the Identity of Indiscernibles is not a necessary truth, it has no actual counterexamples.) But if we consider the properties that in fact uniquely distinguish an actual individual from all other actual individuals, we find that the vast majority of these properties are ones that it is quite implausible to regard as essential rather than accidental. As for the remainder, on close inspection, we typically find that the uniquely distinguishing property is not, strictly speaking unshareable, even in the weak sense. For example, many have found it plausible to say that the property of coming from a particular zygote (or sperm and egg) is an essential property of a particular human individual. But even if this property is actually unshared, it is not unshareable, given the possibility that that zygote should have divided to produce identical twins. But the more we refine the uniquely distinguishing properties, in an attempt to supply properties that are genuinely unshareable (even in the weak sense), the less plausible becomes the claim that such properties are essential properties.[13] In sum: there are relatively few uniquely distinguishing properties of individuals that can with any

[12] Of course, the qualification (introduced in Sect. 2.2 above) that what is under investigation is whether things have *non-trivial* individual essences is still in force.

[13] This is the case, e.g., if, in order to deal with the problem of identical twins, we suppose (following Forbes) that it is essential to an untwinned human being that it came *immediately* from its zygote, rather than coming from one of a pair of daughter cells produced by the mitotic division of that zygote in a twinning process.

plausibility be regarded as essential properties. And if we restrict our attention to those that can plausibly be regarded as essential properties, we find that they do *not* appear to be genuinely unshareable, even in the weak sense, let alone the strong sense.

The problem of finding suitable candidates for the role of individual essences for ordinary persisting things is reinforced by two problems: the 'recycling problem' and the 'tolerance problem'. The recycling problem reinforces the difficulty of finding plausible candidates for essential properties that are also unshareable in the weak sense. The 'tolerance problem' reinforces the difficulty of finding plausible candidates for the essential properties of individuals that are also unshareable in the strong sense.

3.4. THE RECYCLING PROBLEM

A version of the recycling problem can be described as follows.[14] We are considering the suggestion that it is an unshareable essential property of a biological individual A, such as an animal, that it is generated (immediately) from a particular zygote $Z1$, and that this prevents the construction of 'reduplication problems' involving A. However, for consistency, $Z1$ itself must also have some unshareable essential property. Perhaps we could try to supply this by appealing to the fact that $Z1$ is a zygote originally composed of a certain particular piece of matter M with certain other properties S that are not themselves unshareable (for example, certain genetic properties that could in principle be instantiated in different matter). But even if it is plausible to regard this origin property (*being a zygote originally composed of M, with properties S*) as essential to the identity of $Z1$, there seems to be no barrier, in principle, to the 'recycling' of M so that, at a later time, it comes to constitute a second zygote $Z2$ that also has S. Assuming that $Z2$ and $Z1$ are numerically distinct, this shows that *being a zygote originally composed of M, with properties S*, even if it is an essential property, is not a genuinely unshareable property after all. Moreover, even if, in the actual world, the matter of $Z1$ is not so recycled, there will be a possible world in which such recycling takes place. But such a world presents us with a reduplication problem of the type that the

---

[14] The recycling problem is emphasized, in particular, by McKay (1986). See also Robertson 1998. It is discussed by Forbes in his (2002), and also in Forbes 1997.

postulation of (weakly) unshareable essential properties is designed to avoid (see Section 2.8 above). For unless we postulate a suitable further essential property of Z1—for example, that Z1 is not the product of recycling—we must allow that there are some possible worlds in which Z1 is the first in a recycling sequence, and some in which it is the second, and so on.[15,16]

The recycling problem arises even more naturally in the case of artefacts. The possibility of the recycling of matter shows that *being originally composed of a certain parcel of matter according to a certain plan* does not, strictly speaking, represent a weakly unshareable property of any particular artefact, even if it is legitimate to regard it as an essential property of that artefact.[17] So unless some further essential property can be invoked to distinguish two artefacts that come into existence at different times with the same original matter and plan, we face the possibility of 'reduplication worlds' for a given artefact in which two candidates for identification with a single artefact come into existence at different positions in a recycling sequence.[18]

Clearly, if, in the face of the recycling problem, we are still determined to attribute an unshareable essential property to an entity such as a zygote, we must find some further property which, when included

---

[15] Note that it is pointless to try to avoid this problem by claiming that Z1 and Z2 are numerically identical: that is, that Z2 is merely a reconstituted Z1, reappearing after an interval. For this would merely invite the problem that in that case the property of *originating (immediately: i.e., not via a biological twinning process involving the division of Z1) from Z1* is not an unshareable property, and hence will not serve to supply a biological individual that comes from Z1 with an unshareable essential property. For suppose that Z2 produces (immediately) an individual *B* distinct from the individual *A* that was previously generated (immediately) from Z1. It will be undeniable that *these* individuals (*A* and *B*) are numerically distinct if (as is obviously perfectly possible) *B* comes into existence while *A* still exists. Yet if Z1 = Z2, both *A* and *B* originate immediately (in the relevant sense), although at different times, from Z1.

[16] It is the reduplication problem that is most obviously pressing if we start by considering a zygote Z1 whose matter is not in fact recycled in the way described, but could have been. This is important, since it shows that even if the possibility of recycling of the problematic kind is a recherché possibility—one that is perhaps never realized—the fact that it is possible at all represents a serious obstacle to the attempt to find individual essences for things like zygotes. However, if we consider a world in which recycling *does* actually take place, then we can see that recycling can generate an example of the multiple occupancy problem.

[17] Cf. Salmon 1979, sect. III, and Salmon 1982, Appendix 1, sect. 27. The problem is, of course, reminiscent of, and related to, the traditional 'Ship of Theseus' problem concerning identity over time. The adaptation of the problem to the modal case should probably be credited to Hugh Chandler (1975).

[18] See note 16 above.

in the zygote's essence, will transform its essence into an unshareable property. The most obvious move is to add to the property of *being a zygote originally composed of M, with properties S*, as essential to the zygote Z1's identity, some further property concerning Z1's exact time of origin, or Z1's position in a recycling sequence. However, the suggestion that the *exact* time at which a zygote or any similar entity came into existence is an essential property of that individual is so implausible that no one, as far as I know, has seriously suggested this as a response to the problem.[19] It has been seriously suggested, and with rather more plausibility, that the position of an object in a 'recycling sequence' may be regarded as one of its essential properties (Forbes 2002). This proposal is also known as 'predecessor essentialism'. (Of course, if it is to do the work required of it, predecessor essentialism must be taken to imply that in the normal case, where there is just one zygote, and no recycling, this zygote's having no predecessor is one of its essential properties.) However, even its chief proponent, Graeme Forbes, has recently admitted that predecessor essentialism has some consequences that he appears to regard as sufficiently counterintuitive to warrant its rejection.[20] But he does not supply, in its place, an alternative that provides an answer to the recycling problem while preserving the attribution of individual essences.[21]

3.5. THE TOLERANCE PROBLEM AND THE 'FOUR WORLDS PARADOX'

There is a further problem with the attempt to attribute, to ordinary persisting things, individual essences that concern their origins. The difficulty arises from the fact that, in the case of at least some persisting things—in particular, artefacts—we have a very strong intuition that it is not essential to the thing's identity that it have been originally composed of *all* of its original matter, even if we think that it couldn't have been originally composed of entirely different matter, and even

---

[19] In his (2002) Forbes does not even mention this as a possible response to the problem.

[20] The counterintuitive consequences of predecessor essentialism are emphasized by Hawthorne and Gendler (2000). Forbes appears to accept that these consequences render predecessor essentialism unacceptable in Forbes 2002: 333–4.

[21] This is argued in Mackie 2002: 347–8.

if we think that it had to be composed of *most* of its actual original matter. If we respect this intuition of (modal) 'tolerance' in the original constitution of an artefact, then, for example, we must not say that if a ship s1 was originally composed entirely from some portion of matter M1, it is an essential property of s1 that it was originally composed of *precisely* M1, for we concede that s1's original matter could have been slightly different. And this means that *being a ship originating from all of M1* is not a candidate for an essential property of s1; a fortiori, it is not a candidate for an unshareable essential property of s1.[22] Still, on the face of it, it seems that we could provide s1 with an unshareable essential property by holding that it is essential to s1 that it be a ship originally composed of *most* of M1, since (if we ignore the recycling problem)[23] this is also an unshareable property (in the weak sense).

However, it can easily be shown that although this may provide the ship s1 with a weakly unshareable essential property (if we ignore the recycling problem), it does not do so in a way that provides a barrier to bare identities and bare differences, and does not do so in a way that provides an individual essence for the ship. The reason for this is that it is not plausible to regard this property as unshareable in the stronger of the two senses characterized in Section 3.3 above. That is, it is not plausible to suppose that if s1 was originally composed of most of M1, there is no ship *distinct* from s1 that has, in some other possible world, the property of being originally composed of most of M1.

This is easily shown.[24] To simplify, suppose that the ship s1 is constructed from just three parts, A1, B1, and C1—each of these constituting one third of its original matter M1. (If this seems intolerably unrealistic, note that this simplification is inessential to the structure of the argument, which would work if we took M1 to consist of, say, 100 planks or other pieces of matter in a certain arrangement. Alternatively, we could change the example to one that involves a bicycle rather than a

---

[22] Given the recycling problem, it seems that the property is not, strictly speaking, unshareable either. But let us ignore the recycling problem for the moment: the difficulty now being considered is that even if the property *were* unshareable, it would still not be plausible to regard it as essential.

[23] Alternatively, we might suppose that, in response to the recycling problem, we have attributed to the ship s1, as essential to its identity, some further origin property, such as its precise time of origin, or its position in a recycling sequence, that has the right logical characteristics to provide it with an essential property that is genuinely unshareable. The important point is that even if we can produce a genuinely unshareable essential property by this manoeuvre, the tolerance problem still arises.

[24] Cf. Salmon 1979, sect. IV, and Salmon 1982, Appendix 1, sect. 28.

s1: A1 + B1 + C1	s2: A1 + B2 + C2	s3: A1 + B2 + C1
w1 (actual)	w2	w3

Figure 3.3

ship, where A1 is the frame, and B1 and C1 are the two wheels.) In w1, s1 is originally composed of A1 + B1 + C1 (see Figure 3.3). Suppose that we allow that s1 could instead have been originally composed of a combination of any *two* of A1, B1, and C1 together with a substitute third element. Call this concession 'the tolerance principle'. But let us suppose that, in an attempt to provide s1 with a weakly unshareable essential property, we also say that it is an essential property of s1 that it is originally composed of *at least* two out of A1, B1, and C1. Call this 'the restriction principle'. Suppose, now, that there is a possible world w2, containing a ship s2 originally composed of A1 + B2 + C2, where B2 ≠ B1, and C2 ≠ C1. There is no apparent reason why there should not be such a world, and, indeed, nothing to prevent its being the case that in this world the ship s2 is qualitatively identical with s1 as it is in w1 in all relevant respects, in spite of the fact that its original composition includes some numerically different parts. Nevertheless, according to the restriction principle, the ship s2 in w2 cannot be identical with the ship s1. So far, so good. But now consider a further possible world w3, containing a ship s3 originally composed of A1 + B2 + C1. On the face of it, there is no reason to deny that s3 represents a way that s1 could have been. For s3 in w3 shares two thirds of its original parts with s1 in w1, and we may suppose (if this is relevant) that it is otherwise qualitatively identical with s1 (as s1 is in w1). But equally, there appears to be no reason to deny that s3 represents a way that s2 could have been. For s3 in w3 also shares two thirds of its original parts with s2 in w2, and we may suppose that it is otherwise qualitatively identical with s2 (as s2 is in w2). But obviously this creates a difficulty for anyone who wants to appeal to essential properties in order to avoid bare identities. The ship s3 satisfies conditions prima facie sufficient for identity with s1, yet s3 also satisfies conditions prima facie sufficient for identity with s2. But on pain of contradiction, we cannot say that s3 is identical with both s1 and s2, since s1 and s2 are agreed to be distinct. Hence we must deny that s3 satisfies both *genuinely* sufficient conditions for being s1 and also *genuinely* sufficient conditions for being s2.

One response is to recognize *two* worlds like w3, one of which contains s1 with the original composition A1 + B2 + C1, and the other of which contains (the distinct ship) s2 with that same original composition. But this is to embrace a 'bare' difference between the identities of ships across possible worlds. If, instead, we say that there is just one possible world like w3, but that the ship (s3) in it is identical with just one of s1 and s2, and not with the other, we also appear to take on a commitment to a kind of bare (ungrounded) identity or distinctness.[25] For in virtue of what could s3 be identical with s1 rather than s2? Or with s2 rather than s1? We have set up the example in such a way that the relations between s3 and s1, on the one hand, and between s3 and s2, on the other, are exactly parallel. Perhaps, then, s3 is identical with *neither* s1 *nor* s2? But why not? What stops s3 from representing a way that each of s1 and s2 could have been? The conclusion appears to be that we must either admit bare identities, or suppose that our tolerance principle is too tolerant: that we were, after all, too generous in supposing that a ship could have been originally composed of most (rather than all) of the matter of which it was in fact originally composed. To avoid bare identities, it seems that we must attribute to a ship an 'intolerant' essence involving its original material composition, contradicting our initial, and overwhelmingly natural, assumption of tolerance.

The argument just rehearsed is a version of the 'Four Worlds Paradox' discussed by Nathan Salmon (1982, Appendix 1, sect. 28; also 1979, sect. IV). There are four worlds—rather than just three—if we suppose that there are two qualitatively indiscernible worlds corresponding to world w3, one of which contains s1, and the other of which contains s2.[26]

---

[25] Albeit of a rather different kind from the 'bare identities' that have been the focus of my discussion up to now.

[26] This argument may also be reminiscent of Chisholm's Paradox (to be discussed in the next section). Unlike Chisholm's Paradox, however, this argument does not have the form of a *sorites* (*pace* Forbes 1985, ch. 7: 164–5). The unattractive conclusion that is generated by the argument presently under discussion is that to avoid bare identities we must suppose that ships have intolerant essences. But the argument for this conclusion does not rely on the fact that a succession of small changes can add up to a big change, which is characteristic of *sorites* arguments.

Could one react to this argument by suggesting that what it shows is not that we were too *lenient* in our initial verdict about the essential origin properties of the ship, but rather that we were too strict? (That is, that it is the restriction principle, not the tolerance principle, that we should abandon?) It is easy to show that, from the point of view of the opponent of bare identities, to adopt this view is to move from the frying pan to the fire. Suppose we replace our original restriction principle with the weaker restriction principle that a ship could not have existed without being originally composed of *some* of its original matter. The difficulty is that (even if we ignore the recycling problem) *being a ship originally composed of some of matter M1* is obviously not an unshareable property (even in the weak sense of a property that cannot be possessed by two individuals within a possible world). But to abandon the attribution to the ship of a weakly unshareable essential property is immediately to invite versions of the reduplication problem. For example, both of the following are consistent with this weaker version of the restriction principle: (i) in some possible world w4, s1 is originally composed of $A1 + B2 + C2$ (instead of $A1 + B1 + C1$); (ii) in some possible world w5, s1 is originally composed of $A2 + B1 + C3$ (instead of $A1 + B1 + C1$), where $A2 \neq A1$, $B2 \neq B1$, $C2 \neq C1$, $C3 \neq C1$, and $C3 \neq C2$. But now consider a possible world w6 containing two ships, one (*sx*) originally composed of $A1 + B2 + C2$, and the other (*sy*) originally composed of $A2 + B1 + C3$ (see Figure 3.4). Evidently the construction of w6 (in which features of both w4 and w5 have been reproduced) generates an instance of the reduplication problem—precisely the problem that the appeal to unshareable essential properties (such as *being essentially originally composed of at least two of $A1 + B1 + C1$*) was designed to avoid.

s1: A1 + B1 + C1	s1: A1 + B2 + C2	s1: A2 + B1 + C3	sx: A1 + B2 + C2 sy: A2 + B1 + C3
w1 (actual)	w4	w5	w6

Figure 3.4

One significant moral to be drawn from the 'tolerance' problem is that the attribution of essential properties that are unshareable in the weak sense is not enough to guard against bare identities. Even though the attribution of weakly unshareable essential properties rules out reduplication worlds, it need not rule out some examples of what I earlier called 'multiple occupancy' worlds: worlds that contain a single individual that satisfies conditions prima facie sufficient for identity with each of two distinct individuals. To rule out *all* such worlds we must not only attribute to objects essential properties that are unshareable in the weak sense, but also attribute, to pairs of objects (even pairs of objects that are in distinct worlds) incompatible essential properties. The problem demonstrated by the example illustrated in Figure 3.3 is that the property *being a ship originally composed of most of A1 + B1 + C1*, although unshareable in the weak sense,[27] is not *incompatible* with the property *being a ship originally composed of most of A1 + B2 + C2*. (For example, if a ship, such as s3 in w3, is composed of A1 + B2 + C1, then of course it has both properties.) It follows that if we wish to say that any two ships are distinguished from one another by their own peculiar individual essences, weakly unshareable properties like these cannot serve as their individual essences.

It is true that the multiple occupancy problem here generated is unlike the example of, say, Berkeley and Hume of Chapter 2, or the oak trees of Section 3.1 above, in that it does not *immediately* involve the danger that two distinct objects that exist *in the same possible world* will attempt to 'identify themselves' with a single object in another. In my example, the two distinct individuals that are candidates for identification with the ship in w3 are a ship in one possible world that has the property of *being originally composed of A1 + B1 + C1* and a ship in a different possible world that has the property of *being originally composed of A1 + B2 + C2* (see Figure 3.3). Given that these ships have one original part (A1) in common, it is obvious that (in the absence of recycling) there is no possible world in which these two ships coexist with exactly these properties. But as long as there can be two distinct ships in *distinct* possible worlds, one of which has the first property, and the other of which has the second, we appear to have a version of the multiple occupancy problem none the less.

[27] Setting aside the recycling problem, of course.

3.6. CHISHOLM'S PARADOX

If essences are 'tolerant', this also leads to another well-known problem: 'Chisholm's Paradox'.[28] The paradox may be illustrated by adapting the argument of the previous section. If the ship s1 is originally composed in w1 of $A1 + B1 + C1$, and s1 could have been originally composed of any two of these parts with a substitute for the third, then s1 could have been originally composed of $A1 + B1 + C2$, where $C2 \neq C1$. So let us suppose a possible world wn in which s1 has this different original composition (see Figure 3.5). But now, if s1 *had* been originally composed of $A1 + B1 + C2$, surely (by parity of reasoning) it would then have been possible for s1 to have been originally composed, instead (say, in another world $w(n + 1)$), of any two of *those* parts plus a substitute for the third: for example, of $A1 + B2 + C2$, where $B2 \neq B1$. Again, if s1 had been composed of $A1 + B2 + C2$, then it could have been composed (in world $w(n + 2)$) of $A2 + B2 + C2$, where $A2 \neq A1$.

There are now (at least) two problems. First, even by the time we get to $w(n + 1)$ we appear to be committed to the claim that if s1 could have had just two thirds of its original parts, then it could have had just one third of those parts. As David Lewis puts it in discussing a version of the problem, the argument leads 'to the conclusion that [the thing's] essence must be twice as tolerant as we had initially assumed' (1986*a*: 245). Secondly, once we get as far as world $w(n + 2)$, we have an additional problem. For, assuming that no matter is *shared* by any of the parts in

s1: $A1 + B1 + C1$	s1: $A1 + B1 + C2$	s1: $A1 + B2 + C2$	s1: $A2 + B2 + C2$
w1 (actual)	wn	$w(n + 1)$	$w(n + 2)$

Figure 3.5

[28] See Chisholm 1967, and, for discussion, Forbes 1985, ch. 7; Lewis 1986*a*: 243–8. See also Salmon 1982, Appendix I, sect. 28.

question, it seems that A2 + B2 + C2 might be exactly the same as the original composition of some ship, s4, in w1 that is distinct from s1. (s1 and s4 could, of course, exist simultaneously in w1.) But this threatens to generate a case of 'bare identity'. For it now seems that we can postulate two worlds like w(n + 2), that differ only in that in one of them it is s1 that has the original composition A2 + B2 + C2, and in the other of which it is the distinct ship s4 that has this original composition.

Chisholm's Paradox has the form of a *sorites* paradox. For this reason, it is not clear that it can be taken as a satisfactory *argument* for bare identities, even though it obviously has a commitment to bare identities as a consequence.[29] If there is a way of blocking a standard *sorites* argument in order to avoid conclusions such as the conclusion that a man with a million hairs on his head is bald, then one would expect there to be a way of blocking the argument of Chisholm's Paradox in order to avoid the conclusion that an artefact could have been originally composed of less than half—or indeed none at all—of its original matter.[30] If, however, there is no way of avoiding the conclusion of Chisholm's Paradox, then it looks as if one must accept that it is at least possibly possible that s1, in our example, should have been composed of less than half of its original matter, and possibly possibly possible that s1 should have been composed of none of its original matter at all.

A suggestion that has been championed by Nathan Salmon (1982), following Hugh Chandler (1976), is that in these cases a non-transitive accessibility relation between possible worlds can come to the rescue. Salmon's suggestion, applied to my most recent example of the ship, is that the invocation of a non-transitive accessibility relation can solve the paradox by making palatable after all the conclusions (i) that there are possible worlds in which s1 begins its existence with few or none of its actual original parts, and (ii) that there are two possible worlds that differ only in that one of them contains s1 and the other contains s4.[31] The idea is that although w(n + 2) is possible relative to w(n + 1), w(n + 1) to wn, and wn to the original world w1, we need not say that either w(n + 2) or w(n + 1) is possible relative to w1. There are worlds (such as w(n + 2) and w(n + 1)) in which s1 exists and has an

---

[29] Chisholm himself does not take the paradox (which in his version concerns human beings, rather than artefacts) as an argument for bare identities.

[30] In his (1985), Forbes argues that to block the *sorites* in the case of Chisholm's Paradox we should adopt counterpart theory. In his (1997), he suggests that this is not the only serious option.

[31] Cf. Salmon 1982, Appendix 1, sect. 28.3.

original composition very different from its actual original composition. But these worlds are 'isolated' from actuality (from the original world w1) in a sense that makes them *impossible* relative to w1, although they are possibly (or possibly possibly) possible.[32]

Whether Salmon's suggestion provides an adequate solution to the problem may be questioned.[33] However, it is important to note that even if Salmon's proposal is accepted, it does not amount to a denial of bare identities, but rather to a proposal that bare identities may be acceptable on certain conditions. The same is true if Salmon's suggestion is applied (as Salmon suggests that it should be) to the Four Worlds Paradox mentioned in the previous section. Salmon's proposal, applied to that case, is that the suggestion that there are two worlds like w3 (see Figure 3.3), that differ only in that in one of them the ship originally constructed from A1 + B2 + C1 is s1, and in the other the ship originally constructed from A1 + B2 + C1 is s2, can be made more palatable if we say that the first of these worlds is accessible from (possible relative to) w1, but not accessible from w2, and the second of these worlds is accessible from (possible relative to) w2, but not from w1. Again, though, even if Salmon is right in thinking that such 'bare identities' are made more palatable by the invocation of a non-transitive accessibility relation,[34] the proposal still amounts to an admission that there can be 'bare identities'.

3.7. COUNTERPART THEORY AND THE ESSENCES OF ARTEFACTS

In his (1985), Forbes concludes that the 'tolerance' of the essences of individuals such as artefacts means that to artefacts (unlike biological

---

[32] Salmon's solution to Chisholm's Paradox has to deal with two implausibilities. One is that there are worlds that differ only in the identities of the ships that they contain (a standard case of 'bare identity'). The other is the implausibility (quite independently of any duplication problems) of identifying a ship in one world with a ship in another world that shares few or none of its original parts. It should be noted that a proponent of bare identities is not automatically committed to the second of these implausible claims (that there is a world in which the ship is originally composed of little or none of its original matter) although of course, to avoid this commitment, some other solution to Chisholm's Paradox must be found.

[33] Has been questioned, by David Lewis (1986*a*: 246–7).

[34] It seems that the accessibility relation will have to be non-transitive to achieve the desired 'isolation' of words. There is no reason to deny that w2 is accessible from w1. But if w2 is accessible from w1, and the world in which s2 comes from A1 + B2 + C1 is accessible from w2 (which there is also no reason to deny), then, unless transitivity fails, the world in which s2 comes from A1 + B2 + C1 will be accessible from w1.

organisms) we should not attribute individual essences in order to avoid bare identities. (In reaching this conclusion, Forbes relies on a *sorites* argument that is a version of Chisholm's Paradox, rather than the 'Four Worlds' type of argument described in Section 3.5 above. Hence Forbes is particularly concerned to deal with what appears to be vagueness in transworld identities as well as the generation of bare identities (1985, ch. 7).) According to Forbes, the way to avoid bare identities in the case of individuals with 'tolerant essences' is to interpret *de re* modal claims about such individuals in terms of counterpart theory rather than transworld identity. (These counterpart relations are still grounded, but they do not have to obey the logic of identity.) However, this appears to be a larger concession than Forbes explicitly admits. First, if it is the case that wherever there are tolerant essences, we must resort to counterpart theory, the class of individuals to which we should attribute individual essences in the strict sense may shrink dramatically. For example, it may plausibly be argued that Forbes is committed to the view that the essences of biological things are also to some extent 'tolerant'.[35] Secondly, and more important, if it is *coherent* to give a counterpart theoretic interpretation of *de re* modal claims involving ships, why not do so in the case of all persisting individuals (including plants and animals), thus avoiding the commitment to individual essences? Forbes's response to this in his (1985) is as follows:

[I]t may be asked why, having set up the counterpart-theoretic generalization of the standard framework, we do not apply it to entities of every category whose members come from other entities in some suitable sense. A short reply to this is that for e.g. . . . the products of biological growth, there is no tolerance principle analogous to (T) [the principle that an artefact could have originated from a slightly different collection of parts]. (1985: 189–90)

However, this seems an unsatisfactory reply. Even if Forbes is right in thinking that there is no similar tolerance principle concerning the origin of a biological organism (a claim that is disputable), we have seen that there are nevertheless grave problems, of a different kind, for the attempt to find plausible individual essences for biological things,

---

[35] If one adopts a general principle that where a thing's original material composition enters into its essence, its essence will be to some extent 'tolerant' (because it is too much to demand that its *exact* original material composition is part of its essence), then, according to Forbes's account of the essences of zygotes (see, e.g., Sect. 3.4 above), the essences of at least some zygotes must be tolerant. But if the essences of zygotes are tolerant, the essences of individuals whose identities depend essentially on the identities of those zygotes must be (indirectly) tolerant too.

thus attempting to respect the logic of identity while also ensuring that all *de re* possibilities for biological things are appropriately 'grounded'. Evidently, counterpart theory could come to the rescue here too, if it can in the case of artefacts. Why not let it do so? But if counterpart theory is satisfactory as a general theory of *de re* modality, the search for the elusive candidates to play the role of individual essences for biological things may safely be abandoned.

3.8. CONCLUDING REMARKS

The conclusion of this lengthy discussion is this. I have explored, I think exhaustively, the attempt to discover, in the features of the origin of an individual such as an organism or an artefact, distinctive features that have the right logical characteristics to serve as non-trivial individual essences for those individuals while also satisfying the requirement of being plausibly regarded as essential properties of those individuals. My verdict is that the difficulties we have encountered show that the attempt to find such individual essences is doomed to failure. Yet if no distinctive features of the origins of these individuals will satisfy these two requirements, it is clear that no distinctive features of their subsequent histories will do so, given our strong intuitions about the contingency of the continued existence of such individuals. I conclude that, if we are to regard such an individual as preserving its identity in different possible situations or worlds, then we must reject the seductive thought that its identity can be underwritten by an individual essence that supplies conditions that are non-trivially sufficient for its identity: for its being the individual that it is and no other.

4

Extrinsically Determined Identity and 'Best-candidate' Theories

4.1. TAKING STOCK

I have argued that the attempt to provide individual essences for ordinary things in order to avoid 'bare identities' is unsuccessful.[1] At least, it is unsuccessful if what we seek is an attribution of individual essences that does not clash with our intuitions about the essential properties of these individuals. (If we were to drop this requirement of intuitive plausibility, the task would, of course, become a very easy one. But it would be bizarre to adopt a counterintuitive theory of individual essences simply in order to avoid counterintuitive consequences concerning bare identities.) Moreover, as I pointed out in Chapter 3, there appears to be a potential instability in the attempt to find individual essences for ordinary things. If it is conceded—as by Graeme Forbes it appears to be—that there are *some* ordinary things for which suitable individual essences cannot be found, but where we can preserve the coherence of *de re* modal judgements, without accepting bare identities, by interpreting those judgements in terms of counterpart theory, it is unclear why counterpart theory should not be adopted, across the board, as the solution to the problem.

If I am right in thinking that the problem cannot be solved by an appeal to individual essences, how should we respond? Evidently, one reaction—the one that I myself prefer—is to bite the bullet, and accept bare identities. Another (to be discussed in the next chapter) is to abandon the interpretation of *de re* modality in terms of identity across possible worlds in favour of counterpart theory. However, the form of the argument that I have adopted from Forbes suggests that there is

---

[1] Of course, I continue to use 'individual essence' as short for 'non-trivial ("substantial") individual essence', as explained in Sect. 2.2 above.

another possible reaction: a compromise by which the interpretation of *de re* modality in terms of identity may be retained, but which avoids 'bare identities' by taking a liberal view of the facts that may be relevant to a transworld identity. This is the idea that transworld identity can be 'extrinsically determined' (see Section 2.11 above). This option may seem particularly attractive to those who are already committed to a 'best-candidate' account of identity over time. Unfortunately, as I shall show in this chapter, even if the corresponding account of identity over time may successfully be defended, the 'extrinsic determination' solution to the bare identities problem about transworld identity is unsuccessful. I conclude that anyone who wishes to avoid both bare identities and individual essences, without abandoning *de re* modality entirely, must adopt counterpart theory.

4.2. EXTRINSICALLY DETERMINED IDENTITY

Given the structure of the reduplication and multiple occupancy problems discussed in the previous chapters, it seems that one option open to someone who wants to avoid both the attribution of individual essences and the admission of bare identities, while avoiding counterpart theory, is to hold that transworld identities and non-identities can depend on the presence or absence of 'competing candidates' for identity. For example, in the case of the reduplication problem involving Forbes's oak tree, discussed in Section 3.1 above, a non-identity between O1 in w2 and O2 in w4 need not be ungrounded, for it can be grounded in the fact that in w4 there is an extra oak tree; alternatively, a non-identity between O1 in w3 and O3 in w4 could be so grounded. In the case of the 'multiple occupancy' problem involving the trees, a non-identity between O2 in w4 and a tree with the intrinsic features of the trees in w5 and w6 could be grounded in the fact that, in addition to being similar to O2 in w4, this tree also shares significant characteristics with another tree, O3, in w4; the same could be said, *mutatis mutandis*, to justify the non-identification of a tree that has the intrinsic features of the trees in w5 and w6 with O3 in w4.[2]

However, I shall argue that it is a mistake to suppose that an appeal to extrinsically grounded identities can provide a satisfactory general solution to the reduplication and multiple occupancy problems that

[2] See Sect. 3.1 above. See also Figures 3.1 and 3.2.

is a rival to the 'bare identities' solution. There are several reasons for this conclusion. But the most telling point is that the 'extrinsic determination' solution cannot coherently be worked out without its reintroducing a version of the bare identities thesis that it was designed to avoid.

4.3. COUNTERINTUITIVE CONSEQUENCES

The first problem is that to regard these identities as 'extrinsically determined' is to embrace some extremely counterintuitive consequences. If the extrinsic determination theory is applied to the reduplication problem involving the oak tree (Figure 3.1 in the previous chapter), its defender has to deny one or other of the following counterfactuals:

C1. If it is true that O1 could have been exactly as it is in w2, it is true that O1 could have been as it is in w2 except for being accompanied by a tree like O3.

C2. If it is true that O1 could have been exactly as it is in w3, it is true that O1 could have been as it is in w3 except for being accompanied by a tree like O2.

To deny either of these counterfactuals seems highly counterintuitive. It seems quite wrong to say that the mere existence of an extra tree could make such a difference to the possibilities that are available to O1. And if the extrinsic determination theory is applied to the multiple occupancy problem involving the oak trees (Figure 3.2 in the previous chapter), the consequences are no better. It seems that the 'extrinsic determination theorist' must say something like the following about the trees in w4 (with w4 considered as actual): 'If the tree O2 had *not* been accompanied by O3, it would then have been possible for O2 to have existed with a different origin from its actual origin, and to have been like the tree in w5. But as things are, this is not possible. Since O2 is accompanied by O3, it could not have had a different origin from its actual origin.'

It is instructive to compare the 'extrinsically determined identity' response to our modal puzzles with the 'best-candidate' account of identity over time on which it is modelled. In response to various puzzle cases concerning identity, some philosophers have advocated a 'best-candidate' account of identity over time, according to which whether an individual *A* existing at time *t* is identical with an individual

B at time (*t* + 1) may depend on what individuals other than *B* exist
at time (*t* + 1).[3] For example, suppose that an object *A* splits into two
halves, both of which seem to be equally good candidates for identity
with it. According to a best-candidate theorist, we may say that in this
case (represented by w7 in Figure 4.1) neither of the competing halves
is identical with *A*. Nevertheless, according to the theorist, in a case in
which *A* splits as before, yet some accident befalls one of the halves (*C*)
that puts that 'candidate' out of the competition, the other half may be
identical with *A* (as in w8 in Figure 4.1). (In a case that is a favourite
in the literature on personal identity, w7 and w8 might represent two
split-brain transplant operations performed on *A*, in one of which the
operation is a complete success, while in the other the operation is a
success except for the fact that the right half of the brain is injured in
the course of the operation.)

This verdict commits the best-candidate theorist to some modal
consequences that might be thought objectionable. For example, the
best-candidate theorist has to deny the following conditional:

C3. If it is true that *B* could have been as it is in w7, it is true that
    B could have been as it is in w7 even if the right-hand half had
    suffered an accident like the one *C* suffers in w8.

(According to the theorist, *A* in w7 is not identical with *B*, yet *A* in w8 is
identical with *D*; hence, by the transitivity and necessity of identity, we
cannot identify *B* with *D*. Nor can we identify *B* with any left-hand half
that results from the division of *A* and is (like *D*) similar to *B* except for

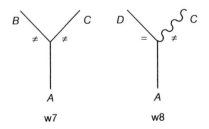

w7   w8

Figure 4.1

[3] See, e.g., Nozick 1981: 27–70; Parfit 1984, Part 3, esp. ch. 12; Shoemaker 1984, chs. 12–13.

lacking a rival.)[4] For similar reasons, the best-candidate theorist must deny the following conditional:

C4. If it is true that A could have been as it is in w8 (i.e., continuing in existence as the left half), it is true that A could have been as it is in w8 even if the right half had suffered no accident.

In denying these conditionals, the best-candidate theorist of identity over time seems committed to some form of 'extrinsic determination' of transworld identity. For example, in an intuitive sense B and D may share all their intrinsic features after the division, and all their intrinsic relations to A as it was before the division, but the theorist says that they are distinct objects, because of the 'extrinsic' fact that in w7 the right-hand half bears certain relations to A as it was before the division.[5]

This discussion shows that although this best-candidate theory is a theory of identity over time, not a theory of identity across possible worlds, it has certain modal consequences, and, indeed, certain consequences about how transworld identities can be determined.[6] Moreover, it might be thought that these modal consequences (e.g., the denial of the counterfactuals C3 and C4) are not significantly different from the modal consequences (the denial of C1 or C2) that led to my rejection of the extrinsic determination solution to Forbes's puzzle of the oak tree.

This issue is disputable.[7] However, as I have argued elsewhere (Mackie 1989), the standard examples where a best-candidate theory of identity over time is attractive may be distinguished from the cases where a 'best-candidate' theory of identity across possible worlds would be relevant by the fact that in the former, but not the latter, the rival

---

[4] As the preceding sentences indicate, it is a mistake to think that the best-candidate theorist is committed to the denial of the necessity of identity. For amplification of this point, see Gale 1984, Shoemaker 1984, ch. 12, and Noonan 1985*a*.

[5] The fact that the theory must deny conditionals like C3 and C4 seems to be closely related to Noonan's ground for criticizing best-candidate theories of transtemporal identity in Noonan 1985*b*.

[6] The best-candidate theory of identity over time cannot be regarded as a theory of transworld identity, since no theory of identity *over time* tells us that A in w7 is to be identified with A in w8. All that a theory of transtemporal identity can tell us is that *if* we identify the subjects of the division in w7 and w8 as some same object, A, the identification has certain consequences for what is, and is not, also identical with A in those worlds.

[7] For more discussion, see Garrett 1988 and Mackie 1989.

candidates for identity are causally connected with one another. For example, in the standard 'split-brain' example, the separated left and right hemispheres of the brain are indirectly causally connected with one another via their individual causal connections with the whole brain before the division. By contrast, there need be no causal connection, however indirect, between the two trees in w4 that are (allegedly) rivals for identity with O1.[8]

However, even if this difference concerning causal connection is not regarded as relevant, there is an important difference between a best-candidate theory of identity over time and a best-candidate theory of identity across possible worlds. This difference is founded on the fact that possible worlds are not ordered in the way that instants of time are.

4.4. AVOIDING INCOHERENCE

In its simplest form, a best-candidate theory of transworld identity would apparently involve principles like the following: for any possible worlds wx and wy, any object A in wx, and any object B in wy, B in wy is identical with A in wx if and only if (i) B in wy is a sufficiently good candidate for identity with A; (ii) B is the best candidate in wy for identity with A, and (iii) there is no object C in wx distinct from A such that B is at least as good a candidate for identity with C as it is for identity with A. However, this simple account has logically disastrous consequences.

For example, going back to the worlds w1–w4 (in Figure 3.1), it is an assumption of the discussion that the best-candidate theorist of transworld identity says that the tree at p1 in w2 satisfies the conditions for identity with O1 in w1, and so does the tree at p2 in (the distinct world) w3. Yet the best-candidate theorist can have no legitimate reason for denying that O2 in w4 satisfies the 'best-candidate' conditions for identity with the tree at p1 in w2, or for denying that O3 in w4 satisfies these conditions for identity with the tree at p2 in w3. But if so, then, given the transitivity of identity, our best-candidate theorist is committed to a contradiction: at least one of O2 and O3 both is and is not identical with O1.

The simple version of the best-candidate theory of transworld identity is incoherent; hence no one should accept it, whether or not that

---

[8] I ignore, as irrelevant, the fact that O2 and O3 will exert some gravitational attraction on one another in w4.

person holds a best-candidate theory of identity over time. However, perhaps the best-candidate theory of transworld identity can take a more sophisticated form. For the theorist can, apparently, preserve the transitivity of identity by denying the transitivity of the accessibility relation between possible worlds.[9] Instead of adopting the principles of the simple theory, which imply that a single world w4 can be the subject of 'best-candidate' comparisons with all of w1, w2, and w3, with the disastrous result that w4 turns out to contain trees with contradictory identities, the theorist may say, instead, that although there is a world *like* w4, which is possible relative to w2, in which O1 occupies p1, and a world *like* w4, possible relative to w3, in which O1 occupies p2, it is not the case that both of these worlds are possible relative to w1, although both w2 and w3 are possible relative to w1. By making the accessibility relation non-transitive, the logic of identity can be respected. However, it is respected only at the price of introducing (at least) two worlds like w4, which differ only in the identities of the trees they contain and in their accessibility relations to other worlds.[10] But this reintroduces a version of the bare identities thesis: the very thesis that the appeal to extrinsically determined identity was designed to avoid. So the apparent advantage of the extrinsic determination theory over the bare identities account is lost. I think that this point is sufficient to show that the extrinsic determination theory does not represent a satisfactory alternative to the bare identities thesis.

4.5. IDENTITY OVER TIME AND IDENTITY ACROSS POSSIBLE WORLDS

For comparison, it is helpful to consider how the best-candidate theorist of identity over time avoids a conflict with the logic of identity. Why does the theorist not face possibilities like the following: of the objects around in the year 2000, z is the best candidate for identity with an object x existing in 1998, and of the objects existing in 1999, y is the best candidate for identity with x in 1998, yet z is not a sufficiently good candidate for identity with y to be regarded as continuing y in existence?

---

[9] Cf. Sect. 3.6 above.

[10] By contrast, the 'standard' bare identities solution would say that there are several worlds like w4, differing only in the identities of the trees they contain, and that each of these worlds is accessible from (possible relative to) all of w1, w2, and w3. Nevertheless, bare identities with a non-transitive accessibility relation are still bare identities.

If such a situation could occur, it would seem that the best-candidate theorist of transtemporal identity could not respect both the symmetry and the transitivity of identity.

It seems undeniable that situations that threaten to exhibit this structure can occur, and they have been discussed in the literature.[11] An example is provided by a case where an object divides into two halves, both of which are reasonably good candidates for identity with it, but one much better than the other; if the inferior half survives for longer than the superior it may apparently become the best candidate for identity with the original after the extinction of its rival. In spite of this, best-candidate theorists of identity over time can avoid a conflict with the logic of identity by appealing to the way in which actual states of affairs are ordered in a temporal sequence, and holding that verdicts about identity over time are not to be based on a direct comparison between states of affairs at times that are remote from one another. In deciding whether an object z in 2000 is the 'best candidate' for identity with an object x in 1998, we do not directly compare the states of affairs in 2000 and 1998; rather, we ask whether there is a chain of *links* of the 'best candidate' relation leading back from z in 2000 to x in 1998.

There is certainly an analogy between the way in which the best-candidate theorist of transtemporal identity manages to respect the logic of identity and the way in which the sophisticated best-candidate theorist of transworld identity does so. The sophisticated transworld theory says that we are not to impose the 'best candidate' comparison on worlds that are inaccessible to one another, whereas the transtemporal theory says that we are not to impose the 'best candidate' comparison on states of affairs that are at times remote from one another.[12] However, although there is a formal analogy here, this is not enough to establish that someone who adopts the transtemporal best-candidate theory should accept the transworld best-candidate theory. It is undeniable that (if we accept the existence of states of affairs) we must accept that the temporal order generates a non-transitive relation of proximity in time between actual states of affairs. But obviously, it does not follow that, if we accept the existence of possible worlds, we must also accept that there is a non-transitive accessibility relation between possible worlds of the kind

[11] See the discussion of the 'branch-line' case in sects. 75 and 97 of Parfit 1984, and the discussion of a similar case in Nozick 1981: 43–7.

[12] The transtemporal theorist may even be committed to saying that there can be two actual states of affairs that differ from one another only in the identities of the objects that they contain and in their distance in time from other states of affairs.

required by the sophisticated best-candidate theory. So a best-candidate theorist of identity over time is fully entitled to reject the idea that there is such a non-transitive accessibility relation between possible worlds, and thus to reject the best-candidate theory of transworld identity in the only form in which it has any chance of being coherent.

4.6. CONCLUDING REMARKS

To sum up the results of the preceding sections: there are at least two problems for the best-candidate (extrinsic determination) theory of transworld identity, considered as a rival to the other responses to the puzzles of transworld identity. First, the best-candidate account is committed to implausible (I would say grossly implausible) verdicts about the kinds of factor that determine whether a certain object could have had a certain history (Section 4.3). Secondly (even if we ignore this problem of implausibility), the best-candidate theory of transworld identity can avoid a conflict with the logic of identity only by reintroducing a version of the bare identities thesis that it promised to avoid (Section 4.4). In addition, it is not even true that someone who adopts a best-candidate theory of identity over time thereby undertakes any obligation to adopt a best-candidate theory of transworld identity (Section 4.5).

We can add a final nail in the coffin of the best-candidate theory. It is significant that the extrinsic determination (or best-candidate) account is applicable only to transworld identity puzzles that involve at least one possible world that contains *two* candidates for identity with a single individual in another world. But there are puzzles that threaten to produce bare identities that are not of this form: for example, my version of the 'Four Worlds Paradox' in Section 3.5 above, in which the problem involved two ships in *different* worlds both of which were candidates for identification with a single ship in another world. If there are puzzles of this form, we must conclude that the 'extrinsic determination' proposal is not equipped to provide a solution to the full range of the relevant puzzles, even if we ignore the other difficulties rehearsed above.

I conclude that anyone who is tempted by the extrinsic determination or best-candidate solution would be better off trying to avoid bare identities by adopting, in the place of transworld identity, a counterpart theory of *de re* modality.

5

Counterpart Theory and the Puzzles of Transworld Identity

Given the results of the previous chapter, our options are narrowed even further. Unless we accept a counterintuitive version of the theory of individual essences (of which the extreme 'Leibnizian' theory of individual essences referred to in Section 2.2 would be an example), then, if we are to preserve *de re* modality, we must either accept bare identities, or adopt counterpart theory as our interpretation of *de re* modal claims. In this chapter, I briefly consider the 'counterpart theory' option.

5.1. COUNTERPART THEORY AND CONCEPTIONS OF POSSIBLE WORLDS

Since its introduction by David Lewis,[1] counterpart theory has been subjected to a barrage of criticisms. I shall not attempt to evaluate these criticisms here, although I shall assume that they do not refute the theory. I shall also assume, however, that counterpart theory has its most natural home in David Lewis's concrete realist theory of modality. If one accepts Lewis's realism, then the claim that ordinary individuals are 'world-bound' (confined to one possible world) is extremely natural, perhaps almost inescapable, and thus, for a Lewisian realist, counterpart theory appears to be the only obvious alternative to Leibnizian 'hyper-essentialism' about ordinary individuals.[2] Of course, it does not follow that the thesis that ordinary individuals are 'world-bound' must be unacceptable to someone who is not a Lewisian realist about

---

[1] Lewis 1968. Lewis responds to criticisms in his 'Postscripts to "Counterpart Theory and Quantified Modal Logic"' (Lewis 1983: 39–46), and in Lewis 1986*a*.

[2] See Lewis 1986*a*, ch. 4, sects. 2–3.

worlds. However, I shall assume that, although counterpart theory may be in principle available, as an alternative to transworld identity, to those who do not accept Lewis's version of realism about possible worlds, its adoption by someone who is not a Lewisian realist is not a natural option. I shall assume (perhaps controversially) that, for the non-Lewisian, the principal, if not the only, reason for adopting counterpart theory would be that the transworld identity puzzles lead one to despair of being able to give a satisfactory interpretation of *de re* modal statements in terms of identity across possible worlds.[3]

The evaluation of Lewis's version of modal realism is far too large a topic for this book. I shall confine myself to the question whether, for someone who does *not* accept Lewis's realism, the puzzles about transworld identity that we have considered provide compelling reasons for adopting counterpart theory. I shall suggest that they do not.

It may, perhaps, be questioned whether the non-Lewisian theorist can legitimately adopt counterpart theory at all. Suppose that we accept that there are possible worlds, but that they are merely abstract objects, such as possible states of affairs. Suppose, for example, that we accept an analysis of discourse about possible worlds of the type advocated by Plantinga, according to which for an individual to exist with certain properties in some possible world is simply for it to be true that, had that possible world (maximal state of affairs) obtained, that individual would have existed with those properties. For example, for Napoleon to be tall in some possible world is simply for it to be true that if that possible world had obtained, Napoleon would have been tall. (And if he had been tall, then, obviously, he would have existed.)[4] If we accept such analyses as these, it is not obvious that we can even make sense of the idea that the 'truth-maker' for the *de re* modal statement 'Napoleon might have been tall' could be the existence of a tall *counterpart* of Napoleon who is not identical with Napoleon. For what could the characteristics of such a counterpart have to do with the truth conditions of the modal statement, under the interpretation suggested above?[5] However, in what follows I

<hr/>

[3] Stalnaker (1986) proposes a combination of counterpart-theoretic semantics with a metaphysics that involves identity across possible worlds. However, a principal motivation for Stalnaker's adoption of the counterpart-theoretic semantics appears to be the existence of 'transworld identity' puzzles of the kind discussed in Chs. 2 and 3 above.

[4] Plantinga 1974; cf. van Inwagen 1985.

[5] Lewis's counterpart theory has been criticized on the grounds that it makes the truth of *de re* modal claims depend on the characteristics of individuals that are not identical with the individuals that those *de re* modal claims are about. If this is taken to be an *ad*

shall set this worry aside.[6] I shall argue that even if the non-Lewisian can make sense of the idea that *de re* modality is to be interpreted in terms of counterpart theory (and the non-Lewisian can give sense to the idea that *de re* modal claims about actual individuals may be made true by the existence of counterparts of those individuals in other possible worlds), there are difficulties with the counterpart-theoretic solution to our transworld identity puzzles that cast doubt on its attractiveness as a rival to the bare identities solution, at least for someone not committed to the acceptance of counterpart theory on other grounds.

5.2. COUNTERPART THEORY AND THE LOGIC OF IDENTITY

If counterpart theory is to solve the reduplication and multiple occupancy problems, it seems that this can only be for one of three reasons: that (in the case of a certain kind of individual) either

(a) the counterpart relation, unlike identity, can be 'bare', or

(b) the counterpart relation, unlike identity, can be 'extrinsically determined', or

(c) the counterpart relation lacks some of the formal properties of identity.

I shall consider these possibilities in turn, referring to the reduplication problem of Chapter 3 concerning the oak tree, but relabelling the trees in the worlds w1–w4 'A', 'B', 'C', and so on, to reflect the fact that the trees in w2 and w3 are now to be counterparts of the tree in w1, rather than being identical with it (see Figure 5.1). Strictly speaking, the acorns and places should also be relabelled; I ignore this for simplicity.

On the face of it, the first proposal, (a), does not seem to be a serious option. If, just by itself, it is supposed to solve the problem, it must rely

hominem criticism of Lewis, then it seems problematic (cf. Lewis 1986*a*, ch. 4; although see also Rosen 1990: 349–54). However, it appears more plausible to say that there is something suspect about the attempt to add, to a non-Lewisian theory of possible worlds, the idea that a Napoleon-counterpart could be relevant to the truth of a *de re* modal claim concerning Napoleon.

[6] In particular, I shall not attempt to discuss the arguments in Stalnaker 1986, mentioned in note 3 above.

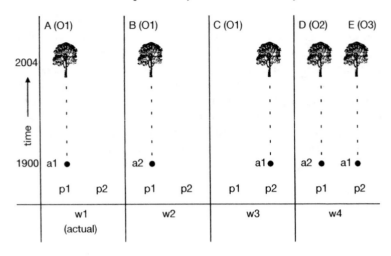

Figure 5.1

on the postulation of a counterpart relation that preserves as many of the logical properties of identity as it can without collapsing into identity, yet can be bare where identity (allegedly) cannot be. But it is hard to see what anyone could suppose to be the advantage of this manoeuvre. (It would not be acceptable to Forbes (see 1985: 188) nor, apparently, to Lewis.)[7]

Proposal (b), however, may look more promising. If we consider a counterpart relation that is like David Lewis's in that it makes the question whether a tree in w4 is a counterpart of some object *O* in another possible world depend on whether that tree is more like *O* than is any other object in w4, we can see how the presence of another tree in w4 could make a difference. However, this account of the counterpart relation would give us no reason to think that D in w4 is not a counterpart of the tree (B) in w2, or that E in w4 is not a counterpart of the tree (C) in w3. Hence if option (b), thus supported, helps with the reduplication problem, this can only be in virtue of the fact that, on this construal, the counterpart relation will not be *transitive*. But this brings us to the third proposal, (c): that the advantage of counterpart theory is that the counterpart relation lacks some of the formal properties of identity.

---

[7] See note 11 below.

Given the structure of the reduplication problem, there seem to be only two ways in which proposal (c) could be supposed to solve it: by appeal to a counterpart relation that either is not transitive, or is such that one object can have two counterparts in a single possible world. If we deny transitivity, we can say that although B and C are both counterparts of A, and D and E are counterparts of B and C respectively, at least one of D and E is not a counterpart of A. Suppose that we say, for example, that D is not a counterpart of A. When we translate back from counterpart theory to ordinary modal discourse, we get the result that although A could have been just as B is, and *if* A had been just like B, then A could have been just as D is, nevertheless, as things are, A could not have been just as D is. There may be cases where a denial of transitivity of this form is plausible, but this is not one of them. If we ask what *stops* it from being possible for A to have had a history like D's, the only thing that the advocate of this proposal has to appeal to is the presence in w4 of an extra tree. But, as we have already seen, in the discussion of the 'extrinsic determination' or 'best-candidate' proposal (Section 4.3 above) this seems to be the wrong sort of ground for the denial of such a possibility.

The final proposal is that the reduplication problem can be solved by the use of a counterpart relation that permits *both* D and E to be counterparts of A. Then a price of accepting the proposal is a denial of the necessity of identity (cf. Lewis 1968). Similarly, if we adapt this proposal to deal with a 'multiple occupancy' problem involving trees, we shall say that a single tree in one world is a counterpart of two trees in another, with the result that we must deny the necessity of distinctness.

I discuss this final proposal in more detail in Sections 5.3–5.5 below. But first, we may also consider what counterpart theory has to say about the 'Four Worlds' paradox discussed in Chapter 3. Here the potential non-transitivity of the counterpart relation apparently comes to the rescue. The counterpart theorist can say that although the ships s1 in w1 and s2 in w2 do not have enough parts in common to be counterparts of one another, nevertheless each of them is a counterpart of the single ship s3 in w3, and it is a counterpart of both of them (see Figure 3.3 in Chapter 3). Thus, for example, s3 is a counterpart of s1, and s2 is a counterpart of s3, although s2 is not a counterpart of s1. In this case, the counterpart-theoretic solution undeniably has some plausibility, matching the plausibility of the combination of the following thoughts: a ship with the original composition of s1 in w1 could have had the original composition of s3 in w3, and a ship that has the original composition of s3 in w3 could have had the original composition of s2 in w2, but a ship with the original composition of s1 in w1 couldn't have had the original composition of s2 in w2. In other words, we have here a plausible case of the non-transitivity of *de re* possibility, which is mirrored in the non-transitivity of the counterpart relation. However, it is not obvious that this is a reason for adopting counterpart theory in preference to a bare identity solution. For, as has been shown, the bare identity theorist can (although this is not compulsory) mirror the apparent non-transitivity of *de re* modality by appealing to a non-transitive relation of accessibility between possible worlds.[8]

5.3. MULTIPLE COUNTERPARTS AND DISTINCT POSSIBILITIES

I have suggested that if counterpart theory is invoked in order to avoid bare identities and differences, this will be by appeal either to the non-transitivity of the counterpart relation, or to the fact that the counterpart relation need not be one-one. The idea envisaged is that by appeal to these features of the counterpart relation (features that distinguish it from identity) the counterpart theorist can avoid having to distinguish two possible worlds that differ only in that they contain different individuals.

However, if I am right in claiming that, when applied to cases of reduplication and multiple occupancy, the denial of the transitivity of the counterpart relation is an unsatisfactory solution to the puzzles, the real contender, it seems, is the counterpart theorist's claim that the counterpart relation need not be one-one: that an object in one world may have multiple counterparts in another, or that a single object in one world may be a counterpart of more than one object in another.

As I have already noted, this proposal involves a denial of the necessity of identity and the necessity of distinctness, a price that many theorists will be unwilling to pay for a solution to the puzzles.[9] But there is more to be said. In an interesting twist to the debate, Lewis (1986*a*) employs the notion of multiple counterparts to argue, in effect, that according to counterpart theory there can be 'bare' differences

---

[8] See Salmon's proposal, referred to in Sects. 3.5–3.6 above.
[9] See Sect. 2.2 above, note 4.

between possibilities even if there are no 'bare' differences between possible worlds. His rationale for introducing this distinction is that he thinks that there are intuitive cases of 'bare differences'—differences in possibilities that consist merely in a difference in identities—but that he can accommodate them without appealing to genuine bare differences between worlds, which he finds unacceptable. (Lewis conducts the discussion in terms of what he calls 'haecceitistic' differences: differences in *de re* representation that do not supervene on qualitative differences. But any discrepancies between this notion and my notion of 'bare identities' are irrelevant here.)[10]

An example that Lewis gives is that I could have been one, or I could have been the other, of a pair of twins. Assuming that this is so (some would deny that I could have been a twin if I am not actually one, of course, but let us leave that aside), then there seem to be two distinct possibilities: one, that I should have been the first-born twin, and the other, that I should have been the second-born twin. So Lewis:

The haecceitist [and the bare identity theorist–PM] says: two possibilities, two worlds. They *seem* just alike, but they must differ somehow. They differ... in what they represent, *de re*, concerning someone. Hence they must differ with respect to the determinants of representation *de re*; and these must be non-qualitative, since there are no qualitative differences to be had. I say: two possibilities, sure enough. And they do indeed differ in representation *de re*: according to one I am the first-born twin, according to the other I am the second-born. But they are not two worlds. They are two possibilities within a single world. The world in question contains twin counterparts of me... Each twin is a possible way for a person to be, and in fact is a possible way for me to be. I might have been one, or I might have been the other. There are two distinct possibilities for me. But they involve only one possibility for the world: it might have been a world inhabited by two such twins. The haecceitist was quite right when he thought that purely qualitative worlds gave us too narrow a range of distinct possibilities. He concluded that worlds must not be purely qualitative. He'd have done better to conclude that *worlds* gave us too narrow a range of possibilities. The parts of worlds must also be put to use. (Lewis 1986*a*: 231)

An obvious question is why we are allowed to treat this as a case of two possibilities, rather than just one possibility: that I should have been *both* of the twins. As Lewis says, the world he envisages has twin counterparts of me, not just a single counterpart of me. So the question

---

[10] See above, Ch. 2, Appendix A.

arises: why are we allowed to consider each of these counterparts in isolation, as representing a separate possibility?

One might think that Lewis could achieve this result by invoking distinct counterpart relations. We know that, according to Lewis's theory, counterpart relations are to some extent independent of the nature of possible worlds, in the sense that different counterpart relations can obtain between the same objects in possible worlds. For example, given two ('world-bound') objects, A in w1, and B in a distinct world w2, A may be a counterpart of B according to one counterpart relation (for example, one that stresses similarity of origins), but not according to another (for example, one that stresses similarity of later history). To put it another way: in Lewis's theory the nature of possible worlds and their inhabitants does not completely fix the counterpart relations that hold between individuals in different possible worlds.

However, the appeal to distinct counterpart relations—invoking distinct similarity relations—must be irrelevant to the present case. This is conclusively shown by the fact that Lewis explicitly says that his theory allows that I might have been the one, or I might have been the other, of two *qualitatively indiscernible* twins (1986a: 239). But it is obvious that if twins B and C in a possible world are qualitatively indiscernible, there can be no counterpart relation—no standard of similarity whatsoever—under which B is a counterpart of an object A in another possible world while C is not, or vice versa.[11]

How, then, is the separation of possibilities without a distinction between possible worlds achieved? It seems that the answer must be just that where there are twin (and hence numerically distinct) counterparts B and C in a world w2 for an individual A that belongs to a world w1, both of the following conditions hold: there is in w2 a counterpart x of A such that x is not identical with C; and there is in w2 a counterpart y of A such that y is not identical with B. The first of these, then, can represent the possibility that of the qualitatively indiscernible twins B and C, A might have been B (and not C), and the second can represent the (distinct) possibility that of the qualitatively indiscernible twins, A might have been C (and not B). In other words, it appears that Lewis is adopting a terminology according to which distinct counterparts within

---

[11] At least, this is so if the counterpart relation is determined qualitatively. But Lewis holds that it must be, and regards a non-qualitative counterpart relation as 'a contradiction in terms' (1986a: 229).

a world may be regarded as representing distinct *de re* possibilities for no other reason than that the distinct counterparts *are* distinct.

Lewis's appeal to distinctions between possibilities may be applied to some of our other examples of haecceitistic or 'bare' differences. Lewis himself applies it to a case like Adams's (1979), where we start by envisaging two objects *A* and *B* that are exactly alike in one world, and then contemplate two possible ways in which *A* and *B* might have been discernible: ways that differ only in that in one of them *A* has different properties, whereas in the other it is *B* that has different properties.

Reverting to our reduplication problem concerning the oak tree, the problem was that if we allow that there are two ways for the tree to be different that are 'intrinsically' composible, we are confronted with the embarrassing 'reduplication' world w4, containing replicas of trees each of which is alleged to be identical with the original tree in w1. The solutions that are suggested by counterpart theory are: non-transitivity, and multiple counterparthood. According to the non-transitivity solution, one or other of the trees in w4 is not a counterpart of the tree in w1, although they are counterparts of the trees in w2 and w3, which are in turn counterparts of the tree in w1; allegedly this is not a problem, because the counterpart relation is not transitive. My objection to this was that it made the *de re* possibilities for an individual such as a tree depend on irrelevant factors (such as the presence of an extra tree). According to the 'multiple counterparts' solution, both the trees in w4 are counterparts of the tree in w1. But according to Lewis's (1986*a*) elaboration of the 'multiple counterparts' theory, corresponding to the fact that the trees in w4 can both be regarded as counterparts of the tree in w1, we can take w4 to represent two distinct possibilities for that tree, in one of which it is at p1 (and not at p2) and in the other of which it is at p2 (and not at p1).

Turning to our 'multiple occupancy' problem involving trees, the problem was that, unless we adopt strict requirements on the essential properties of a tree, the very same tree-history seems to be a possible history for *two* trees.[12] The bare identity theorist concludes that there are two possible worlds that differ only in that they contain different

[12] See Figure 3.2 in Ch. 3. The problem is that O2 and O3 in w4 are undeniably different trees, yet if w5 represents a possible history for O2, and w6 also represents a possible history for O3, then there is a single possible tree-history (the one that is common to O2 in w5 and O3 in w6) that is a possibility for each of the two trees O2 and O3.

trees. According to the version of the counterpart-theoretic solution that exploits the idea that the counterpart relation need not be one-one, however, instead of these two qualitatively indiscernible worlds, there is just one world, containing a tree that is a counterpart of two trees in another.[13] Again, though, according to Lewis's (1986*a*) elaboration of such cases, it seems that we can take this single world to represent two distinct possibilities: one that is a possibility for the tree O2, and another that is a possibility for the tree O3.

5.4. MULTIPLE COUNTERPARTS AND BARE IDENTITIES

However, once Lewis's theory is elaborated in this way, there is a question why the invocation of multiple counterparts for a single individual (and a single counterpart for a multiplicity of individuals) and the corresponding distinctions between possibilities, should be preferred to an account, such as the 'bare identities' account, according to which the distinct possibilities correspond to distinct but indiscernible worlds.

It is interesting that although Lewis has theoretical objections to genuine 'haecceitistic' (non-qualitative) differences between worlds (and hence to bare identities)[14], he thinks that the intuitions in favour of some kind of haecceitistic differences are sufficiently respectable that it is worth finding some way of accommodating them. The reason he does

---

[13] It seems that a counterpart theorist might, instead, provide a non-transitivity solution to the multiple occupancy problem, but apparently only by adopting a non-standard version of counterpart theory according to which x is a counterpart of y only if there is no other object in y's world (*sic*) to which x is more similar than it is to y. (This would represent a departure from the version of counterpart theory given in Lewis 1968, for example.) Note that the history that the trees have in w5 and w6 (in Figure 3.2) is just like the history that the tree A has in w1 (in Figure 5.1). So this counterpart theorist might say, for example, that although B in w2 is a counterpart of D in w4, and A in w1 is a counterpart of B in w2, nevertheless A in w1 is not a counterpart of D in w4, since there is another object, E, in w4 to which A is more similar (in relevant respects) than it is to D. As in the case of the non-transitivity solution to the reduplication problem, I find this unconvincing: why should the fact that D happens to be accompanied by another tree (the tree E) make it impossible for D to have the history represented by A in w1?

[14] In Ch. 2, Appendix A, I argued that although one could accept 'haecceitism' in the sense here under consideration (non-qualitative differences between worlds) without accepting bare identities, the rejection of haecceitism involves the rejection of bare identities.

not want to take the intuitions at face value is that he objects to the theories that make haecceitistic differences intelligible, rather than to the alleged haecceitistic differences themselves:

> The principal thing to say against haecceitism is just that when we survey the various forms of genuine or ersatz modal realism, we find that the ones that are congenial to haecceitistic differences are the ones that we have already seen to be in serious trouble on other grounds. What's more, it turns out that there is a cheap substitute for haecceitism.... So we should reject haecceitism not for any direct reason, but rather because its intuitive advantage over the cheap substitute—if indeed it has any advantage at all—costs us far more trouble than it's worth. (Lewis 1986*a*: 228)

Lewis's way of accommodating the intuitions means that he does, in effect, allow that there can be haecceitistic or 'bare' differences between *possibilities*: for example (Case 1) that we can recognize a distinction between the possibility of *A*'s having a history H and the possibility of *B*'s having a history H, even if there is no qualitative difference between the way the world would have been had *A* had H and the way it would have been had *B* had H. We do this, according to Lewis, by taking one possible world, containing an individual, *C*, that has H, and considering separately *C*'s being a counterpart of *A* and *C*'s being a counterpart of *B*. Similarly (Case 2) the distinction between my being the first-born of a pair of twins and my being the second-born is to be got by taking a single possible world containing a pair of twins, T1 and T2, and considering separately the possibility represented by T1's being my counterpart and the possibility represented by T2's being my counterpart.

To think of the possibilities in Case 1 as separate possibilities is, *inter alia*, to think of the first as the possibility that *A* has H *while B does not*, and the second as the possibility that *B* has H *while A does not*. Similarly, to think of the possibilities of my being the first and my being the second of a pair of twins as separate is to think of them as the possibility of my being the first *and not being the second*, and of my being the second *and not being the first*.

Perhaps it is true that a Lewisian realist has good reasons for thinking that haecceitistic differences between possibilities are acceptable in a way that haecceitistic differences between possible worlds are not. However, I do not see why anyone who is *not* a Lewisian realist about possible worlds should regard the first as more acceptable than the second. Hence I do not see why anyone but a Lewisian realist should see this allegedly 'cheap' substitute for haecceitism as significantly cheaper than the full-blooded haecceitism (or 'bare identities' theory) that it replaces.

5.5. MULTIPLE COUNTERPARTS AND DISTINCT COUNTERPART RELATIONS

It may be objected that this still leaves open the possibility that we might use one world, and different counterpart relations, to distinguish possibilities for which the haecceitist or bare identity theorist wants to recognize two different worlds. For example, in the case of my reduplication problem concerning the oak tree, it may seem plausible that it is in virtue of *different* properties that D and E represent possible histories for the tree A (= O1) in w1: roughly, E has the same biological origin as A, but not the same location; D the same location, but not the same biological origin (see Figure 5.1). So in this case it appears that the separate invocation of two different counterpart relations (one that stresses biological origin—'propagule-origin', to use Graeme Forbes's terminology—and another that stresses original location) might enable the one world w4 to represent the two distinct possibilities for the tree A (O1), whereas the genuine haecceitist or bare identity theorist has to resort to two separate qualitatively identical worlds to do this.

However, if it is employed in this way, then I think that Lewis's theory faces a different objection. Take the counterpart relation that emphasizes propagule-origin, and hence takes E in w4, but not D in w4, to be a counterpart of the tree A in w1. Now, either this counterpart relation assigns so much weight to propagule-origin that it does not allow *any* object to be a counterpart of the tree A unless it comes from the same acorn (or rather, strictly speaking, a counterpart of the same acorn) as does A, or it does not assign as much weight as this to propagule-origin. Suppose that it does not. Then, according to this counterpart relation, the tree B in w2 may be a counterpart of A in w1, and thus w2 may represent a possible history for A in which A grows from a different acorn from its actual acorn. But if D in w4 is not a counterpart of A although B in w2 is a counterpart of A, we have the counterintuitive consequences cited earlier (Section 5.2) in connection with the 'non-transitivity' solution to the reduplication problem. Suppose, on the other hand, that the counterpart relation in question *does* assign such weight to propagule-origin that, according to this counterpart relation,

A could not have come from a different acorn from its actual acorn, so B in w2 is not a counterpart of A in w1. Since there is, *ex hypothesi*, another counterpart relation (one that emphasizes original location, but puts relatively little emphasis on propagule-origin) according to which B in w2 *is* a counterpart of A, then the proposal forces us to concede that there is some way of correctly thinking about the possibilities for the oak tree that implies that it could not have originated from a different acorn, even though there are other (equally acceptable) ways of doing so that imply that it could. Even if such 'inconstancy' is coherent, I do not think it represents a plausible reaction to this reduplication problem.[15]

My conclusion is that if one does not already have reasons for adopting counterpart theory, the puzzles of transworld identity do not provide compelling reasons for accepting it. In its 'non-haecceitistic' form, the counterpart-theoretic response to the puzzles posed by the reduplication problem and the multiple occupancy problem involves counterintuitive restrictions on the ways that individuals such as trees could have been different from the ways that they actually are. In its 'haecceitistic' form, it is doubtful that it has any advantages over the bare identities solution except to a Lewisian realist about possible worlds. It seems that the advocate of a counterpart-theoretic solution to the transworld identity puzzles will preach only to the converted.

5.6. CONCLUSION TO CHAPTERS 2–5

I have argued that, whatever essential properties things may have, they do not, in general, have (non-trivial) individual essences that distinguish them from all other things. In the case of most of the individuals that are the subjects of our counterfactual speculations, it is a mistake to think that we can capture their individuality in terms of properties that uniquely distinguish them from all other individuals in all possible worlds. However, I have also argued that Graeme Forbes is right in supposing that to reject the conception of an individual as distinguished by its own unique modal nature or essence is to pay a price. Either we must conclude, as the counterpart theorist does, that a possible-worlds interpretation of *de re* modal statements about individuals must deny that the same individual has different properties in different possible worlds, or we must allow that there can be 'bare identities'. But a

---

[15] For the claim that *de re* modality is 'inconstant' see Lewis 1986*a*, ch. 4, sect. 5.

commitment to bare identities is a commitment to the thesis that a possible world, including, apparently, the actual world, may have a 'duplicate' that differs from it only in the identities of some of the objects that it contains. And, as I pointed out in Section 2.5, this commitment is paradoxical. It apparently forces us to accept that the total history of the world, up to the time that a particular individual (you, for example) came into existence at a certain place was insufficient for the individual that then and there came into existence to be *that* individual, rather than something else. Nevertheless, I have suggested that, unless one is a Lewisian realist about possible worlds, the commitment to 'bare identities', paradoxical though it may seem, should be preferred to counterpart theory.

However, even if it is no part of an object's being the object that it is that it have its very own set of uniquely distinguishing essential properties—even if all its (non-trivial) essential properties are either shared or shareable—it could still be the case that many individuals differ from one another in their essential properties. (Even if there are no conditions that are non-trivially sufficient for an individual's identity in all possible worlds, there might nevertheless be non-trivial necessary conditions for its identity in all possible worlds.) But is this really true of ordinary persisting individuals such as people or animals or plants or artefacts? Do they really have any interesting essential properties at all?

In the following three chapters, I begin to answer this question by considering two versions of the thesis that such individuals have non-trivial essential properties: the view that certain features of an individual's origin are essential to its being the individual that it is, and the view that for every individual there is some sortal kind to which it belongs essentially.

6

The Necessity of Origin

In a famous passage, Kripke wrote, of possibilities concerning the Queen of England:

How could a person originating from different parents, from a totally different sperm and egg, be *this very woman*? One can imagine, *given* the woman, that various things in her life could have changed... One is given, let's say, a previous history of the world up to a certain time, and from that time it diverges considerably from the actual course.... And so it's possible that even though she were born of these parents she never became queen.... But what is harder to imagine is her being born of different parents. It seems to me that anything coming from a different origin would not be this object. (1980: 113)

This is an instance of Kripke's 'necessity of origin' thesis, already mentioned several times in this book. The crux of the thesis is that, as a matter of metaphysical necessity, an individual is essentially tied to particular features of its origin in a way that it is not essentially tied to particular features of its subsequent history. As for what the essential features of a thing's origin are, Kripke suggested that, in the case of a human being, they concern the identity of its biological antecedents (as indicated in the passage quoted above); in the case of an artefact, its original material composition (1980: 113–15).

It is generally agreed that Kripke's thesis (with its contrast between necessity of origin and contingency of development) has intuitive support, although there is debate about how firm the relevant intuitions are. And even those who reject the necessity of origin thesis may concede that to envisage an individual as having a different origin is harder, or involves a greater departure from actuality, than to envisage its having a different subsequent history. This weaker thesis might be called 'the tenacity of origin'. It would, for example, be exhibited by a version of counterpart theory that gave greater weight to match of origins than to match of subsequent history in determining the counterpart relation.[1]

If Kripke's necessity of origin thesis (as opposed to the weaker 'tenacity of origin' thesis) is correct, then even if ordinary persisting individuals do not have individual essences, each of them nevertheless has essential properties that distinguish it from many, and even from most, other individuals of the same kind. In this chapter I shall argue that although the intuitive appeal of the necessity of origin thesis can be explained, the explanation tends to cast doubt on the thesis, rather than confirming its acceptability.

6.1. NECESSITY OF ORIGIN AND SUFFICIENCY OF ORIGIN

I have rejected the view that 'ordinary' persisting things have individual essences: essential properties that are strictly sufficient for their identity in all possible situations or worlds; properties that *constitute* (in a strong sense) their being the particular individuals that they are.[2] In addition, however, I have pointed out that if we *were* to insist on attributing individual essences to such ordinary persisting things, we should inevitably have to appeal to distinctive features of their origins, on pain of contradicting deeply held intuitions about the contingency of an individual's development.[3]

My contentions obviously raise a question about the status of Kripke's necessity of origin thesis. Admittedly, as I have pointed out before, the features of a thing's origin to which Kripke's thesis appeals are not, strictly speaking, necessarily unique features. But they are close enough to having this status to make one wonder whether his necessity of origin thesis relies on principles about sufficient conditions for identity across possible worlds that I have argued that we should reject.

This suspicion may be reinforced by the fact that there is a well-known account that derives the necessity of origin thesis from a 'sufficiency of

---

[1] Cf. Lewis 1986a. Although Lewis does not adopt the version of counterpart theory mentioned above, he does say that 'match of origins often has decisive weight' (1986a: 88). See also Lewis's 'Postscript' to 'Counterpart Theory and Quantified Modal Logic' in Lewis 1983: 43.

[2] See Sect. 2.2 above for clarification of the notion of an individual essence that I reject. In particular, remember that I admit that things have individual essences in a 'trivial' sense, although not in a non-trivial sense.

[3] See above, Sect. 3.1.

origin thesis', an account inspired by Kripke's own discussion.[4] (Forbes's argument for the necessity of origin, discussed in Chapter 3, may be regarded as a variant of this account.) The account begins with the claim that it is plausible to regard the origin of an individual (such as a human being or an artefact) as *sufficient* for its identity in all possible worlds. It is then argued that this 'sufficiency of origin' thesis leads to incoherence unless it is combined with a necessity of origin thesis that implies that in every possible world in which the individual exists, it has that same origin.

In this chapter I argue that we can explain the intuitive appeal of Kripke's necessity of origin thesis without supposing that the thesis relies on 'sufficiency' principles of the type that I have tried to discredit in Chapter 3. According to the alternative explanation of the appeal of the necessity of origin thesis that I propose, the thesis can be seen as relying on a weaker principle about identity across possible worlds, which I call 'the overlap requirement'. Nevertheless, I do not take this to show that the necessity of origin thesis is to be accepted. For the 'overlap requirement', although less demanding than the sufficiency principles that it replaces, is nevertheless open to sceptical attack. I conclude that it is doubtful that any necessity of origin thesis that relies on the overlap requirement is defensible.

6.2. THE NECESSITY OF ORIGIN AND THE BRANCHING MODEL OF *DE RE* POSSIBILITIES

Following the passage quoted at the beginning of this chapter, Kripke added, in a footnote:

Ordinarily when we ask intuitively whether something might have happened to a given object, we ask whether the universe could have gone on as it actually did up to a certain time, but diverge in its history from that point forward so that the vicissitudes of that object would have been different from that time forth. (1980: 115, note 57)

Here Kripke associates his thesis of the necessity of origin with what may be called a 'branching model' of possibilities concerning particular individuals. According to the branching model suggested by Kripke,

---

[4] See Kripke 1980: 115, note 56. For discussions of the argument, see, e.g., Salmon 1979 and 1982, Noonan 1983, and Robertson 1998. See also Ch. 3 above.

ways in which the Queen might have been different are restricted to *divergences* from actual history. In addition, according to this branching model, these divergences are in one direction only: 'forward' into the future, not 'backward' into the past. The model says that we are to consider how the world might have gone on differently after a certain point in time. It does not suggest that it will do equally well to consider, instead, how the world might have been different before a certain point in time.

In terms of possible worlds, Kripke's branching model puts a restriction on what a possible world has to be like if it is to contain the Queen. A possible world in which the Queen exists must be the same as the actual world up to some point in its history. There is a possible world in which the Queen is childless, for example, only if there is a possible world which is the same as the actual world up to a certain time, and then diverges from it in such a way that the Queen has no children.

I want to maintain not only that Kripke was right in associating the necessity of origin thesis with a branching model of possibilities, but also that the thesis can be regarded as a consequence of a version of the branching model.[5] However, there is an obvious difficulty about how to get from the branching model of possibilities adumbrated by Kripke to the necessity of origin claims that he wants to make. The difficulty takes the form of a dilemma (cf. McGinn 1976: 130).

Are we to suppose that a non-actual possible world contains the Queen only if it branches off the actual world at some time *after* the Queen actually came into existence? Whether we answer 'yes' or 'no' to this question, we seem to be in trouble.

Suppose that we answer 'yes'. Possible worlds that contain the Queen must be exactly the same as the actual world up to, and including, the time that the Queen actually came into existence. If we say this, then we can certainly draw the conclusion that the Queen's origin is essential to her identity, in both of two senses of 'origin'. It will be essential to the Queen that she have her actual origin in the sense of her actual original state, by which I mean the set of properties that she had when she actually came into existence. And it will be essential to the Queen that she have her actual origin in the sense of her actual causal antecedents, including her biological parents, the sperm and egg that produced her, and so on.

---

[5] This additional claim is suggested by Kripke, although not explicitly endorsed by him.

However, this version of the branching model makes all of the properties of the Queen's actual original state essential to her. And this seems much too strong. For example, no one wants to say that the exact location of the Queen's birth or conception is essential to her, or that no feature of the surroundings in which she came into existence could have been different.[6] Worse, this proposal makes it essential to the Queen's identity that the entire history of the world, before she came into existence, should have been exactly the same as it actually was in every particular. And it implies, for example, that, given that the Queen didn't actually have an older brother, it is absurd to wonder what her life would have been like if she had had an older brother (cf. Coburn 1986: 179).

We must conclude that it is wildly counterintuitive to say that possible worlds containing the Queen must be exactly the same as the actual world up to the time that she actually came into existence. Moreover, it is a view that Kripke explicitly rejects.[7] He implies that certain changes to the world, occurring before the Queen actually came into existence, would have resulted in her coming into existence with different properties.

Suppose, then, that, following Kripke, we say that although the Queen exists only in possible worlds that are the same as the actual world up to some point, some of these possible worlds that contain the Queen diverge from the actual world at times before the Queen came into existence. The problem with this is that we are in danger of losing the connection between the branching model of possibilities and the necessity of origin. For if we do make this concession, what is to preclude the existence of a branching possible world in which the Queen comes into existence from quite different biological antecedents from those that actually engendered her? Why can't there be a possible world that is exactly the same as the actual world up until (say) 1900, and then diverges from it, in which the Queen results from a different sperm and egg, and different parents, from those that actually produced her?

The dilemma arises because Kripke's thesis of the necessity of origin (and the thesis that commands intuitive support) is not the thesis that

---

[6] Cf. McGinn 1976: 130, and Coburn 1986: 179.

[7] 'Note that the time in which the divergence from actual history occurs may be sometime before the object is actually created' (Kripke 1980: 115, note 57). Kripke implies that it is not even true that all of a human being's intrinsic (in the sense of 'non-relational') origin properties are essential properties.

all features of an individual's origin are essential to it. Rather, it is a selective thesis: some of an individual's origin properties are essential; others are not. The question thus arises whether there is a version of the branching model from which this selective thesis can be derived.

Evidently, what is required is the following compromise. In order to contain the Queen, a possible world does not have to be *exactly* the same as the actual world up to the time that the Queen came into existence. What it must do, however, is to match the history of the actual world up to the time that she came into existence *in certain respects*. In particular, according to Kripke, it must be like the actual world in containing certain actual biological entities (for example, the Queen's parents, and the sperm and egg from which she came) and certain biological events (in particular, the fusion of that sperm and egg to generate a new individual).

It may be objected that even if we can formulate a version of the branching model that is consistent with Kripke's (selective) necessity of origin thesis, this will not *explain* the selective aspect of the thesis. Suppose that I am puzzled about why certain biological features of the Queen's origin should be regarded as essential, whereas other features of her origin (such as its location) are not. Merely to point out that we require the 'trunk' of a branching possible world that contains the Queen to match the actual world in respect of these biological features, but not in respect of the others, appears to be of no help to me at all.

I agree that although the branching model can be made to accommodate the selective aspect of Kripke's necessity of origin thesis, it does not explain this aspect of the thesis. However, this does not mean that the branching model does no explanatory work.

Kripke's necessity of origin thesis involves two distinct contrasts. One is an asymmetry between origin and development. The second is a contrast between those features of a thing's origin that are essential to it and those that are not. Hence, the thesis invites two distinct questions, which can be abbreviated as follows. One question is: why *origin* (rather than development)? The second question is: why *these* features of origin (rather than others)? I concede that the branching model of possibilities does not help to answer the second of these questions. However, in order to answer the first question—'why *origin*?'—I believe that an appeal to a branching model of possibilities is inescapable.

It may be objected that this is to ignore the 'sufficiency of origin' argument, and Forbes's variant of it, mentioned in Section 6.1 above. My answer is that the 'sufficiency of origin' argument does not *answer* the question 'why *origin*?'; it merely relocates it. The question reappears as the question why it should be features of a thing's origin, rather than features of its later history, that are regarded as sufficient for its identity in all possible worlds. Similarly, Forbes's account of the necessity of origin as based on a theory of individual essences needs to explain why the properties that constitute a thing's individual essence should have to do with its origin rather than its later history.[8] I believe that any plausible answer to this question must involve an appeal to the considerations that underlie the branching model of possibilities.

However, to defend this claim I must briefly discuss what appears to be a rival explanation of the necessity of origin thesis: an explanation proposed some years ago by Colin McGinn.

6.3. McGINN'S ACCOUNT

In his (1976), Colin McGinn offers a quite different argument for the necessity of origin, one that appeals to an analogy between the continuity involved in the identity over time of a single biological entity and the continuity involved in biological generation. This argument appears to bypass the need to base the necessity of origin thesis on the branching conception of possible worlds. Indeed, McGinn offers it as an alternative to basing the necessity of origin thesis on that branching conception, which he thinks cannot serve as a satisfactory basis for the thesis because of the dilemma outlined above (McGinn 1976: 129–31). As indicated above, I do not think that the dilemma is decisive against the association of the necessity of origin with the branching conception. However, I shall also argue that McGinn's alternative explanation is untenable, in part because it fails to accommodate the temporal asymmetry inherent in the necessity of origin thesis.[9]

McGinn offers a version of a 'sufficiency of origin' argument as a ground for accepting that it 'seems essential that you come from the gametes you actually came from' (p. 132). However, he undertakes to give an explanation of the 'sufficiency of origin' thesis, or, at least, for the slightly weaker thesis that in any possible world in which an individual

---

[8] See Mackie 1987: 186, and Mackie 2002: 342. This issue is discussed by Forbes in his (2002), where he calls it 'The Bias Problem'. See also Sect. 3.1 above, and note 26 below.

[9] I should add that I have no idea whether McGinn still endorses the explanation of the necessity of origin that he gave in McGinn 1976.

comes from A's actual gametes (sperm and egg), that individual will be a stronger candidate for being A than an individual that does not. 'The reason for preferring the actual gametes of a person as a criterion of [transworld] identity is, I surmise, a matter of a certain sort of spatiotemporal *continuity*' (ibid.). This kind of continuity McGinn labels 'd-continuity' (which I take to be an abbreviation for 'diachronic and developmental continuity').

Either McGinn's explanation of the necessity of origin relies on an appeal to an analogy with cases involving identity over time, or it does not. But there are problems either way. First, suppose that, in arguing for the necessity of a human being's origin, McGinn does appeal to an analogy between the developmental continuity involved in identity over time and developmental continuity that does not involve identity. That McGinn is making such an appeal is suggested by the following passage:

Just as you must have come from the zygote you came from because you are diachronically and developmentally continuous with it, so you must have come from the gametes you came from because you are similarly continuous with them. (1976: 133)

Since McGinn believes that you are *identical* with your original zygote (p. 132), this passage evidently involves an appeal to an analogy between a case of identity over time and a case of a developmental continuity (from gametes to person) that is not a case of identity, because it involves a relation between two entities and one entity. Further, in the discussion preceding this remark, McGinn argues, first, that a person had to develop from its actual zygote because the person is identical with the zygote, and identity over time is necessary. He then appeals to the fact that we can 'extend biological continuity beyond the zygote' (pp. 132–3) to argue that the zygote (i.e., the person) had to come from the particular gametes from which it actually came. This looks like an appeal to the following argument:

Argument from Analogy with Identity (AAI):

(1) The adult person is identical with the zygote from which it developed.

(2) Identity over time is necessary.

(3) The identity of the zygote with the adult person is constituted by a certain sort of spatio-temporal and developmental continuity.

(4)   A similar sort of spatio-temporal and developmental continuity is exhibited in the relation between the gametes and the zygote that develops from them.

Therefore:

(5)   The relation between gametes and the zygote that develops from them is necessary—in the sense that the zygote necessarily comes from those gametes.

This argument must be rejected. My objection is not that the argument is invalid: as an argument from analogy it is not intended to be strictly valid. My objection is not that it is wrong to say that the zygote is identical with the adult person. It would be pointless to dispute premise (1) of the argument, since the argument could easily be modified by replacing this premise with one that is more readily acceptable: for example, that the adult person is identical with the infant from which it developed, in order to derive, in place of (5), the conclusion that the relation between person and zygote is necessary (rigid) even if it is not identity. The similarity between the developmental continuity that leads from zygote to person and the developmental continuity that leads from gametes to zygote could then be invoked in order to derive the original conclusion (5) that the relation between gametes and zygote is necessary (rigid). Rather, my objection is this. If the argument AAI is to work, we must suppose that it is the fact that identity over time involves a kind of spatio-temporal and developmental continuity that provides the reason why identity over time is necessary. Argument AAI requires not only that you are identical with your zygote because you are spatio-temporally and developmentally continuous with it, but also that the *necessity* of your identity with your zygote arises from your being spatio-temporally and developmentally continuous with it. But the second claim doesn't follow from the first claim together with the necessity of identity. And it also seems quite untrue. The necessity of your identity with your zygote (if such identity there is) arises simply from its being identity: if identity is necessary, then identity is always necessary, regardless of what are, in any particular case, the constituting facts or criteria for the identity.[10]

It is difficult to state this objection clearly, partly because if we speak in the way that is suggested by the premises of AAI, we shall say both

---

[10]   As mentioned before, I take the necessity of identity to be a true principle, although this is contested (see Sect. 2.2).

that I am identical with my zygote and that I came from and am developmentally continuous with it. Which commits us to saying that I came from myself and am developmentally continuous with myself. It is possible that the use of the language of continuity and 'coming from', which suggests that the zygote and the person are somehow two, even though identical, may help to give the argument AAI a spurious plausibility. If identity over time were a relation between two distinct objects, one of which develops into the other, and if a similar kind of development were exhibited in the case where a zygote comes from two gametes, and if identity over time were necessary, then there might, indeed, be a case for concluding that the relation between zygote and gametes is also a necessary one. But if identity over time were a relation that held between two distinct objects, what reason would we have to believe in the necessity of identity over time?

The pointlessness of the appeal to the necessity of identity is also brought out by the fact that 'd-continuity' is supposed to give rise to certain *asymmetrically* rigid relations, whereas identity is symmetrical.[11] If identity is necessary, and I am identical with the zygote from which I came, then, if it is correct to say that I had to come from that zygote, it must also be correct to say that that zygote had to become me. Of course it (i.e., I) didn't have to survive long enough to become an adult, but then again I (i.e., it) didn't have to survive long enough to be an adult that came from it. The situation is supposed to be different when we consider me and the two gametes from which I came: they didn't have to produce me, but I had to come from them in order to exist at all. However, the argument from analogy with identity not only fails to explain this asymmetry, but also makes the asymmetry extremely puzzling. For if we really were to rely on the analogy with the necessity of identity to support the conclusion that d-continuity gives rise to rigid relations, we should expect d-continuity always to give rise to symmetrically rigid relations.

I conclude that the appeal to the necessity of identity must drop out of the picture as an irrelevance. But if so, McGinn's proposed explanation of the necessity of origin is in trouble. For suppose that

---

[11] McGinn describes 'rigid' relations as ones of which it is true that 'when entities stand in these relations they necessarily do, . . . in any world in which they exist these entities are related as they are in the actual world' (1976: 131). However, as my remarks in the text indicate, this characterization of 'rigidity' is problematic, since it does not appear to accommodate the asymmetry that is involved in the thesis of the necessity of origin.

McGinn does not rely on the analogy with identity over time to support the necessity of origin. Then his explanation of the necessity of origin for human beings and other organisms reduces to the general claim that d-continuities (excluding cases of identity over time) are rigid. However, as an explanation, this is pretty thin. The response 'But what explains the d-continuity principle?' is all too pressing. It is true that if we already had intuitions to the effect that relations of d-continuity (excluding identities over time) are rigid in a wide variety of cases, then this fact would increase the potential of the general d-continuity principle to serve as an explanation of the necessity of a human being's (biological) origin. But I do not think that the antecedent of this conditional is fulfilled. Perhaps those who have the intuition of the necessity of a human's origin have a similar intuition about the necessity of the origins of various higher animals. But is it true that these people also have the required intuitions about the origins of lower animals, and the origins of spermatozoa and ova, not to mention the origins of tree branches, foliage, hair, teeth, and toenails? I find it hard to believe that McGinn could find a set of sufficiently strong intuitions, about a sufficiently wide variety of cases, to convince a sceptic that his d-continuity principle has significant explanatory power.[12]

In short: to appeal to d-continuity alone as the explanation of the necessity of origin for human beings is unsatisfying; to appeal to an analogy with identity over time is fallacious. McGinn's proposed alternative account of the necessity of origin thesis is unsuccessful.

6.4. THE APPEAL OF THE BRANCHING MODEL

I have argued that the difficulties discussed in Section 6.2 above do not present an insuperable obstacle to regarding the necessity of origin thesis as the product of a branching model of possibilities. I also think that Kripke was right in suggesting that the branching model has considerable intuitive appeal. It is, I agree, very natural to think of ways that actual individuals might have been different in terms of divergences *into the future* from 'the actual course of events', even if we are not very strict or precise about the extent of match that is involved when we speak of 'the actual course of events'.

---

[12] McGinn presents, as evidence for the rigidity of d-continuity, a variety of judgements that he claims are intuitively plausible (1976: 133–4). These judgements do not seem to me to have very strong intuitive appeal.

However, if this is correct, it raises the question why this branching model of *de re* possibilities, with its consequent asymmetry between origin and development, should be so appealing.

Before I embark on my account, a caveat is needed. Throughout the discussion in the remainder of this chapter, my principal question is not 'Is the branching model correct?', but 'Why do we find it attractive?' What I say may sometimes appear to embody the objectionable assumption that it is up to us to determine by fiat the answers to questions about *de re* modality (such as the question whether Queen Elizabeth could have had different parents), by adopting certain modal principles in preference to others. However, I do not think that my procedure is really committed to this form of subjectivism about *de re* modality. Nothing that I say entails that the reasons why we find certain modal principles appealing cannot also be reasons for thinking that those principles are true.

In considering why the branching model is attractive, I shall simplify things by ignoring what I have called the 'selective' aspect of Kripke's necessity of origin thesis (an aspect that I shall not attempt to explain) and adopt two pretences. First, I shall pretend that the branching model of *de re* possibilities that we find natural is a simple one that restricts the ways in which an individual could have been different to divergences from its actual history that occur only *after* the individual comes into existence, and not before. In conformity with this, I'll pretend that the necessity of origin thesis that Kripke and others find plausible is the thesis that an individual's origin could not have been different in any respect whatsoever.[13]

In addition, for ease of exposition I shall apply the branching model to an individual who has now ceased to exist: Julius Caesar. The branching model of *de re* possibilities (in its simplified form) can then be exemplified by the following principle:

> *Being F* is an unrealized possibility for Julius Caesar (Julius Caesar wasn't, but might have been F) if and only if:

---

[13] This is not a change of subject; merely a harmless idealization. I argued in Sect. 6.2 that the simple branching model can be modified to accommodate what I call the selective aspect of Kripke's necessity of origin thesis. Thus there is no harm in my ignoring this selective aspect when I use the branching model to explain the asymmetry between origin and development that is a feature of the necessity of origin thesis. (Recall that it is only the question 'why *origin*?' and not the question 'why *these* features of origin?' that I am attempting to answer by appeal to the branching model.)

(a)   Julius Caesar was not F, but

(b)   there was some time in Julius Caesar's existence at which it was a future possibility that he should be F.[14]

Obviously, this won't generate any unrealized possibilities for Julius Caesar unless we assume that there were times in his existence at which various alternative futures were open to him. But if we do make this assumption—I'll call it '*the assumption of open futures*'—we shall get the picture of possibilities for Caesar illustrated by diagram (i) in Figure 6.1. The central horizontal line is intended to represent Julius Caesar's actual history, and the branching lines some of the various possible futures that Caesar had at different times in his existence.

I am claiming that we find it natural to think of possibilities for Julius Caesar in terms of this branching model, and that it is because of this that we find it hard to envisage that Julius Caesar's origin could have been different from what it actually was.[15] The question I now address is: why are we attracted to this branching model, with its consequent asymmetry between necessity of origin and contingency of development?

One suggestion that has been made[16] is that the intuitive appeal of this way of thinking about possibilities for Julius Caesar derives from its intuitive appeal as a way of thinking about metaphysical possibilities in general, whether or not they concern actual individuals. In addition to our branching model of *de re* possibilities, there is a more general branching model, based on the following principle:

A state of affairs S is, at time t, an unrealized possibility if and only if:

   (a) S has not occurred at or before t,

and

either   (b) S is a future possibility at t,

or   (c) there was some time, prior to t, at which S was a future possibility.[17]

If, as before, we assume that the future is open, in the sense that there is, at any given time, a variety of possible futures, this gives us the branching model of possibilities illustrated by diagram (ii) in Figure 6.1.

---

[14]   Cf. Prior 1960; p. 70 in the version reprinted in Prior 1968. But see also ibid.: 77.

[15]   In describing my claim in this way, I am, of course, employing my two simplifying pretences.

[16]   By J. L. Mackie (1974).

[17]   Cf. Prior 1960, p. 69 in the version reprinted in Prior 1968.

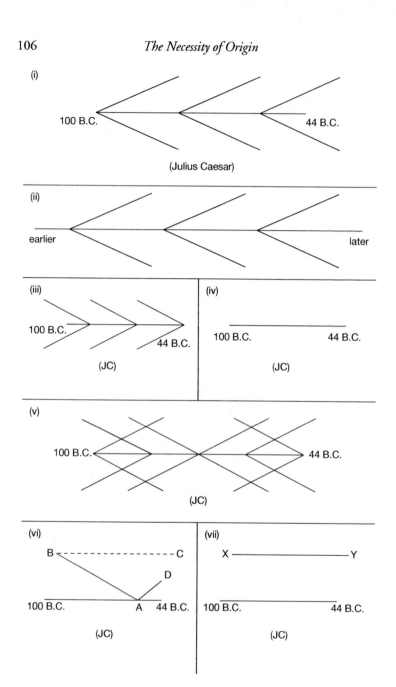

Figure 6.1

The central horizontal line represents the actual history of the world, and the branches represent various possible divergences into the future from the actual course of events.

This model allows that what is now past could have been different in certain respects. For example, it allows that although there were, in actual fact, no dodos alive in 1900, it is now possible that there *should have been* dodos alive in 1900. For presumably there was a time, before the extinction of the dodos, at which their continued existence until 1900 was a future possibility.

In general, this model allows us to say that anything that was, at some past time, a future possibility, is still a possibility, in the sense of something that *might have been*, or *could have been*, the case, even if it actually was not. But what the model does not allow is that there are any unrealized possibilities that are not, at some time in the history of the world, future possibilities. In particular, it does not allow that our world could have had an entirely different past.[18]

The suggestion we are to consider is this: the plausibility of the branching model of *de re* possibilities derives from the plausibility of the general branching model as a model of metaphysical possibilities. I doubt that this can be the whole story. My reason is this. It seems to me that a branching model of *de re* possibilities has some plausibility quite independently of the general branching model.

This is illustrated by the fact that there would be nothing strange about someone's rejecting the general branching model of metaphysical possibilities, while accepting a branching model of those metaphysical possibilities that concern actual individuals. Suppose that I reject the general branching model, because I think that it is metaphysically possible that the whole of the past should have been radically different from what it actually was. There would, I think, be nothing odd about my adding that if there had been such a radically different past, none of the individuals that actually exist would then have existed. That is, there would (I think) be nothing odd about the claim that although there are

---

[18] We adopt this model of possibilities, J. L. Mackie suggests in the article cited above (1974), because we hold the following combination of beliefs: determinism is false, but the past is fixed merely by having occurred, whereas the future is not fixed in advance. (Without the fixity of the past, indeterminism would yield open pasts as well as open futures, and hence backward branching as well as forward branching.) Admittedly, this model has its genesis as a model of thinking about causal possibilities. But—Mackie suggests—we find it natural to extend the model to metaphysical possibilities that go beyond the causal possibilities.

possible worlds, and possible states of affairs, that do not conform to the branching model, there are no possible states of affairs *in which actual individuals exist* that do not conform to it.

If I am right about this, we need to explain why the branching model of possibilities that concern particular individuals has this extra appeal, over and above that of the general branching model. Not surprisingly, I shall suggest that the explanation depends on questions concerning the existence of actual individuals in merely possible situations: hence questions concerning identity across possible worlds.

6.5. THE OVERLAP REQUIREMENT

We need to distinguish two features of the branching model of *de re* possibilities. This I shall do with reference to my example of Julius Caesar.

The first feature is that unrealized possibilities for Julius Caesar are represented by divergences (branches) from his actual history. It follows that any *complete* alternative possible history for Julius Caesar must have some segment (however small) that is the same as some portion of his actual history. I'll call this '*the overlap requirement*' on possible histories for Caesar. The idea behind the overlap requirement is, roughly, this: when you are considering how Julius Caesar might have been different, you have to take Julius Caesar as he actually was at some time in his existence, and consider what possibilities there are for him that are consistent with his being as he actually was at that time in his existence. (I intend the overlap requirement to represent a principle about *de re* modality that has some intuitive plausibility, corresponding to the idea that we can 'keep hold' of an actual individual in a possible situation only by 'anchoring' it to its actual history. This obviously raises the question how strict the notion of 'sameness' involved in the overlap requirement is supposed to be. For example, does anyone suppose that we can 'keep hold of' Julius Caesar in a possible situation only by keeping fixed *all* the properties that he had at some time in his actual existence?[19] However, having noted this point, I can, for my purposes

---

[19] One obvious problem with this is that if 'the same' were to mean 'sharing *all* properties, including past-tensed and future-tensed properties', then a possible history could not be the same as Julius Caesar's actual history at any one time without being the same as his actual history at all times. For the present I shall simply assume that some

in this part of my discussion, set it aside. Just as I can pretend, for simplicity, that the necessity of origin thesis is the thesis that all of a thing's origin properties are essential to it, so I can, for my present purposes, pretend, for simplicity, that the overlap requirement that we find plausible is the principle that any possible history for Julius Caesar must involve a complete coincidence with the properties of his actual history at some time.[20] I shall return to this issue in the penultimate section of this chapter.)

The second feature of the branching model is that it permits possible divergences from Julius Caesar's actual history to be in one direction only: a 'forward' direction; that is, into the future.

If there were no overlap requirement, then there would be nothing to stop Julius Caesar from having a completely different history, with a different origin and a different subsequent history as well: for example, as represented by the line XY in diagram (vii) in Figure 6.1.

But even given the overlap requirement, it would still be possible for Julius Caesar to have a different origin if the model allowed unrealized possibilities for Julius Caesar to include *backward* divergences from his actual history. For example, if we adopted the models of possibilities for Julius Caesar represented by diagram (iii) or diagram (v) in Figure 6.1, we should obey the overlap requirement, while allowing Caesar to have a different origin from his actual origin.

Hence, when we ask why we might accept what I call 'the branching model', we need to distinguish two questions. First, given the assumption that any possible history for Julius Caesar must overlap his actual history, why suppose that the possible divergences from his actual history go into the future, but not into the past? Why not, instead, adopt a model of possibilities for Caesar that allows backward divergences but no forward divergences, as in diagram (iii) in Figure 6.1, or allows both forward and backward divergences (as in diagram (v))?

A second, quite separate, question is: why accept the overlap requirement? Why suppose that the only possible histories for Julius Caesar are ones that include some portion of his actual history?

version of the overlap requirement can be formulated that avoids this consequence (cf. Mackie 1994: 317, and Ch. 7 below).

[20] Or at least, to accommodate the point in the previous note, a complete coincidence of non-tensed properties. For more discussion of what I am calling 'the overlap requirement' and the notion of 'anchorage', see Ch. 7 below. See also Mackie 1994, sects. 3–4, Wiggins 1980: 105–6, and Brody 1980: 114–23. The terminology of 'anchorage' is taken from Ayer 1973: 197–8; quoted in Wiggins 1980: 105.

6.6. FORWARD BRANCHING, BACKWARD BRANCHING, AND THE OVERLAP REQUIREMENT

Why not accept the overlap requirement, but allow for *backward branching*, and thus abandon the necessity of origin thesis?

First, why not allow backward branching, and no forward branching? Why not take the view represented by diagram (iii) in Figure 6.1, and say that the *only* possibilities for Julius Caesar are represented by backward divergences from his actual history?

If we took this view, we would have to abandon what I have called 'the assumption of open futures'. This assumption has, of course, been challenged, by those who embrace a strict metaphysical determinism or fatalism about the future. However, although this doctrine has its adherents, it would be extremely odd to combine this denial of the assumption of open futures with the assertion that there is a variety of different *pasts* that an individual could have had. In other words, if you deny the assumption of open futures, then diagram (iv) in Figure 6.1 (with no branching at all) seems more plausible than diagram (iii).

But why not backward divergences *as well as* forward divergences? Take Julius Caesar as he was at a certain time, say, just before he crossed the Rubicon. We can, no doubt, suppose that a variety of alternative futures then lay open to him. But what is to stop us from contemplating, in addition to this, a variety of *past* histories, including ones in which he had a quite different origin, that could have led him to that point in his career? For example, why not take Julius Caesar at point A in diagram (vi) in Figure 6.1, and treat him as having not only possible futures such as AD, but also possible pasts such as AB?

This would mirror our situation with respect to epistemic possibilities. If we are confronted with a person whose past history is unknown (a stranger on the train, say, or a foundling child, or the man who claims to be Martin Guerre) and we are trying to work out what that history is, then we are forced to consider a variety of alternative 'possible' past histories for that individual—histories that are possible, in the sense of being consistent with what we know.

Backward branching thus seems to be an inescapable feature of epistemic possibilities that concern actual individuals.[21] So why, when

---

[21] The fact that epistemic possibility seems to generate backward branching just as easily as it does forward branching represents an obstacle to the attempt that P. F.

we consider metaphysical, as opposed to epistemic, possibilities that concern actual individuals, should we exclude backward branching?[22]

The explanation, I suggest, is this. Taken just by itself, backward branching is not particularly counterintuitive. It is not particularly counterintuitive to ask questions like: given the way that Julius Caesar was in 49 BC, what are the various ways in which he might have started from a different origin and ended up at that point in his career? But what we cannot comfortably do is to combine the acceptance of backward divergences with both the overlap requirement and the possibility of forward divergences.

For suppose that we allow that Caesar could have had a different origin—say, the origin B in diagram (vi) in Figure 6.1—on the grounds that this is compatible with his leading a life that converges with his actual life at point A, in 49 BC. If, in general, we allow that forward divergences are possible as well as backward ones, we shall be inclined to say that if Caesar had had this different origin, he could have had a history that never converged with his actual history. For example, we shall say that he could have had the history represented by the line BC in diagram (vi) in Figure 6.1. But if Caesar could have had a history like BC, then there are possible histories for Caesar that do not obey the overlap requirement. In other words: if we accept that forward divergences are possible, then we cannot comfortably accept *both* the overlap requirement *and* the claim that backward divergences are possible.

At this point, I expect that the following objection will be made. Histories for Julius Caesar (like the one represented by BC in diagram (vi)) that flout the overlap requirement can be generated only if we allow a *combination* of backward branching and forward branching to produce a possible history for Julius Caesar. But someone could hold both that possible histories for Julius Caesar can be generated by forward branching alone (to give histories like AD in diagram (vi)), and also by backward branching alone (to give histories like AB in diagram (vi)), but refuse to accept that backward branching and forward branching can legitimately be combined to generate possible

Strawson makes to ground Kripke's 'metaphysical' possibilities in epistemic possibilities in Strawson 1979.

[22] More accurately, why can we treat backward branches as real (metaphysical) possibilities only if they arise out of previous divergences from an individual's actual history? (cf. J. L. Mackie 1974: 558).

histories like BC in diagram (vi). Evidently, such a person could accept both forward branching and backward branching possibilities for Julius Caesar without abandoning the overlap requirement.

However, although this is true, I do not think that it undermines my proposed explanation of the necessity of origin intuition. For the suggested restriction, to the effect that we can allow both AB and AD to be possibilities for Caesar, while excluding BC, seems an extremely unnatural one. This point can be reinforced by considering some quotations from writers who are arguing *against* Kripke's necessity of origin thesis. For example, according to Michael Dummett:

> [T]he antecedents of counterfactuals are not restricted to possibilities of the kind Kripke is interested in: we may quite intelligibly . . . for example . . . wonder what difference it would have made to Franz Kafka's outlook if he had not been of Jewish descent and upbringing. (Dummett 1973: 132)

And David Wiggins expresses doubts about the necessity of origin thesis in the following terms:

> Perhaps the speculator has to be able to *rebut* the charge that he has lost his subject of discourse [Julius Caesar] if he changes its parents or origin. But now I ask: can he not rebut the charge by claiming to speculate about how *the man whom Brutus murdered in 44 B.C.* would have fared if (say) Marius had been his father? (Wiggins 1980: 116, note 22)

A striking feature of these examples is that the authors are using the supposition of an individual's having a different origin as the antecedent of a counterfactual about how things would have been different *later* if the individual's origin had been different.[23] The supposition that the thing could have had a different origin is employed in order to explore what the later consequences of this would have been. But if the point of supposing that Caesar, say, should have had a different origin is precisely to explore how this would have affected his subsequent history, it seems absurd to insist on retaining, within the scope of this supposition, the idea that he is to have a career that converges, at some later point, with his actual career. If, to take Wiggins's example, I am speculating about how Julius Caesar would have fared if Marius had been his father, I shall not want to restrict myself to cases in which, in spite of this different origin, he still ends up being murdered by Brutus in 44 BC.

---

[23] See also D. H. Mellor's 'If John hadn't been a Kennedy, he wouldn't have been shot' (Mellor 1977: 310).

This, I think, reinforces the idea that we cannot comfortably allow *both* backward divergences *and* forward divergences without abandoning the overlap requirement. Assuming that forward divergences (and the associated 'assumption of open futures') are obligatory (although I admit that I haven't explained why), those who deny the necessity of origin must reject the overlap requirement. If we want to say that Julius Caesar could have had a quite different origin, then we had better also be prepared to say that he could have had, not only a different origin, but also a history entirely different from his actual history.[24]

6.7. NECESSITY AND SUFFICIENCY AGAIN

I have argued that if we accept both the overlap requirement and the assumption of open futures, then we shall be led to accept a branching model of *de re* possibilities that entails the necessity of origin thesis. Schematically, my argument has been:

> [Overlap requirement + assumption of open futures (i.e., forward branching)] → no backward branching → necessity of origin.

Moreover, I want to employ this argument to explain the intuitive appeal of the necessity of origin thesis. The explanation, I suggest, is (roughly) as follows. If we were to give up the necessity of origin thesis, we should have to give up either the overlap requirement or the assumption of open futures. But it is counterintuitive to give up the overlap requirement, and it is extremely counterintuitive to give up the assumption of open futures. Hence intuition recommends that we accept the necessity of origin thesis.

A distinctive feature of my account is that, as indicated in Section 6.1, it makes no appeal to any principle to the effect that some individual in a

---

[24] It may be objected that the use of the counterfactual reasoning described above to generate a possible world in which Julius Caesar has the history BC need not, strictly speaking, involve a violation of the overlap requirement on possible histories for Caesar. It need not do so, as long as BC is regarded as a history for Julius Caesar that is merely 'possibly possible': a history that *would* have been possible for him if he had had a different origin, but actually is not. However, although this is technically correct, I do not think it undermines my argument. This attempt to insulate the history BC from conflict with the overlap requirement seems intolerably ad hoc. I agree that there are some cases where it may be plausible to distinguish what is possible from what is merely possibly possible (see Chandler 1976; also Sects. 3.5–3.6 above). However, I do not think that this is one of them.

possible world can be Julius Caesar only in virtue of possessing properties *sufficient* to make him Julius Caesar. In particular, as I characterized the overlap requirement, it is the principle that an individual in a possible world can be Julius Caesar *only if* it has a history that matches some portion of Caesar's actual history. I was careful not to make the overlap requirement entail that *if* any individual in a possible world has a history that matches a portion of Julius Caesar's actual history, that individual is Caesar.[25]

I admit that if one were to interpret the overlap requirement as a sufficiency thesis, this would provide the starting point for a rival explanation of the necessity of origin intuition.[26] However, I think it is of interest to show that the necessity of origin thesis can be explained as a consequence of principles about *de re* modality that are independent of any such sufficiency assumption. This is especially so if, as I have argued in the previous chapters, the appeal to such sufficiency assumptions (and the associated appeal to individual essences) in the case of ordinary persisting things, including persons, is untenable.

6.8. IS THE OVERLAP REQUIREMENT INDISPENSIBLE?

However, although I propose this as an explanation of why people *do* accept the necessity of origin thesis, I do not take this to show that they *should* accept it. If my argument is correct, one who accepts the assumption of open futures has a choice: either accept the necessity of origin thesis, or reject the overlap requirement. But I do not think it is obvious that the acceptance of the necessity of origin thesis is the correct choice.

---

[25] The distinction I am making here echoes one made by Wiggins (1980: 116, note 22).

[26] The explanation (anticipated in Chs. 2–3 above) would go as follows. Interpreted as a sufficiency thesis, the overlap requirement has intolerable consequences. 'Having a history that overlaps *some* portion of Julius Caesar's actual history' cannot, as a matter of logic, be a genuinely sufficient condition for identity with Caesar, since it is a property that can be possessed by two distinct individuals in one possible world. An obvious remedy for this 'reduplication problem' is to modify the overlap requirement, so that it selects just *one* portion of Julius Caesar's actual history as the one that he must retain in all possible worlds. But which portion of his actual history is to be favoured? Here what I have called 'the assumption of open futures' comes into play. If there is to be any one portion of Julius Caesar's actual history that he must retain in all possible worlds, then, given the assumption of open futures, it can only be his origin (cf. Sect. 3.1).

I admit that the rejection of the overlap requirement may seem paradoxical. How can we allow Julius Caesar the liberty of being unconstrained in other possible worlds by the anchorage to his actual history that is provided by the overlap requirement? If we do this, won't we be in danger of—as David Wiggins puts it—*losing* Caesar altogether? Suppose that I say: there is a possible world in which *I* exist, although in this possible world I am born to different parents, lead a life that is utterly different from my actual life, and end up becoming the Emperor of China. Can there really be any reason to distinguish this from a possible world from which I am absent, and in which some other person becomes the Emperor of China?

Nevertheless, I doubt that the overlap requirement should be regarded as sacrosanct. I think that the requirement represents an unstable intermediate position between, on the one hand, the theory that the most that is essential to an actual individual is that it retain, in any possible world, some subset of its actual properties—although not necessarily the same subset in every possible world—(a requirement that is met in the scenario envisaged above in which I am the Emperor of China), and, on the other hand, the theory, which I have argued (in Chapter 3) to be untenable, that it is essential to an individual that it retain, in every possible world, some subset of its actual properties that is non-trivially sufficient for its being the individual that it is. The overlap requirement appears to represent an attempt to capture the particularity of a given object in terms of its properties, while simultaneously attempting to avoid the commitment to supply a non-trivial individual essence for the object. But no such compromise remains plausible on close inspection.

Problems with the overlap requirement emerge when we revisit an issue that I raised in Section 6.5, but have deliberately ignored throughout most of the subsequent discussion: if we are tempted to accept the overlap requirement, what properties should we take the 'overlap' to involve? As we shall see in the next chapter, to get off the ground at all, the overlap requirement must, it seems, exclude from the requirement certain relational properties. But must the extent of overlap include all of a thing's *intrinsic* properties? Not if, as I argue in Section 7.4, we should admit that things have what I there call 'accidentally permanent intrinsic properties'. And should the required overlap exclude all of the thing's relational properties? Apparently not, if the requirement is to explain the intuition that it is essential to an individual that it came into existence from certain particular antecedents, since its coming from those antecedents seems undeniably to be one of its relational properties (cf. Chapter 3, note 5). But it now appears that the overlap requirement, thus interpreted, is in danger of dwindling to some such requirement as this: that, in order to be identical with a particular individual—let us again take Julius Caesar as our example—an individual in a possible world must share with Caesar, at some time in its existence, some set of significant properties that at some time in Caesar's existence happens to distinguish him from all other things, perhaps including some (but not all) of the relational properties that he then has, while excluding any properties that he merely happens to possess throughout his existence (his accidentally permanent intrinsic properties). I shall have more to say, in the next chapter, about the overlap requirement and its interpretation. But here my interim conclusion is that if the overlap requirement is qualified as suggested above, it is hard to see that it can provide a principled, non-ad hoc, basis for the attribution of essential properties to persisting individuals.

6.9. NECESSITY OF ORIGIN AND TENACITY OF ORIGIN

It seems undeniable that, when we consider how a persisting individual such as a human being might have been different, we normally have a tendency to assume it to retain some of the properties, and even some of the distinctive properties, that are associated with its origin. Kripke was surely right to recognize this fact. It seems clearly correct that 'match of origins', in some sense, is a feature to which we often give considerable weight when considering the ways in which such an individual could have been different from the way that it actually is, and to which we typically give much greater weight than we do to match of later history. However, the proposal that these facts about our *de re* modal intuitions can be enshrined in a defensible version of something as strong as the necessity of origin thesis does not, I think, survive careful scrutiny.

I suggest that we have an alternative: the 'tenacity of origin' thesis mentioned at the beginning of this chapter. The tenacity of origin thesis does not attempt to insist that Julius Caesar *could* not have had a quite different origin—that he *could* not have had different parents, for example. The most that it need maintain is that his having something similar to his actual origin in certain respects (including, for example, his having his actual parents) is a feature that is *normally* kept fixed in counterfactual speculations about him. I think that we may explain the intuitive plausibility of this relatively modest thesis, by appeal to a combination of the influence of the branching model of *de re* possibilities and some version of the overlap requirement, without undertaking the much more demanding—and, I suspect, ultimately impossible—task of defending the full-blooded necessity of origin thesis.[27,28]

[27] I develop the suggestion that some essentialist claims may be replaced by claims to the effect that certain properties are 'tenacious' rather than essential in Ch. 9 below.

[28] One might even suggest that the 'tenacity of origin' thesis better represents (than does the necessity of origin thesis) the tentative form of Kripke's remarks when, in the passage quoted at the beginning of this chapter, he says that 'what is *harder to imagine* is her being born of different parents' (1980: 113; my emphasis). However, elsewhere in the work Kripke commits himself more definitely to the necessity of origin thesis that is associated with his name.

7

Sortal Concepts and Essential Properties I: Substance Sortals and Essential Sortals

7.1. SORTAL ESSENTIALISM

There is a pretty general consensus that if the notion of an essential property has any application at all, the essential properties of an individual involve the fact that it could not have belonged to a *radically* different kind from the kind (or kinds) to which it actually belongs.[1] If this view is correct, then if a thing, A, belongs to a given kind, there are certain other kinds such that A's *not belonging* to those other kinds is an essential property of A. For example, it would be generally agreed that although Aristotle could have been and done many things, Aristotle could not have been a centipede, or a giraffe, a parsnip, a paper clip, or the number 17.

Later in this book, I shall try to defend the thesis that this widespread consensus is, in fact, mistaken. But in order to justify the claim that my (apparently wildly eccentric) view should be taken seriously, I must undermine a popular theory that purports to explain and justify the claim that Aristotle could not have been any of these things by appeal to the thesis that there is some sortal kind or category to which Aristotle essentially belongs. I call this theory 'sortal essentialism'.

The view that I have in mind says that the impossibility of Aristotle's having been a centipede is grounded in two facts. The first is the fact that there is some sort, corresponding to a *sortal concept*, such that Aristotle is essentially a thing of that sort. The second is the fact that belonging to that sort is incompatible with being a centipede. If we ask what sort of thing Aristotle is essentially, sortal essentialists do not give a unanimous answer. But *person* and *man* (in the sense—if there still is

---

[1] For some representative examples, see Adams 1979: 24–5; Kirwan 1970: 49; Forbes 1997: 520–1. For more details, see Ch. 9 below.

one—of 'human being') are popular (although apparently competing)[2] candidates. A sortal essentialist, then, might argue as follows. *Man* is a sortal concept that Aristotle falls under essentially. So Aristotle is essentially a man. In other words, he is a man in all possible worlds in which he exists. Nothing in any possible world is both a man and a centipede. Therefore there is no possible world in which Aristotle is a centipede—in other words, he could not have been one.

Sortal essentialism is not, of course, restricted to claims about the essential properties of human beings. Sortal essentialists are likely to say that any animal, plant, or artefact is essentially confined to a certain sortal kind, and essentially debarred from membership of certain other sortal kinds. However, there is no consensus about exactly which sortal kinds these are. For example, sortal essentialists may disagree over whether or not an animal's species is essential to it, and over whether such concepts as *machine* or *knife* correspond to essential sorts.

These remarks give only a sketch of sortal essentialism. But they serve to introduce the topic that is the subject of this chapter and the next.

If sortal essentialism is true, we should expect to be able to say why it is true. In particular, we should expect to be able to answer the following two questions:

(1) Why are *any* sortal properties essential, rather than accidental, properties? and

(2) What are the principles that determine *which* are the 'essential sortals'—the sortal concepts under which things essentially fall?

I shall examine two very different theories of sortal essentialism, both of which might be expected to answer these questions. The first theory, formulated by Baruch Brody (1980), bases sortal essentialism on the notion of a property that an individual must possess throughout its existence if it possesses it at any time in its existence. The second theory, proposed by David Wiggins (1980, 2001), bases sortal essentialism on the notion that a thing's principle of individuation is essential to it. I shall argue that neither theory succeeds in giving satisfactory answers to the two questions raised above.[3] Brody's theory is the topic of the current chapter. Wiggins's theory will be discussed in Chapter 8.

---

[2] e.g., if a foetus is a human being but not a person, and every adult human being was once a foetus, it seems that Aristotle cannot be both essentially a human being and also essentially a person. See, e.g., Olson 1997 and D. Mackie 1999.

[3] I think that many contemporary philosophers are sortal essentialists. Some years ago P. F. Strawson remarked, of a version of sortal essentialism, that it is 'now widely

7.2. TERMINOLOGY

Before proceeding, I need to say something about the notion of a sortal concept. I shall not try to define it. Instead, I shall appeal to the way in which the notion has been used in the literature.[4] Although it has been employed in slightly different ways, a common thread is provided by the idea that sortal concepts have a special role in *individuation*: they are concepts that provide *criteria of identity* or *principles of individuation* for the things that fall under them.[5] Thus:

> A concept is a *sortal concept* only if it provides a criterion of identity (principle of individuation) for the things that fall under it.

The following statement is, I think, a fairly orthodox expression of this view about the role of sortal concepts:[6]

> If 'F' is a sortal term (a term corresponding to a sortal concept), then expressions of the form 'this F', 'that F', or 'the F that is so and so' can be used to single out an individual in such a way as to determine what counts (both at the time of singling out and at earlier and later times) as *the same individual* as the one singled out. By contrast, if 'C' is not a sortal term, then the attempt to single something out as 'this C', 'that C', etc., will fail to determine what counts as the same individual as the one picked out, unless some sortal term is implicitly being invoked, in which case it is the sortal term, and not 'C', that is really doing the work.

---

regarded as scarcely contentious' (1981: 604). I shall argue that sortal essentialism *should* be contentious.

[4] The term 'sortal' was coined by Locke, in the context of his doctrine of nominal essence (1975/1690, III. iii. 15). For some modern discussions, see: Strawson 1959: 168 and part 2, *passim*; Wiggins 1967, parts I–III, *passim*; Wiggins 1980 and Wiggins 2001, esp. chs. 2 and 3; Dummett 1973, chs. 4 and 16, esp. pp. 73–6 and 546–50. For a comparison between Strawson's use of 'sortal' and Wiggins's, see Wiggins 1967, note 2, or Wiggins 1980: 7. Dummett (1973: 76) defines 'sortal' in a way that amounts to Wiggins's definition of 'substance sortal'.

[5] I shall take it for granted that this view about the role of sortals does not imply Geach's thesis of the relativity of identity (e.g., Geach 1967). For a defence of this assumption, see Wiggins 1980, chs. 1–2. In fact, I shall ignore relative identity theories, and assume that criteria of identity are always criteria for absolute identity.

[6] I do not mean to suggest that the view is universally accepted. For a denial that individuation requires sortals, see Ayers 1974.

The application of this test for being a sortal is not an easy matter. But it is plausible to say that *red thing*, for example, is not a sortal concept, although *brick, tomato*, and *flamingo* all have some claim to be sortals. (From now on I shall use the term 'sortal', as a noun, as short for 'sortal concept'.)

I define 'essential sortal' as follows:

> A sortal concept S is an *essential sortal* if and only if the things that fall under S could not have existed without falling under S.[7]

Finally, 'sortal essentialism' I define simply as the view that there are essential sortals.

With these preliminaries over, I proceed to the first of the two theories of sortal essentialism that I shall examine: that given by Baruch Brody.[8]

7.3. SUBSTANCE SORTALS, ESSENTIAL SORTALS, AND THE OVERLAP REQUIREMENT

The first element in Brody's theory is the claim that some sortal concepts represent properties that an object must have throughout its existence if it has them at any time in its existence (1980, ch. 4, sect. 1). Brody gives *person* as an example of such a sortal. According to Brody, if something is a person, it must have been a person from the first moment of its existence, and it cannot cease to be a person without ceasing to exist. Sortal concepts answering to this description have been called 'substance sortals'.[9] I characterize the notion as follows:

> A sortal S is a *substance sortal* if and only if an individual that falls under S at any time in its existence must fall under S throughout its existence.

We may also express the main idea loosely, by the following slogan:

> If F is a substance sortal, then 'once an F, always an F'.

---

[7] I ignore the possibility that there might be a sortal such that some, but not all, of the things that fall under it fall under it essentially. This can hardly weaken my criticisms of sortal essentialism, since such a possibility would be an embarrassment to a sortal essentialist.

[8] In Brody 1980, ch. 4, sect. 2, and ch. 5, esp. pp. 114–23. All references in the remainder of this chapter are to this work, unless otherwise indicated.

[9] See Wiggins 1980: 24; also p. 64. The notion is derived from Aristotle's distinction between substantial change and alteration.

For example, if *parrot* is a substance sortal, then if something is once a parrot, it is always a parrot (as long as it exists). If *parrot* is a substance sortal, then being a parrot is not a temporary occupation.

The notion of a substance sortal is a modal notion. However, several writers (including Brody himself) have pointed out that it does not *immediately* follow, from the fact that something is a substance sortal, that it is an essential sortal.[10] There is a logical gap between the claim that something cannot change from being an F to not being an F, or vice versa, and the claim that something that is actually an F could not have passed its entire existence as something other than an F. Hence, even if we accept that *person* is a substance sortal that applies to, say, Socrates, we cannot immediately infer that Socrates could not have existed as anything other than a person.

Nevertheless, Brody has an ingenious argument to bridge this gap. He shows that if we adopt a model of counterfactual possibilities that I shall call 'the overlap model', we must conclude that any substance sortal is also an essential sortal.

Brody holds that counterfactual possibilities for actual individuals are to be understood in terms of possible extensions of portions of their actual histories. This is connected with his treatment of identity across possible worlds. Brody accepts a possible worlds account of *de re* modality that implies that actual individuals, such as Socrates, exist in other possible worlds (pp. 87, 103, 108–16). But he holds that Socrates exists in a possible world—a possible world contains Socrates—only if it shares, with the actual world, some portion of Socrates' actual history (pp. 114–16, 120). (According to Brody, this allows us to reduce the conditions for identity across possible worlds with Socrates to the conditions for identity over time with Socrates (pp. 115, 121).)

One way of satisfying this requirement would be to restrict possible histories for Socrates to ways in which he might have developed from his actual original state (the state he was actually in when he came into existence). Evidently, this would yield the result that if some sortal is a substance sortal for Socrates, it is an essential sortal for Socrates.[11] If Socrates was a person from the first moment of his existence, and *person* is a substance sortal, *and* all possible histories for Socrates have to

---

[10] See Kirwan 1970: 50; Kripke 1980, note 57; Wiggins 1980: 215–16, longer note 4.24; Brody 1980: 116–23.

[11] See Brody's 'proposal (3)', pp. 117–19.

be possible developments from his actual original state, then obviously *being a person* must be one of his essential properties.

However, Brody acknowledges that this constraint is too strong (pp. 119–20). It makes every detail of the beginning of Socrates' existence essential to him, and this, as we have seen in Chapter 6 above, is extremely counterintuitive. For example, no one wants to say that the exact location of Socrates' birth or conception is essential to him.

In response to this problem, Brody proposes a model of counterfactual possibilities that has the following implication: Socrates could have been F at *t* if and only if *either* there was, at some time in Socrates' actual existence, a possible future for him in which he was F at *t*, *or* there was, at some time in Socrates' actual existence, a possible past for him in which he was F at *t* (cf. pp. 120, 125). Socrates' non-actual possible pasts and futures can be represented by lines branching out like the broken lines in Figure 7.1 from a solid line representing his actual history. For example, the broken line RS is intended to represent something that was, at point R in Socrates' actual history, a possible future for Socrates. And the broken line PQ is intended to represent something that was, at point Q in Socrates' actual history, a possible past for Socrates: one in which he had a different origin from his actual origin.

According to this version of a branching model, possible pasts and futures for Socrates are possible extensions of parts of his actual history.

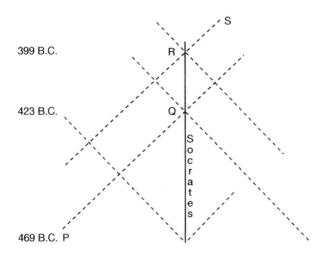

Figure 7.1

The idea, roughly (as we shall see in the next section, this needs refinement to deal with non-intrinsic properties) is that something is a possible past or future that Socrates had at $t*$ only if it is one that is *compossible* with his actual state at $t*$. It is, roughly, a past or future that he could have had, while *also* having the properties that he actually had at $t*$.

Finally, to satisfy Brody's requirement that possible worlds that contain Socrates must contain some portion of Socrates' actual history, we must add the following restriction: something is a *complete* possible history for Socrates only if it incorporates some segment (however small) of his actual history.[12] This segment need not, however, include Socrates' actual original state. For example, one possible complete alternative history for Socrates is represented by the path in Figure 7.1 consisting of the broken line PQ followed by the portion of his actual history QR and concluding with the broken line RS.

Brody's model is committed to a version of what I earlier called (in Chapter 6) 'the overlap requirement' on counterfactual possibilities for individuals. Brody's version may initially be represented as follows:

> *Brody's Overlap Requirement*: If something is a possible (complete) history for an individual, there must be some segment of that possible history that is exactly the same as some segment of the individual's actual history.

It can easily be seen that an 'overlap model' of counterfactual possibilities: that is, a model that includes Brody's Overlap Requirement, has the consequence that all substance sortals are essential sortals. For example, if *person* is a substance sortal that applies to Socrates, then Socrates was a person throughout his actual history. According to Brody's Overlap Requirement, any possible complete history for Socrates must therefore include his being, at some time in that history, a person. But if *person* is a substance sortal, then any possible Socrates who is a person at some time in his history must be a person throughout that history. It follows—if *person* really is a substance sortal—that Socrates is a person throughout all of his possible histories, and thus *being a person* is one of his essential properties.

This attempt to generate sortal essentialism will work only if two conditions are fulfilled. First, there must be substance sortals. Secondly,

---

[12] In using the term 'segment' I do not intend to imply that a 'segment' of an individual's history need have any significant temporal extent.

the Overlap Requirement must be an acceptable restriction on counterfactual possibilities.

I shall now argue that, even if the first condition is fulfilled, the
second is not. Brody's Overlap Requirement is too restrictive, partly for
reasons touched on in Chapter 6 above. Moreover, although Brody's
Overlap Requirement can be modified to meet these difficulties, the
modified versions are still unacceptable, unless the modifications weaken
the principle to such an extent that it no longer supports the generation
of sortal essentialism.

7.4. BRODY'S OVERLAP REQUIREMENT REJECTED

As Brody is aware (p. 122), the overlap model of counterfactual
possibilities is unsatisfactory unless certain properties that make reference
to the past are excluded from the Overlap Requirement. For example,
if Socrates actually originated in Athens, he has, throughout his actual
existence, the property of *having an Athenian origin*. As it stands, Brody's
Overlap Requirement will carry this property over to Socrates' history
in every possible world in which he exists. And this will generate the
unwelcome conclusion that it is essential to Socrates that he originated
in Athens. Moreover, tensed properties are not the only ones to cause
problems. For example, unless we want to say that Socrates could not
have existed unless the Pyramids also existed, we must exclude, from
the Overlap Requirement, the relational property that Socrates had,
throughout his existence, of *living in a world that contains the Pyramids*.
If the Overlap Requirement is to be plausible at all, it must be restricted
to 'intrinsic' properties, in an appropriate sense.

However, I do not want to make much of this problem. Let us
suppose that unwanted tensed properties and relational properties
can be exempted from the Overlap Requirement, and the Requirement
restricted to intrinsic properties (in some appropriate sense of 'intrinsic'),
in a way that is not merely ad hoc. For reasons not noted by Brody, the
overlap model will still be too restrictive.

To back up this claim, I offer two examples. First, if Socrates *always*
actually had a mole on his left foot, then, according to the overlap model,
there is no possible history for Socrates in which he *never* had a mole
on his left foot. For obviously, an individual who never has such a mole
does not, at any time, have exactly the same intrinsic properties as any
individual who always has such a mole. We might call this problem 'the

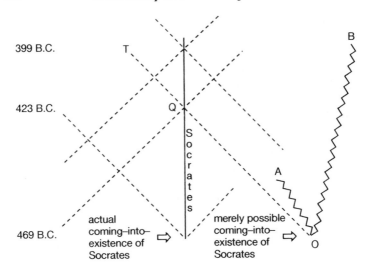

Figure 7.2

problem of accidentally permanent intrinsic properties'. (I assume that the property of having a mole on one's left foot is an intrinsic property.) Secondly, the overlap model has the following implausible implication: although Socrates could have had a different origin, he could have done so only if he had *also* gone on to lead a life that converged completely, at some later time, with his actual life. For example, the model allows that the line OQT in Figure 7.2, which converges with Socrates' actual life at 423 BC and then diverges again, represents a possible history for Socrates. What it does *not* allow is that the zigzag line OA, which starts from the same origin as OQT, represents a possible history for Socrates. For OA never converges with, and hence never shares a segment with, Socrates' actual history. But this restriction imposed by the overlap model seems unsatisfactory, for reasons explained in the previous chapter. As I there emphasized (Section 6.6), if we suppose that Socrates could have had a different origin, we shall be reluctant to suppose that he could have had that different origin only if he had also gone on to lead a life that converged at some point with his actual life. So, for example, surely we want to say that *if* Socrates could have originated at O and had the history OQT, then he could have originated at O and had some history like OA that never converged with his actual history.

These difficulties are, to my mind, sufficient to show that Brody's
Overlap Requirement must be rejected, even if it is restricted to intrinsic
properties, and that it cannot be used to support the thesis that substance
sortals are essential sortals.

7.5. OVERLAP, SIMILARITY, AND SUBSTANCE SORTALS

The second of my two objections to Brody's Overlap Requirement
turns on the apparent instability, noted in Chapter 6, that results if
one attempts to combine the view that an individual could have had
an origin different from its actual origin with the requirement that it
must nevertheless have, in any possible world, a history that overlaps its
actual history, an instability that is connected with what I called 'the
assumption of open futures'. However, it seems that Brody might modify
his Overlap Requirement to meet this objection. We saw in the previous
section that Brody is forced to restrict his Overlap Requirement to an
overlap of intrinsic properties, in order to avoid making certain relational
properties of Socrates, such as his property of originating in Athens,
or his property of coexisting with the Pyramids, essential properties
of Socrates. However, once the restriction to intrinsic properties is
imposed, it is no longer clear that Brody should have abandoned his
original suggestion that it is an overlap of *origin* that is required for
identity with Socrates in another possible world. As we have seen, the
most obvious counterexamples to the claim that Socrates could not
have come into existence with different properties concern what appear
to be *relational* properties of his original state, such as its location.
And this suggests that Brody might do better to abandon the Overlap
Requirement described above, and substitute for it something like the
following 'Overlap of Origin Requirement':

> *Overlap of Origin Requirement*: If something is a possible (complete)
> history for an individual, the initial segment of that history must
> be exactly the same, in its intrinsic properties, as the initial segment
> of the individual's actual history.

However, even if this Overlap of Origin Requirement represents an
improvement, it does nothing to answer my first objection, concerning
the mole on Socrates' left foot: my 'problem of accidentally permanent
intrinsic properties'. As long as there can be—as surely there can
be—such properties, *any* theory that requires, for transworld identity

with Socrates, a complete coincidence of intrinsic properties with Socrates at *any* time in his existence must be in trouble.

Nevertheless, there is a further modification of Brody's Overlap Requirement that appears to meet both my objections, while still delivering the result that substance sortals are essential sortals. The modification is as follows:

> *Indirect Overlap Requirement*: If something is a possible (complete) history for an individual *x*, then *either* there must be some segment of that possible history that exactly matches (in its intrinsic properties) some segment of *x*'s actual history, *or* the original segment of that possible history must exactly match (in its intrinsic properties) the original segment of some *other* possible (complete) history that has a segment that itself exactly matches (in its intrinsic properties) some segment of *x*'s actual history.

This modification still yields the result that any of Socrates' substance sortals is an essential sortal for Socrates, and, in general, that all substance sortals are essential sortals. The paths represented by the zigzag lines (OA and OB) in Figure 7.2 are now allowed to be possible histories for Socrates. But they are allowed only because they share their origin with a possible history, such as OQT, that does converge with Socrates' actual history. We have already established that, if *person* is a substance sortal, then Socrates is a person throughout the possible history OQT, including its origin O. But if Socrates is a person at O, and *person* is a substance sortal, then Socrates must be a person throughout any possible history—such as the zigzag lines in Figure 7.2—that begins with O.

However, I shall now argue that even this modified, 'indirect', version of the Overlap Requirement is unwarranted.

The Indirect Overlap Requirement allows, as the previous two versions of the Requirement did not, that even if Socrates always actually had a mole on his left foot, he could have existed even if he had never had a mole on his left foot. And the Indirect Overlap Requirement allows, as the first version of the Overlap Requirement did not, that Socrates could have led a life in which he has not only an origin different (in its intrinsic respects) from his actual origin, but also a history that never converges with (so as temporarily to match in its intrinsic respects) his actual history. But the Indirect Overlap Requirement implies that in each case these things are possible only because *another* history for Socrates, a history that does converge with (and hence does 'overlap' with, in the sense of 'matching in its intrinsic respects') his actual history, is also possible. For example, the Indirect Overlap Requirement implies that a history for Socrates in which he lacks a mole on his left foot throughout his existence is possible only because another history for Socrates is also possible: one in which, although Socrates comes into existence without a mole on his left foot, he later acquires such a mole, and becomes intrinsically exactly like the actual Socrates at some later stage in his existence. I think this is absurd. Perhaps there will always *be* such a possible history. But the idea that it is required to underwrite the possibility that a Socrates who always had a mole on his foot should have lacked one throughout his existence seems ludicrous. The reason that we can envisage the possibility that Socrates should always have lacked such a mole is, rather, that the precise distribution of moles about Socrates' person is an utterly trivial feature when it comes to envisaging alternative possible histories for Socrates.

The moral that I draw from this is that anyone tempted by the considerations that appear to support any of the overlap requirements so far mentioned should retreat to the following *Similarity Requirement* on counterfactual possibilities:

> *Similarity Requirement*: If something is a possible (complete) history for *x*, then *either* there must be some segment of that possible history that is *similar in important respects* to some segment of *x*'s actual history, *or* the possible history must share its original segment with some other possible (complete) history that itself has some segment that is *similar in important respects* to some segment of *x*'s actual history.

I suspect that the Similarity Requirement is still too strong. But the important point, for my purposes here, is that, unlike any of the overlap requirements, the Similarity Requirement does *not* automatically guarantee that substance sortals are essential sortals. It implies that a substance sortal that Socrates falls under is essential to him only if the sortal also represents a property that is important when it comes to envisaging alternative histories for Socrates.

At this point, someone might make a final attempt to defend a proposal in the style of Brody's, as follows. 'When it comes to considering what it takes for something to be similar to the actual Socrates in important respects, the fact that Socrates was actually a person is so very important that nothing could count as sufficiently similar unless it were a person.'

However, even if it is true that *person* has the requisite importance, this will not do as a defence of anything in the spirit of Brody's proposal. The ground has been shifted. What is now being claimed is no longer that a substance sortal is essential because it is, by definition, a concept that must apply to an object throughout its existence if it applies to the object at all. It is being argued that it is essential because, in *addition* to this, it represents a feature that is important when it comes to envisaging possible alternatives to actuality.

I conclude that Brody's model of counterfactual possibilities cannot be exploited to provide a sound basis for sortal essentialism. I suggest that the proponent of sortal essentialism will have to appeal to the idea of the 'importance' of certain sortals in the context of speculations about how an individual might have been. This brings me to my next topic: David Wiggins's defence of sortal essentialism.

8

Sortal Concepts and Essential Properties II: Sortal Concepts and Principles of Individuation

8.1. PRINCIPLES OF INDIVIDUATION AND ESSENTIAL SORTALS

In this chapter, I turn to a discussion of the second of the two theories of sortal essentialism cited in Section 7.1, the theory proposed by David Wiggins. Wiggins presents a version of sortal essentialism that is independent of Brody's overlap model.[1] In Wiggins's version, the claim that certain sortal concepts represent essential properties is justified by appeal to the role that sortal concepts play in providing *principles of individuation*. Summarizing the connection, he writes:

[T]he whole justification of our criterion for essential properties is the claim that there can be no envisaging this or that particular thing as having a different principle of individuation ... from its actual principle. (1980: 122)

In the quoted passage Wiggins employs a principle that we can formulate as follows, labelling it 'EPI' (an acronym for 'Essentiality of Principles of Individuation'):

EPI: If an individual x has a principle of individuation P, then x could not have existed without having P.

EPI says that things have their principles of individuation essentially. And, according to Wiggins, a thing has a principle of individuation

---

[1] Wiggins 1980, ch. 4. All references in this chapter are to this work, unless otherwise indicated. (In ch. 4 of his (2001), Wiggins provides what is substantially the same account, with minor modifications that are not relevant to the argument of the current chapter. See also Sect. 8.7 below.)

by virtue of falling under a sortal that supplies that principle. It does not immediately follow that any sortals are essential sortals: sortals that represent essential properties of the things that fall under them.[2] For one thing, in Wiggins's system many sortals supply the same principles of individuation. In fact, several additional principles are needed to generate Wiggins's sortal essentialism, and the route from EPI to sortal essentialism is not a simple one. I do not want to try to trace the details of that route here.[3] It is enough, for my purposes, to note that, in Wiggins's system, the only sortals that can be guaranteed to be essential sortals are what we can call 'ultimate sortals'. This notion can be characterized as follows:

> S is an *ultimate sortal* if and only if S is *the most general* sortal corresponding to some principle of individuation.[4]

As long as a thing retains its principle of individuation, it must fall under the ultimate sortal that supplies that principle, if there is such an ultimate sortal.

However, my primary concern is not with the notion of an ultimate sortal. Rather, I want to focus on the thesis—EPI—that things have their principles of individuation essentially. Even if we ignore ultimate sortals, we can still consider the bearing that EPI has on certain counterfactual questions.

Suppose that it is true that Aristotle could not have been a centipede instead of a man. Why is this so? Wiggins's theory suggests the following as an explanation. *Man* and *centipede* are sortals that supply different, and incompatible, principles of individuation. Hence Aristotle could have been a centipede only if he could have had a different principle of individuation from his actual principle. By EPI, this is impossible. Therefore Aristotle could not have been a centipede. QED. Similar pieces of reasoning could be invoked to explain why it is that there are

---

[2] See Sect. 7.2 above.

[3] In fact, I do not know of any published account of this. Wiggins does not supply one in his (1980).

[4] Cf. 1980: 65, note 8. Wiggins also refers to these as 'highest autonomously individuative sortals'. In addition, he suggests that there may be no such thing as *the highest* autonomously individuative sortal (i.e., the ultimate sortal) that a thing falls under (1980: 65). I find this puzzling, given that he appears to have such confidence in the principle that an individual must have at least one essential sortal (see 1980: 117). For I see no way in which Wiggins's principles can lead to the conclusion that there are essential sortals that does not rely on the assumption that there are ultimate sortals.

other sorts of thing, animal, vegetable, mineral, and so on, such that Aristotle could not have been a thing of one of those sorts.

I shall argue that the attempt to explain, in this fashion, why Aristotle could not have had certain properties faces a serious challenge. The challenge takes the form of a dilemma. Either the proposed explanations rely on a principle that is unwarranted, or they are vacuous. In either case, they are unsatisfactory as explanations.

Before proceeding, I want to emphasize two points.

First, the principle EPI, that a thing's principle of individuation is essential to it, must be distinguished from another principle, also held by Wiggins, which we may call 'the Absolute Identity Principle':[5]

> *The Absolute Identity Principle*: An individual cannot change its principle of individuation over time, nor can it have two different principles of individuation simultaneously.

For reasons that should by now be familiar, EPI is not equivalent to, nor is it entailed by, the Absolute Identity Principle. The Absolute Identity Principle rules out the possibility that a thing that starts out with one principle of individuation should later acquire a different one. It does not rule out the possibility that a thing that actually has one principle of individuation should have had a different one throughout its existence. Although I intend to cast doubt on the validity of EPI, nothing that I say will be in conflict with the Absolute Identity Principle.

Secondly, although Wiggins is a sortal essentialist, he does not believe that every *substance sortal* is an essential sortal. Recall that (as explained in the previous chapter) a substance sortal is a sortal that must apply to an object throughout its existence if it applies to it at all (see Section 7.3 above). Wiggins explicitly allows that one individual may fall under two substance sortals, one of which is more general than the other (pp. 64–5). According to his Absolute Identity Principle, these two substance sortals must supply the same principle of individuation. It follows that the less general sortal cannot be an ultimate sortal, in the sense I have defined. And it follows that EPI can provide no grounds for saying that this less general substance sortal is an essential sortal. An example, not Wiggins's own, might be this. Suppose *leopard* is a substance sortal; it follows that if anything is once a leopard, it is always a leopard. Suppose that *feline* is also a substance sortal; it

---

[5] See Wiggins 1980: 205, longer note 2.10 (last paragraph); 115, paragraph 2; 215, longer note 4.24.

follows that if anything is once a feline, it is always a feline. Since leopards are felines, Wiggins's Absolute Identity Principle entails that *leopard* and *feline* supply the same principle of individuation. Since not all felines are leopards, it follows that *leopard* cannot be an ultimate sortal. It also follows that it is consistent with EPI that a thing that is actually a leopard could have passed its entire existence as a feline of a different kind.

8.2. PRINCIPLES OF INDIVIDUATION AS PRINCIPLES OF DISTINCTION AND PERSISTENCE

I shall now substantiate my claim that there is a dilemma facing anyone who wants to appeal to EPI to explain why individuals could not have belonged to certain sorts or kinds. Whether or not we should accept EPI depends on which of two interpretations we give to the notion of a 'principle of individuation'. On one of these interpretations, EPI is unwarranted. On the other interpretation, there is no difficulty in securing the truth of EPI, but it becomes vacuous. On either interpretation, EPI cannot play a legitimate role in explanation.

EPI says that a thing could not have had a principle of individuation that is different from its actual principle of individuation. But what is a principle of individuation? On one interpretation, a principle of individuation is what has traditionally been called a 'criterion of identity': a principle that determines answers to questions about identity and distinctness at a time and over time. Let us call this a *'principle of distinction and persistence'*. The idea is that if the concept *frog* supplies a principle of distinction and persistence for frogs, then this principle will determine, among other things, whether a given portion of matter constitutes, at a given time, one frog or two; whether spatio-temporal continuity is a requirement on the continued existence of a frog; whether the relation between a live (and kicking) frog and its corpse is that of identity; and, in general, what sorts of alterations are compatible with the survival of an individual that is a frog.[6] (Readers who are uncomfortable with the term 'principle of distinction and persistence' should note that in the discussion that follows it can be glossed as 'criterion of identity', as long as 'criterion of identity' is understood in the sense indicated above.) Corresponding to this interpretation of 'principle of

[6] Cf. Wiggins 1980, chs. 2–3, esp. ch. 2, sects. 1, 4, 5, 7.

individuation', we have the following interpretation of EPI, which I label 'EPI(1)':

EPI(1): If an individual x has a *principle of distinction and persistence* P, then x could not have existed without having P.

In the next two sections, I shall argue that we have no reason to accept EPI(1). If a principle of individuation is a principle of distinction and persistence, there is no reason to regard a thing's principle of individuation as essential to it. Having disposed of EPI(1), I shall turn (in Section 8.5) to the second interpretation of 'principle of individuation'. I shall argue that under this second interpretation EPI is vacuous, and can provide no explanation or justification for sortal essentialism.

8.3. DISTINGUISHING PRINCIPLES OF INDIVIDUATION

The idea behind EPI(1) is as follows. Let us call questions about the extent to which an object could, counterfactually, have been different from the way that it actually is, questions about what its *counterfactual existence conditions* are. These are, if you like, questions about the necessary conditions for its identity across possible worlds. Such questions are not questions about identity *at a time*. Nor are they confined to questions about identity over time. (For example, although the counterfactual question whether Aristotle could have turned into a centipede can be regarded as a question about the conditions for his identity over time, the counterfactual question whether he could have been a centipede throughout his existence cannot be so regarded.)[7] However, according to EPI(1), it is a constraint on the 'counterfactual existence conditions' of an individual that it must retain the same principle of distinction and persistence in every counterfactual situation. In other words, it is a constraint on the conditions for identity across possible worlds that an individual retain the same principle of distinction and persistence in every possible world in which it exists.

One obstacle to the acceptance of EPI(1) is a difficulty about its interpretation. To know what EPI(1) amounts to, and hence what its

---

[7] Cf. Wiggins 1980: 215, longer note 4.24.

essentialist implications are, we need to understand what it means for principles of distinction and persistence to be the same or different. Wiggins claims (pp. 122–3) that not all animals have the same principle of individuation, while conceding that human beings may share their principle of individuation with some other animals (although he does not specify which these are). Let us assume that his notion of a principle of individuation is that of what I have been calling a principle of distinction and persistence.[8] Then Wiggins will be suggesting that although perhaps some animals of different species have the same principle of distinction and persistence, there is no single principle of distinction and persistence shared by animals of every kind. But how are we to decide, of two animals, whether or not they share a principle of distinction and persistence? Do cats share their principle of distinction and persistence with tigers? With dogs? With humans? Do they share it with frogs, or with butterflies, or with amoebas? For that matter, does our cat have the same principle of distinction and persistence as the cat next door?[9] Wiggins does not explicitly tell us how to decide these questions. His discussion suggests that the answers are to be found by comparing the patterns of activity and development that are characteristic of the life histories of animals of different kinds.[10] However, I do not understand how this is supposed to work. For example, we know that the developmental process that leads from caterpillar to adult butterfly is strikingly different from anything that happens to a kitten or a tadpole in its transition to an adult cat or frog. But I do not see how to employ this information to decide whether or not these differences in the developmental process suffice for a difference in principles of distinction and persistence. (Wiggins implies that this will depend on whether or not the developmental differences suffice to make a difference to the 'point at issue' in matters of survival.[11] However, I do not see how to determine whether the point at issue in matters of a cat's survival is the same as the point at issue in matters of the survival of, say, a tiger, frog, butterfly, or amoeba.) Yet until we can decide this, we have no way of knowing whether EPI(1) implies

---

[8] For the justification for this interpretation, see note 20 below.

[9] Compare the difficulties about the notion of 'same criterion of identity' discussed in Strawson 1976, esp. at p. 211.

[10] See 1980, ch. 3: 77–90, esp. pp. 80–4.

[11] 1980: 122, note 30. See also Wiggins's remarks about 'what is at issue, what the matter turns on [in an identity question]' (p. 77), and 'what is *involved* in persistence' (p. 88).

that nothing that is actually a cat or a frog could have been a butterfly throughout its existence.

8.4. AGAINST EPI(1)

However, let us suppose these difficulties solved. And let us also suppose, for the sake of argument, that a comparison between their typical life histories has persuaded us that cats and butterflies have different principles of distinction and persistence.[12] *If* we also accept EPI(1), then we shall draw the conclusion that our cat could not have been a butterfly. But why should we accept that there is any such connection between principles of distinction and persistence and counterfactual possibilities? If we are wondering whether our cat could have been a butterfly, why should we suppose that it is even *relevant* to consider—as EPI(1) says that we must—whether or not cats and butterflies share a principle of distinction and persistence? I see no reason to regard it as relevant. I can think of several arguments that might be offered in support of EPI(1), but none of them is satisfactory. I shall set out the arguments, and my replies to them, in turn.

First Argument for EPI(1): 'A thing cannot *change* its principle of persistence over time, for a principle of persistence is, by definition, something that puts constraints on the possible changes that a thing can undergo. Questions about how an individual could have been different are limited to questions about how it could have *become* different. So a thing's principle of persistence is essential to it.'

Reply: The argument is unsound. In rejecting Brody's overlap model of counterfactual possibilities, I have already rejected the thesis that the counterfactual possibilities for an individual are limited to the ways in which it could have *become* different, given the way it actually was at the beginning of its existence. In any case, this first argument is not available to Wiggins for the defence of EPI(1), for two reasons. First, Wiggins commits himself to the rejection of the view that we can derive the

---

[12] Nothing turns on this choice of example. If Wiggins does not believe that cats and butterflies have different principles of distinction and persistence, this does not affect my argument. However, on p. 122 of his (1980) Wiggins claims that insects are not animals. And this does suggest (in conjunction with other remarks) that he thinks that cats and insects have different principles of individuation.

conclusion that x could not have *been* F from the premise that x could not have *become* F (1980: 217–18). Secondly, if sound, the argument would be an argument for the conclusion that all substance sortals, and not merely all ultimate sortals, are essential sortals, a conclusion in whose derivation EPI(1) can play no role.[13]

Second Argument for EPI(1): 'Counterfactual possibilities for (actual) individuals have to be anchored in some way in the actual characteristics of those individuals. To suppose that an individual could have been without its actual principle of distinction and persistence is to lose all ties with the actual object. So a thing's principle of distinction and persistence is essential to it.'[14]

Reply: Let us grant that counterfactual possibilities for individuals have to be anchored in their actual characteristics, if this just means that, for any counterfactual situation in which an actual individual exists, there must be some set of its actual properties that it retains in that counterfactual situation. Why should we suppose that the properties required to 'anchor' the individual must include its having its actual principle of distinction and persistence (and hence its remaining under some sortal that supplies that principle)? This would be legitimate if, like Brody, we thought that any possible history for an individual must overlap its actual history, and thus include its having all the intrinsic properties that it had at some time in its actual existence. But if, like Wiggins, we reject this overlap model (and Wiggins's claim that substance sortals need not be essential sortals commits him to its rejection), why should we suppose that the anchorage must include the thing's principle of distinction and persistence? For example, why shouldn't we be able to 'anchor' an individual by the property of *being a material object*, even if, as Wiggins suggests (p. 64, note 6), *material object* is compatible with a variety of *different* principles of distinction and persistence?

Third Argument for EPI(1): 'A set of properties can provide the "anchorage" for an actual individual x in a counterfactual situation only if it

---

[13] Cf. Sect. 8.1 above. As I emphasized in that section, Wiggins allows that two substance sortals may supply the same principle of individuation, although one is more general than the other, from which it follows that EPI does not imply that all substance sortals are essential sortals.

[14] Compare with Wiggins 1980: 150–6.

includes properties sufficient to *individuate* x in the actual situation. But to individuate x, we must classify it under a sortal that supplies a principle of distinction and persistence, a principle that determines its conditions for identity at a time and over time. So a thing's principle of distinction and persistence is essential to it.'[15]

Reply: This version of the anchorage argument begs the question. Why should we accept that a set of properties cannot 'anchor' x in counterfactual situations unless the properties individuate x in such a way as to determine its identity conditions at a time and over time? Because otherwise we can't make sense of its being the *same* object in the counterfactual situation? Whether or not this is so is precisely the point at issue.

Fourth Argument for EPI(1): 'The idea that a cat could have been a butterfly is ridiculous. What could make it the same individual if it were as different as that?'

Reply: True, perhaps, but insufficient to support EPI(1). It would need to be shown that the reason that the supposition is ridiculous is that we are trying to envisage the cat as having a different principle of distinction and persistence from its actual principle.

With the possible exception of the fourth, the arguments that I have rebutted so far share a common feature. They attempt to defend EPI(1) by claiming that something about the notion of a principle of distinction and persistence compels, or at least justifies, our treating such principles as essential. However, there is a quite different way in which EPI(1) might be defended. One might abandon the attempt to argue that we *ought* to treat a thing's principle of distinction and persistence as essential to it, and argue merely that we *do*.[16] In other words:

Fifth Argument for EPI(1): 'There is no good reason why anyone *should* accept EPI(1). Nothing in the notion of a principle of distinction and

[15] Cf. Wiggins 1980: 105, 115–17. However, given his insistence on the role of demonstration (as opposed to description) in individuation, I am not sure that Wiggins could endorse this version of the anchorage argument with its requirement that anchorage must be provided by *properties* sufficient to individuate x (see p. 115, and p. 116, note 22).

[16] I was prompted to formulate this argument by comments on an earlier version of this material from David Wiggins and David Charles. However, I do not know whether either of them would accept my formulation of the argument.

persistence makes EPI(1) compulsory, or even peculiarly appropriate, as a constraint on counterfactual possibilities. The fact remains that we *do* accept EPI(1). And the evidence that we accept it is that we make essentialist judgements—such as the judgement that Aristotle could not have been a centipede—that conform to it, and can be explained by our acceptance of it.'

Reply: First, note how substantial a concession is made by abandoning the claim that we *should* accept EPI(1) in favour of the claim that we do. For example, the proponent of the fifth argument must concede that an individuative practice that agreed with ours in its judgements about the distinctness and persistence of cats would not thereby be debarred from disagreeing radically with ours in its judgements about the essential properties of cats. Thus the fifth argument embodies the concession that EPI(1) figures in our individuative practice as an optional extra. A sortal essentialist who appeals to this argument can respond to the question 'why are certain sortals essential?' with the answer: 'because principles of distinction and persistence are essential'. But to the question 'why is it that principles of distinction and persistence are essential?' the proponent of the fifth argument has nothing to say.

However, even apart from this, the fifth argument is subject to a very serious objection. For it is not clear that we *do* accept EPI(1). It is not clear that we regard sameness and difference of principles of distinction and persistence—of 'criteria of identity'—as *relevant* to counterfactual questions in the way that EPI(1) requires. To establish that we do, it would have to be shown, at the very least, that our essentialist judgements do conform to EPI(1). For example, it would have to be shown that the things that we can envisage Aristotle's having been and done all involve his retaining his actual principle of distinction and persistence. And it would have to be shown that we regard as impossible any speculation that would involve his having a different principle of distinction and persistence. I do not believe that anyone has come close to demonstrating that this is the case.

A major obstacle to doing so is the difficulty, noted in Section 8.3 above, of determining when principles of distinction and persistence are the same, and when they are different. One consequence of this is that the fact—if it is a fact—that we think that a man could not have been a giraffe or a centipede is scant evidence that we accept EPI(1). For it is not obvious that men and giraffes, or men and centipedes, have different principles of distinction and persistence: different 'criteria of identity'.[17] (In this context it would, of course, be question begging to regard the fact that we have difficulty in supposing that a man could have been a giraffe as our reason for thinking that men and giraffes have different principles of distinction and persistence. To support the fifth argument some independent evidence for a difference in principles of distinction and persistence is required.)

I conclude that the arguments I have considered fail to establish even the claim that we do accept EPI(1) as a constraint on counterfactual possibilities. Still less do they succeed in showing that we are rationally required to accept it. I have been unable to think of any further arguments for EPI(1) that are not mere variants of these. Unless some better argument can be produced, we cannot legitimately appeal to EPI(1) to explain the counterfactual constraints there are on the kinds to which things could have belonged. If Aristotle could not have been a paper clip or a centipede, we have as yet found no reason to say that this is because he could not have had a different principle of individuation from his actual principle.

8.5. PRINCIPLES OF INDIVIDUATION AS PRINCIPLES OF COUNTERFACTUAL EXISTENCE

I now turn to the second interpretation of EPI. I have claimed that if a principle of individuation is merely a principle of distinction and persistence, then there is no justification for EPI, the thesis that a thing's principle of individuation is essential to it. However, this difficulty can apparently be circumvented by the following manoeuvre.

Suppose that we make it true by definition that a principle of individuation for Fs includes, as well as a principle of distinction and persistence for Fs, a principle that determines what the counterfactual possibilities are for things that are actually Fs. In other words, suppose that we say that, by definition, a principle of individuation for Fs includes, not only a principle of distinction and persistence, but also a *principle of counterfactual existence* for Fs. The idea would be that a principle of individuation has three roles to play: it supplies conditions

---

[17] Cf., e.g., Dummett's assertion that 'the very same criterion of identity that is used for horses is also used for, e.g., cows, and, if not for quite all animals, at any rate for all vertebrates' (1973: 76).

for identity at a time, it supplies conditions for identity over time, and it supplies conditions for identity across possible worlds. In rejecting EPI(1), I have, in effect, concluded that the counterfactual existence conditions for Fs are independent of the conditions for identity at a time and over time for Fs, and that if Fs and Gs have different principles of distinction and persistence, it does not follow that they have different principles of counterfactual existence. However, this leaves open the following possibility: we might interpret EPI as the claim that an individual could not have existed with a *principle of counterfactual existence* that is different from its actual principle of counterfactual existence. We should then have the following interpretation:

> EPI(2):   If an individual *x* has a *principle of counterfactual existence* P, then *x* could not have existed without having P.

In EPI(2), we have a thesis that is hard to deny. A principle of counterfactual existence for Fs is something that, *by definition*, determines the ways that a thing that is actually an F could and could not have been different. It seems absurd to suggest that these ways that it could and could not have been different could themselves have been different.

So adopting EPI(2) as an interpretation of EPI does mean that we have a reason to accept it. But there is a price to be paid. Under this interpretation, EPI is very nearly a tautology. As such, it can tell us absolutely nothing about what the limits imposed by a thing's principle of counterfactual existence are likely to be. We shall get the result that it is true that some particular cat could not have existed without its principle of counterfactual existence. But this statement, by itself, tells us nothing about what limits are laid down by this principle.

In particular, it tells us nothing about what restrictions there are on the *sortals* that this thing that is actually a cat could have fallen under. All that is specified is this: it is restricted to those sortals, whichever they may be, that are compatible with its principle of counterfactual existence. Moreover, EPI(2) provides no grounds for the conclusion that any sortals are essential sortals. For example, it is perfectly consistent with EPI(2) to claim that although cats and tortoises share their *principle of counterfactual existence*, there is no *sortal concept* under which both cats and tortoises fall. Hence EPI(2) fails to rule out the following possibility: any particular cat could have lived its entire life as a tortoise, even if there is no sortal concept that it actually falls under that it would then have fallen under, and thus no sortal concept under which it essentially falls. It follows that EPI(2), by itself, gives no support whatsoever to sortal essentialism.

This conclusion could apparently be avoided by legislating that any group of things that share their *principle of counterfactual existence*—however diverse their principles of distinction and persistence may be—is, *by definition*, a sort, to which some one sortal concept corresponds. But the gain would be illusory. The proposed piece of legislation involves a perversion of the notion of a sortal concept. If, as the proposal demands, we allow that a sortal need determine no single principle of distinction and persistence, we abandon the fundamental principle that a sortal concept must provide a criterion of identity capable of determining answers to questions about identity at a time, and identity over time, for the things that fall under it.[18] We shall no longer be able to argue that a concept that fails to supply such a criterion of identity is not a sortal concept.[19]

I conclude that the thesis EPI(2), that everything has its principle of counterfactual existence essentially is not much more than a grandiose way of saying that the ways an object could have been are restricted to the ways it could have been. No one could regard this as playing a role in a substantial explanation of why it is that things are essentially confined to certain sorts or kinds, and essentially debarred from membership of others.

On neither of the interpretations that I have considered is it legitimate to appeal to EPI to explain why certain sortals should be essential. I do not see what other interpretation of EPI could be invoked to serve this purpose. Whatever utility the notion of a principle of individuation may have, the claim that things have their principles of individuation essentially can apparently neither explain nor justify the doctrine of sortal essentialism.[20]

8.6. THE CASE AGAINST SORTAL ESSENTIALISM

I conclude that neither of the theories of sortal essentialism that I have discussed gives adequate answers to the questions that I raised in

---

[18] See Sect. 7.2 above.

[19] Cf. Wiggins's argument that *material object* is not a sortal (1980: 64, note 6).

[20] The text of Wiggins 1980 suggests that the principle upon which Wiggins bases his sortal essentialism is EPI(1), not EPI(2). See ch. 4, pp. 103, 115–17. In private correspondence Wiggins has confirmed that he wished to defend EPI(1).

Section 7.1. Neither Brody's theory nor Wiggins's gives a satisfactory explanation of why any sortals should be essential sortals, or a satisfactory account of why some sortals should be essential while others are not. I know of no other theories that attempt to do so. It may be suggested that even if the theories do fail in these explanatory tasks, it may nevertheless be true that some sortals—perhaps, as Brody suggests, all substance sortals, or perhaps, as Wiggins suggests, all ultimate sortals—are essential sortals. That is, it may be suggested that, in spite of the problems that I have discussed, we may nevertheless be justified in supposing that there is *some* sortal kind to which a persisting individual such as a person or an animal essentially belongs, and which therefore constrains the ways that it could have been different from the way that it actually is.

However, I think that this response fails to do justice to the arguments that I have presented in these two chapters. True, some version of sortal essentialism *could*, for all that I have said, be correct. But why should we suppose that it is? We may have strong intuitions that an individual could not have belonged to kinds radically different from the kinds to which it actually belongs: for example, the intuition that Aristotle could not have been a centipede, a giraffe, a parsnip, a paper clip, or the number 17. But, as I have tried to show, even if such intuitions are taken at face value, they fall short of supporting the thesis that there is some *sortal* kind to which the individual essentially belongs. Whatever role sortal concepts play in individuation (and I do not deny that they have an important role to play), we should be sceptical about drawing from this the conclusion that any sortals represent essential properties of the things to which they apply. To reinforce this claim, in the final section of this chapter I shall argue that even someone sympathetic to the spirit of Wiggins's principal claims about the role of sortals in individuation may consistently refuse to hold that any sortals are essential sortals.

8.7. ESSENTIAL KINDS WITHOUT ESSENTIAL SORTALS?

In response to an earlier presentation of the arguments of this chapter (Mackie 1994), Wiggins has suggested that, in order to make plausible my rejection of the principle that I call 'EPI(1)', I need to supply an alternative explanation of why certain hypotheses to the effect that things could have belonged to kinds radically different from their actual kinds are 'idle or baseless' (2001: 121, note 22). It is safe to assume that Wiggins would include, in the scope of such idle or baseless hypotheses, the suggestions that Aristotle could have been a centipede, a vegetable, an artefact, or a number.

Wiggins argues that his version of sortal essentialism may be seen as based on a principle that he calls 'the anchor constraint':

> A handy way of summing up [the principles] (Δ) (E) and (Z) [pp. 109–12] as they combine with the conception of individuation just illustrated is this: x could have the property φ, or it is possible for x to have φ, if and only if it is genuinely possible to conceive of x's having φ; and a thinker genuinely conceives of x as having φ only if there is *some* sortal concept f such that: (i) f adequately answers the Aristotelian question what x is, and commits anyone who singles a thing out as an instantiation of f to an identity-cum-persistence condition for x; (ii) f and φ are cosatisfiable by x, and if x had the property φ that would not preclude x's being singled out as this very instantiation of f. Let us call this the anchor constraint. (Wiggins 2001: 121; bold type emphasis mine. Cf. the very similar passage in Wiggins 1980: 115–16.)

Wiggins's 'anchor constraint', thus characterized, can be seen to imply the principle that I have called 'EPI(1)'. Clause (i) in the quoted passage, together with the first part of clause (ii), implies that any property that x could have had must be a property that is compatible with x's being an f, for some sortal f *that determines an identity-cum-persistence condition for x*. But this implies that it is essential to x that x be an f, for some such sortal f that determines an identity-cum-persistence condition (since the property of *not being an f* is obviously incompatible with the property of *being an f*). Since it is evident that by 'determines an identity-cum-persistence condition for x' Wiggins means 'determines a single identity-cum-persistence condition' (rather than a variety of them), this version of the 'anchor constraint' implies that a thing could not have existed with a different 'identity-cum-persistence' condition from its actual one. But an 'identity-cum-persistence condition' is equivalent to what I have been referring to in this chapter as a 'principle of distinction and persistence'. Hence this version of the 'anchor constraint' implies the principle EPI(1) that has been the subject of my sceptical attack.

Following the passage quoted above, where Wiggins characterizes his 'anchor constraint', he adds:

> What would refute this contention [i.e., refute the combination of claims characterized as 'the anchor constraint'] …? A weaker requirement that arose equally naturally from a theory of particular identification, respected the

absoluteness of identity, and represented the substantial requirement that [principle] (Δ) puts upon the *de re* relation of conceiver, object and attribute. The case for this requirement is that it makes sense of our more reflective practice when we make suppositions. (Our practice, I mean, where it does not idle or substitute fantasy for the careful conceiving, the careful thinking right through, of the alternatives to the actual.)

It follows that the proper response to the proposal is dialectical: to propose a weaker or different principle that promises the same sort of friction or impedance upon claims of possibility that are idle or baseless. This is one part of the reply to Penelope Mackie (1994). (Wiggins 2001: 121, note 22)[21]

In the next chapter, I shall suggest that it is possible to explain why the hypothesis that Aristotle could have been, say, a centipede or a paper clip seems so bizarre and absurd without commitment to the thesis that, strictly speaking, Aristotle belongs essentially to *any* sort or kind that is incompatible with his being a centipede or a paper clip. The strategy will be to substitute, for the thesis that these hypotheses represent genuine impossibilities, the thesis that they represent possibilities so remote as to be unworthy of serious consideration.

However, it is worth noting that Wiggins's challenge can apparently be met, for a large class of the relevant cases, without adopting this extreme position. Consider the following modification of Wiggins's own anchor constraint:

Modified Anchor Constraint (MAC):

> ... x could have the property φ, or it is possible for x to have φ, if and only if it is genuinely possible to conceive of x's having φ; and a thinker genuinely conceives of x as having φ only if there is some sortal concept f, and some kind concept K (where K may or may not satisfy the requirements for being an 'autonomously individuative' sortal concept), such that: (a) f adequately answers the Aristotelian question what x is; (b) f determines an identity-cum-persistence condition for the things that fall under f; (c) necessarily, all fs are Ks; (d) K determines a substantial counterfactual existence condition for the things that fall under K; (e) K and φ are cosatisfiable by x; and (f) if x had the property φ, x could still be singled out as an

---

[21] Except for its last sentence, this paragraph is almost identical with a passage in Wiggins 1980: 116, note 21.

instantiation of some sortal g such that, necessarily, all things that fall under g fall under K.[22]

This modified version of Wiggins's anchor constraint ('MAC', for short) entails that everything belongs to *some* kind essentially. It also entails that this thesis is not completely trivial. According to MAC, a thing must belong essentially to a kind that 'determines a substantial counterfactual existence condition': this precludes, for example, treating *object* as the only essential kind to which a thing belongs. MAC also entails that however different a thing had been, it would have fallen under some sortal or other. And it entails that in order to single something out one has to single it out under a sortal that determines an identity-cum-persistence condition for it.

However, unlike Wiggins's own version of the anchor constraint, MAC does not entail that any sortals are essential sortals, for it does not entail that everything belongs essentially to some *sortal* kind. The relevant kind K may be too broad to count as a sortal kind, because it may fail to determine a single 'identity-cum-persistence' condition (even though K must be specific enough to 'determine a substantial counterfactual existence condition for the things that fall under K'). And MAC, unlike Wiggins's version of the anchor constraint, does not entail EPI(1): for it does not entail that a thing's 'identity-cum-persistence condition' is essential to it. The Modified Anchor Constraint leaves open the possibility that the relevant kind K may include things that have *different* identity-cum-persistence conditions. So if to have a different identity-cum-persistence condition is to have a different principle of individuation, MAC allows that something could have existed with a different principle of individuation from its actual principle.

A potential worry about my proposed Modified Anchor Constraint is, I suppose, that even if it is not completely trivial as a constraint on counterfactual possibilities, it may seem in danger of *approaching* triviality. For it looks as if MAC could be satisfied by taking K to be an extremely general kind—say, *material thing*. Once we break with the idea that a thing belongs essentially to some kind all of whose members share the same *principle of distinction and persistence*, perhaps we open

---

[22] Obviously, this passage is not a quotation; rather, it is a modification of the passage from Wiggins quoted in the first paragraph of this section. In characterizing my Modified Anchor Constraint, I have, however, retained the wording of Wiggins's original passage as far as possible.

the door to a far too liberal (and possibly close to vacuous) conception of essential kinds or categories?

In response to this worry, however, it should be noted that a concept may be too general to supply a single principle of distinction and persistence (in Wiggins's sense) but still not *so* general that it fails to be individuative at all. Consider, for example, the fact that although Wiggins says that *animal* is not an autonomously individuative sortal, because it fails to determine a single persistence condition, he still sometimes calls it a sortal - presumably in an extended sense of that term.[23] Let us use the term 'quasi-sortal' for a term that is too general to be an ultimate sortal in Wiggins's sense, and yet still plays the individuative role that Wiggins attributes to terms such as 'animal' or 'mammal'.[24] Then it is hard to see what principled objection Wiggins could have to my Modified Anchor Constraint, as long as the relevant kind K is restricted to a kind that is at least as specific as a 'quasi-sortal' kind. Yet MAC, even with this restriction, evidently does not entail EPI(1), and does not entail the sortal essentialism that Wiggins advocates. At most, it would entail that each individual belongs essentially to some 'quasi-sortal' kind.

I think that MAC may be regarded as arising out of a theory of particular identification no less naturally than does Wiggins's own anchor constraint; hence may be regarded as meeting this part of Wiggins's challenge in the passage quoted above. My Modified Anchor Constraint also satisfies Wiggins's further desiderata of respecting the absoluteness of identity, and of consistency with his principle (Δ), which embodies the original idea of 'anchorage'.[25]

I conclude that the Modified Anchor Constraint successfully meets Wiggins's challenge to provide an alternative principle that could explain why at least some 'allogeneous' hypotheses (as we might call them),

---

[23] On p. 128 of his (2001), Wiggins describes *animal* and *mammal* as 'unspecific sortal specifications'. On p. 69 (ch. 2) of his (2001), however, he describes *animal, machine,* and *artefact* as 'predicates. . . that have the appearance of sortal predicates but are purely generic'.

[24] See the passages cited in the previous note.

[25] MAC is of course, inconsistent with Wiggins's suggestion that the requirement of anchorage, together with the rest of the theory of particular identification will 'exclude the conceiving of an individual as having a different principle of individuation from its actual principle' (2001: 110). But obviously Wiggins cannot intend to demand that an alternative account be consistent with this claim, since the claim entails his own version of sortal essentialism. It should be noted that MAC is also consistent with Wiggins's (E) and (Z) (2001: 111–12).

such as the hypotheses that Aristotle could have been a vegetable or an artefact or an abstract object, are 'idle or baseless'. And it does so without commitment to the more radical views that I shall advocate in the next chapter. Yet the possibility of the adoption of the Modified Anchor Constraint suggests that even someone who is broadly in agreement with Wiggins's theory of individuation may reasonably reject his thesis that a thing's principle of individuation (in the sense of its principle of distinction and persistence) must be preserved in all counterfactual situations, and hence may reject Wiggins's version, and indeed any other version, of sortal essentialism.

9

Essential Properties and Remote Contingencies

9.1. ESSENTIAL KINDS AND INTUITIVE JUDGEMENTS

If an appropriate version of sortal essentialism—the thesis that there are sortal concepts that represent essential properties of the things that fall under them—were correct, it would provide an explanation (and justification) of the intuition that even if a particular thing has no unique essential properties that distinguish it from all other things, nor any essential properties that distinguish it from other things of its kind, nevertheless it could not have belonged to a kind that is radically different from the kinds to which it actually belongs: an intuition exemplified by the conviction that Aristotle (or, for that matter, any other human being) could *not* have been a giraffe, a centipede, a parsnip, a paper clip, or the number 17.[1]

However, I have argued that we have no good reason to accept sortal essentialism, and hence no good reason to accept its proposed explanation of the intuition in question. But what, then, *does* explain the intuition? In the final section of Chapter 8 I offered, as a compromise to the proponent of Wiggins's version of sortal essentialism, the suggestion that even if there are no essential sortals, there may yet be 'quasi-sortals' that do represent essential properties of the things that fall under them. So perhaps some such theory could be developed, and employed to explain the intuition that Aristotle could not have belonged to kinds that are radically different from the kinds to which he actually belongs?

[1] I say 'an appropriate version of sortal essentialism', because of the problem, noted in Sect. 8.4, that if it were to turn out that the only essential sortals are rather general sortals, sortal essentialism would lack the resources to explain some of the relevant intuitions. For example, if *mammal* were the most specific essential sortal that Aristotle falls under, then sortal essentialism would, obviously, fail to explain why Aristotle could not have been a giraffe.

Perhaps, but I am doubtful. One reason for scepticism is that even if such a theory could explain why Aristotle could not have been, say, a vegetable or an artefact or an abstract object such as a number, it is doubtful that it could explain why he could not have been a giraffe or a frog or a centipede. For a 'quasi-sortal' concept is, by definition, a concept that is too *general* to be a genuine sortal concept. If the kinds to which Aristotle belongs essentially are no more specific than quasi-sortal kinds, it seems unlikely that *any* kind to which he belongs essentially will be one that is incompatible with his being a giraffe or a frog (or even a centipede). Perhaps this conclusion could be resisted by someone who holds a 'Lockean' view of personal identity according to which Aristotle is not a human animal, but rather a person numerically distinct from any animal, and hence denies that Aristotle belongs to a ('quasi-sortal') kind—perhaps the kind *animal*—that includes ruminants and amphibians and arthropods as well as members of the species *Homo sapiens*. However, even if this response evades the difficulty as it concerns our intuitions about the kinds to which Aristotle (and other persons) could have belonged, analogous difficulties will still arise in the case of things other than persons. For example, if cats belong to the 'quasi-sortal' kind *animal*, and *animal* is an essential kind, then this would provide an explanation of the intuition that our cat could not have been, say, a vegetable or a teapot or an event or a number.[2] But obviously it would fail to explain the intuition that our cat could not (any more than could Aristotle) have existed as a giraffe or a frog. And this would represent a failure to explain a large body of the intuitions that one would expect a theory of essential kinds to explain.

Partly for this reason, I am not confident in placing reliance on *any* theory of essential kinds as an explanation of the relevant intuitions. I propose that, instead, we consider seriously the suggestion that we should explain the intuition that Aristotle could not have belonged to certain radically different sorts or kinds without supposing that, strictly speaking, his not belonging to these kinds is among his essential properties.

9.2. 'EXTREME HAECCEITISM'

Most philosophers appear to accept that if *de re* modality is coherent at all, there are some qualitative constraints on the ways that individuals

---

[2] As I pointed out in Sect. 8.7, Wiggins doubts that *animal* is sufficiently specific to be a genuine sortal, suggesting that it is, at best, what I am calling a 'quasi-sortal'.

could have been different, and that these constraints include the prohibition of certain 'allogeneous' hypotheses (as I called them in Section 8.7) such as the hypotheses that Aristotle could have been a giraffe, a centipede, a paper clip, a number, and so on.

Adams uses the term 'Moderate Haecceitism' for the view that 'thisnesses and transworld identities are primitive, but logically connected with suchnesses' (1979: 25–6). Moderate Haecceitism is therefore consistent with a belief in 'bare identities', as that notion has been described in this book,[3] but entails that there are qualitative constraints on the ways that things could have been different. It amounts to the view that although, for a given individual, there need be no qualitative *sufficient* conditions for its identity across possible worlds—its 'thisness' may be in this sense 'primitive'—there are nevertheless qualitative *necessary* conditions for its identity across possible worlds. By contrast, 'Extreme Haecceitism would involve the rejection of all logical connections between suchnesses and the thisnesses of such beings as persons' (Adams 1979: 26, note 29). And Extreme Haecceitism, Adams maintains, is absurd:

[I]f we cannot trust our intuition that we could not have been . . . [plutonium atoms, noises, football games, places, or times] then it is probably a waste of time to study *de re* modalities at all. (1979: 24)

adding:

If there are any transworld identities and non-identities, there are necessary connections between thisnesses and some suchnesses. (1979: 25)

These necessary connections, Adams suggests, are best regarded as synthetic, although resting on analytic connections:

It is a fact, which we understand very well to be true, although not analytic, that Jimmy Carter is a person. And there are necessary conditions of intra- and transworld identity which follow (analytically, indeed) from the concept or property of being a person and which entail that no individual that is in fact a person could under any circumstances be a musical performance. (ibid.)

Christopher Kirwan remarks that although 'it must surely be conceded that the distinction between essential and non-essential attributes is rarely *easy* to make' (1970: 49), nevertheless, there are some clear cases:

---

[3] Chs. 2–5 above. See esp. Ch. 2, Appendix A, on the notions of 'haecceitism' and 'bare identities'.

'That George is a bishop is certainly not essential to him, that he is not the Latin word for "bishop" certainly is . . .' (ibid.), although Kirwan adds:

In between these clear cases, however, there are plenty which are unclear . . . Yet this vagueness at the boundary between the essential and the non-essential is exactly like the vagueness which exists at the boundary between the analytic and the synthetic. Just as it is impossible, perhaps, to specify exactly what is logically necessary for being a tiger, so it may be impossible to specify exactly what is logically necessary for being identical with any given tiger. In both cases it is arguable that the facts are best represented by an open-ended disjunction of conjunctions of conditions. (ibid.)

Graeme Forbes associates the type of view that Adams calls 'extreme haecceitism' with an objectionable commitment to a version of the notion of a 'bare particular':

The problem . . . is that for it to be a possibility for a pot of marmalade to be a railway station, or for {0} to have been a tree, we have to be able to conceive of two different states of affairs in which one and the same thing figures, in the first as a pot of marmalade or singleton zero, and in the second as a railway station or item of flora respectively. However, this in turn means that we would be conceiving of objects and their properties on the model of bare particular and inherence, according to which a thing is a propertyless substratum and can take on any nature you please via the inhering of appropriate properties. But this, if it makes sense at all, is at any rate not the conception which we employ. Articulating our actual conception is another problem, but whatever the right story is in this area (see Wiggins, 1980, ch. 3), one constraint is that it must imply the fundamental unintelligibility of hypotheses which make the broad kind to which a thing belongs an accidental feature of it. (Forbes 1997: 521)[4]

Nevertheless, I shall propose that something approaching extreme haecceitism is much more defensible than it may appear to be.[5] I suggest that the individuals about which we conduct our *de re* counterfactual suppositions are much closer to 'bare particulars' than is usually admitted.

---

[4] Forbes here suggests that to explain why an individual thing (e.g., a set or a pot of marmalade) essentially does not belong to certain kinds, we should suppose that there is some kind to which it *does* belong essentially. By contrast, Kirwan's remarks in the previous passage suggest a different account: that the explanation of why, e.g., Bishop George could not have been a Latin word may involve his belonging essentially to an 'open-ended disjunction' of kinds. (I assume that such a disjunction of kinds would not itself be a kind in any natural sense of that term.)

[5] If we take 'extreme haecceitism', strictly speaking, to be exactly as Adams defines it in the passage quoted earlier (from Adams 1979: 26) the view is clearly indefensible,

I should emphasize, however, that in attempting to defend a version of extreme haecceitism, I am going well beyond the defence of 'bare identities' attempted earlier in this book. Although the 'bare identities' thesis involves a commitment to the 'haecceitistic' (non-qualitative) element in moderate haecceitism, the bare identities thesis, by itself, involves no commitment to anything like 'bare particulars': individuals whose modal nature is compatible with just about any properties you please. By contrast, 'extreme haecceitism' involves a commitment not only to 'bare identities', but also to something like 'bare particulars' in this sense. To put it another way, to believe in 'bare identities' is to believe that individuals have no non-trivial *sufficient* conditions for their identity in all possible worlds. But this belief in bare identities is perfectly compatible with the view, which the most extreme haecceitist rejects, that these individuals have non-trivial essential properties that represent non-trivial *necessary* conditions for their identity in all possible worlds.

9.3. EXTREME HAECCEITISM AND QUASI-ESSENTIAL PROPERTIES

David Lewis describes the most extreme form of 'extreme haecceitism' as the view that 'qualitative character does nothing at all to constrain representation *de re*: anything could have any qualitative character, for instance there is a [possible] world according to which you are a poached egg' (1986*a*: 239). He adds: 'A fairly extreme haecceitism is more defensible than it may seem. Further, it has the obvious advantage over moderation: the less we believe in qualitative limits to haecceitistic difference, the less we need an account of how those limits are imposed' (ibid.).[6]

---

because it rules out even the attribution to Aristotle of the essential property of *being either a number or not a number* (assuming that this is a qualitative property). The version of 'extreme haecceitism' that I shall attempt to defend does not go as far as this, but does deny Aristotle such essential properties as *not being a centipede* and *not being a poached egg*.

[6] Lewis (who credits Pavel Tichý with persuading him that extreme haecceitism deserves serious attention) rejects what he calls haecceitism. His main point is that an extreme haecceitism may be more defensible than a moderate version. However, Lewis's counterpart theory, although not 'haecceitistic' in his sense, is not friendly to the attribution of (non-trivial) essential properties. According to Lewis, *A* could have

Lewis is clearly right in saying that extreme haecceitism has this advantage. The question is whether the price is acceptable.

The strategy for the defence of extreme haecceitism suggested by Lewis is that what other theorists would regard as impossibilities are to be reconstrued, by the extreme haecceitist, as genuine possibilities, but ones that are so remote from actuality that they are, for normal purposes of counterfactual speculation, ignored (1986*a*: 239 ff.). So, for example, although it is, in fact, a genuine possibility that Aristotle should have been a poached egg, this possibility is too far-fetched to be treated as relevant in any normal context of counterfactual speculation.[7] Hence the acceptability, in all normal contexts, of 'Aristotle could *not* have been a poached egg', and the remarkable prevalence of the intuition that to suppose that he could have been one is an absurdity.

Going beyond Lewis, let us call a property of an object 'quasi-essential' (or 'tenacious') if to suppose that the object lacks this property is to envisage a very remote possibility, one that would be ignored in all but abnormal contexts. Then, I suggest, the role that is typically accorded to essential properties may be played, without significant loss, by quasi-essential ('tenacious') properties. Nor need a quasi-essentialist be vulnerable to the charge that this theory is merely a terminological variant of genuine essentialism. Admittedly, we stand in need of an account of *why* some properties of a thing are quasi-essential to that

---

been F if *A* has a counterpart that is F. According to Lewis's (1968) exposition, to be a counterpart of *A*, *x* has only to be 'sufficiently similar' to *A*, as well as being at least as similar to *A* as is anything else in *x*'s world. But, given the varying standards of similarity (what Lewis calls 'inconstancy'), plus the fact that similarity is vague, it is doubtful that there is *no* context, and *no* standard of similarity, according to which a centipede (for example) is sufficiently similar to Aristotle to be his counterpart. Further, there appears to be no obstacle to a centipede's also being more similar to Aristotle than is anything else in its world. Admittedly, Lewis's introduction of 'inconstancy' into counterpart theory also complicates the interpretation of the claim that it is an essential property of Aristotle that he is not a centipede. This might mean that there is no context, and no standard of similarity, according to which Aristotle has any counterpart that is a centipede. But according to another interpretation, the claim that it is an essential property of Aristotle that he is not a centipede has itself to be understood relative to a context—a context that determines what it takes to be a counterpart of Aristotle—and it may be true with respect to one such context, and false with respect to another, that no centipede is among Aristotle's counterparts.

[7] This description suggests that Lewis thinks that the role of the context is to determine, from a range of possibilities already ordered in terms of remoteness or nearness, which possibilities are to be included and which ignored. However, I take it that Lewis's theory should be interpreted as also giving the context some role in determining the ordering of possibilities as 'near' and 'remote'.

object while others are not. But it is not clear that the results of this account can simply be appropriated by a theory that makes the properties in question essential rather than quasi-essential. For one thing, the quasi-essentialist can very naturally construe a property's being quasi-essential (or tenacious) as a matter of degree.[8] By contrast, the standard notion of a genuinely essential property does not admit of degrees.

9.4. THE DEFENCE OF EXTREME HAECCEITISM

Perhaps the most important element in the defence of extreme haecceitism is the fact that *all* modal theorists, whether or not they are extreme haecceitists, must agree that there are many standard contexts in which the range of *de re* possibilities under consideration falls short of the full range. With respect to these contexts, it seems that there need be no disagreement between extreme haecceitists and their rivals.

(a) First, in many—perhaps the overwhelming majority—of everyday contexts in which we discuss the ways in which an individual could have been different, we restrict our enquiry to the ways in which it could have *become* different, given the way that it actually was at some time in its existence. If I am asked, outside a seminar on modality, whether Aristotle could have been a dictator, the natural assumption (unless contradicted), is that—assuming that the issue is not one of epistemic possibility—the relevant question is whether he could have *become* a dictator. That is, it is the question whether, given the way that he actually was at some time in his existence, he could have gone on to *acquire* the property of being a dictator. Yet the overwhelming majority of contemporary modal theorists accept that the notion of 'could have *been* different' that is relevant to questions about *de re* modality and essential properties is broader than this notion of 'could have *become* different'.[9] Hence, according to these theorists, when we do (as I think we very often do) restrict our attention to the 'could have

---

[8] This would require only a slight amendment to the characterization of a 'quasi-essential' or 'tenacious' property that I have given above.

[9] See, e.g., the philosophers mentioned in note 10 of Ch. 7 above. This is, of course, connected with the point (emphasized throughout Chs. 7–8) that, according to the standard notion of an essential property, it does not follow, from the fact that a property is a 'substance sortal property' (and hence both 'unacquirable' and 'unlosable') that it is an essential property.

become' variety of the 'could have been', there is a large number of *de re* possibilities—genuine *de re* possibilities—that we thereby ignore.

Here, then, there need be no disagreement between the extreme haecceitists and their opponents. For there is no reason why extreme haecceitists should not agree with their opponents about the range of *de re* possibilities that is included in the ways in which Aristotle could have *become* different (from the way that he actually was), even though they hold contentious views about the range of ways in which he could have *been* different. In particular, there is no reason why an extreme haecceitist should not believe in substance sortals; that Aristotle falls under some substance sortal—perhaps *human being*—that is incompatible with his being a centipede or a poached egg, and hence that the only way in which he could have been a centipede or a poached egg is if he had never been human at all.

It is perhaps a testament to the prominence, in our counterfactual thinking about individuals, of questions about how they could have *become* different, that in spite of the fact that so many philosophers have insisted on the distinction between the 'could have been' and the 'could have become', the expression '*A* is essentially (an) F' (or '*being (an) F* is an essential property of *A*') is still sometimes used in philosophical discussion to *mean* something like '*A* is (an) F and *A* could not continue to exist without being (an) F'. This notion of an essential property is derived from Aristotle, as explained, for example, in the following quotation (from Jonathan Lowe's book on Locke):

> A further important ingredient in Aristotle's later writings on substance is his notion of essence. He distinguishes between the 'accidental' and the 'essential' properties or qualities of things like men, rocks and trees. Although a primary substance . . . can persist through some qualitative changes, it cannot persist through all: some changes are 'substantial' changes, because they involve the ceasing-to-be or coming-to-be of an individual substance . . . A property which a substance cannot lose without thereby ceasing to exist is an *essential* property of that substance—and the sum total of a thing's essential properties constitutes its essence or nature. (Lowe 1995: 69–70)[10]

Using this as a basis, we may define a '*Weak Aristotelian* conception' of an essential property as follows: *being F* is an essential property of

---

[10] In employing this quotation from Lowe to illustrate what I call the 'Weak Aristotelian' conception of an essential property, I do not suggest that Lowe himself shows any tendency to conflate the Weak Aristotelian notion and the 'modern' notion.

A in the Weak Aristotelian sense if and only if: *A* is F, and necessarily, anything that is F at any time in its existence is F at all times in its existence. Now, I do not deny that this is a perfectly respectable conception of what it is for something to be an essential property. And clearly, according to *this* usage of 'essential property', it is trivially true that substance sortals are what in Chapters 7–8 I called 'essential sortals': sortals that represent essential properties of the things to which they apply. However, it should by now be abundantly clear that this Weak Aristotelian conception is *not* the same as the standard modern notion of an essential property that has been employed throughout this book. For to say that *A could not have existed* without being an F is to say *more* than merely: '*A* is an F and, necessarily, anything that is an F at any time in its existence is an F throughout its existence.'[11]

(b) Very often the *de re* possibilities that interest us concern, not simply how individuals *could* have been different, but how they *would* have been different if certain other features of the world had been altered. But where the antecedents of these counterfactual speculations do not concern remote possibilities, remote possibilities are irrelevant to their consequents too. (This is obvious if we assume, following David Lewis, that 'If P had been the case, would Q would have been the case?' is roughly equivalent to: 'In the closest possible world in which P is true, is Q also true?') One does not have to be an extreme haecceitist to suppose that it is a genuine possibility, albeit a remote one, that Aristotle should have been born in the twentieth century. But this remote possibility is clearly irrelevant to a counterfactual question such as: 'If Aristotle had not gone into philosophy, what career would he have followed?' It would be perverse to answer this question by suggesting that, if he had not been a philosopher, he would have been an astronaut or a computer programmer. Even if these are genuine ways that Aristotle *could* have been, they are not ways that he *would* have been in the counterfactual situation envisaged, assuming (as is surely plausible) that possible worlds in which Aristotle lives in the twentieth century are not among the closest possible worlds in which he pursues a different career. Evidently, the fact that extreme haecceitists believe in a wider range of genuine possibilities for Aristotle than do their opponents provides no reason why the extreme haecceitists should disagree with their opponents about what subset of the total range of

---

[11] See the works cited in note 9 above.

possibilities is relevant to the assessment of a counterfactual conditional whose antecedent is agreed by both parties to represent a possibility.[12]

(c) Many of the *de re* possibilities that interest us are cases where certain causal powers or potentialities of the individuals in question are kept fixed in the envisaged counterfactual situation. Evidently, in these cases also, we restrict our attention to a subset of what we regard as the total range of *de re* possibilities, whether or not we are extreme haecceitists about what this total range comprises. For according to the standard conception of *de re* modality and essential properties, most of the causal powers of an individual are not among its essential properties. Thus, it is true that the extreme haecceitist's possibility in which Aristotle is a cheetah, if such possibility there be, is irrelevant to the question whether, *assuming his causal powers unchanged*, Aristotle could have run a mile in four minutes. But equally irrelevant to this question is the possibility—which most philosophers who are not extreme haecceitists would readily admit to be such—that Aristotle could have existed with the muscular powers of a modern Olympic athlete.

David Wiggins issues a useful reminder that *de re* modal locutions are often used to express notions of possibility that are more restricted than the ways in which an individual could have been different 'consistently with its being the individual that it is':

Of course the locutions 'can' and 'must' are normally put to other, more specific, work. The range of available meanings of these modalities is highly various. *De re* modal claims are usually based upon people's abilities and inabilities, their capacities or incapacities as of some time and in relation to the circumstances of that time, or upon their obligations or debts or compulsions of that time … But the proposal that is put forward in this chapter is that we should see the *de re* necessity of essence as the limiting case of the other *de re* necessities with which their form appears to group them. The essential necessity of a trait arises at that point of unalterability where the *very existence of the bearer is conditional* upon the trait in question. Here, at this point, a property is fixed to its bearer by virtue of being inherent in the individuation of it—inherent in the very possibility of the drawing of a spatio-temporal boundary around the object in the light of some principle of activity of the thing. The closer the source of the attribute to the singling out of the thing itself—the more it is

---

[12] Of course, extreme haecceitists may disagree with their opponents about the evaluation of counterfactuals with antecedents such as 'If Aristotle had been a poached egg', and about the evaluation of counterfactuals such as 'If all actual human beings had been poached eggs, then Aristotle would have been a poached egg'.

bound up with the whole mode of articulating reality to discover such an object there—the more exigent, obviously, is the necessity that, *if there is to be any such thing as the bearer*, it should have the feature in question. The *de re* 'must' of causal inflexibility here passes over at a certain threshold into the inflexibility of the metaphysically necessary or the (in one defensible sense) conceptual (the concept being the *a posteriori* concept of being identical with that very thing). (Wiggins 2001: 127)

I think that the extreme haecceitist can agree with, and applaud, much of the content of this passage, surprising as this may seem.[13] But what I want to emphasize is the point that, as regards the *restricted de re* modalities (as opposed to the 'metaphysical' or 'conceptual' ones) to which Wiggins here refers, extreme haecceitists have no reason to disagree with their opponents about what is included in the range of *de re* possibilities.

9.5. ESSENTIAL PROPERTIES AND PHILOSOPHICAL ARGUMENTS

It may be objected that the acceptance of extreme haecceitism would render pointless a standard type of philosophical argument that employs the notion of an essential property. Even where there is no obvious difference between the non-modal properties of *A* and *B* (or none that can be invoked without begging the question), philosophers may appeal to a difference in the *essential* properties of *A* and *B* in order to establish the non-identity of *A* and *B*, via Leibniz's Law. Thus, for example, if Descartes and his body have different essential properties, they are distinct entities; similarly for pain and C-fibre firing (cf. Kripke 1980: 144–55), and for the statue and the lump of clay with which it happens to coincide throughout its existence. Extreme haecceitism apparently threatens to undermine all such arguments, since it implies that there are no interesting distinctions between the essential properties of any two individuals.[14]

---

[13] The context of the passage is Wiggins's defence of sortal essentialism, to which, of course, the extreme haecceitist must be adamantly opposed. Hence the extreme haecceitist must either disagree with Wiggins about which properties are 'inherent in the individuation' of their bearers, or disagree with Wiggins's claim that a property's being inherent in the individuation of its bearer is a ground for its being an essential property. See also the later sections of Ch. 8, above.

[14] Excluding properties such as *identity with A* and *identity with B*, of course, which (for familiar reasons) the extreme haecceitist can consistently treat as genuinely essential properties.

Now, some philosophers may regard it as no objection to extreme haecceitism if it were to undermine such arguments, since they think that these arguments are typically fallacious. According to these philosophers, an apparent 'difference in essential properties' need be no such thing, since a predicate of the form '*x* is essentially F' or '*x* is accidentally G' is a predicate that may attribute different modal properties to an object depending on how that object is described or referred to.[15] However, I do not want to appeal to this as a defence. I am sceptical about whether the apparent differences in essential properties in these cases should be explained away in this fashion.

Instead, I claim that it is not true that extreme haecceitism must undermine the basis for these arguments. The most it would require is that they be slightly modified in form. Even if extreme haecceitists cannot say that there is a difference between the *essential* properties of *A* and *B*, they may still hold that there can be *some* modal difference between *A* and *B*: for example, that there is some property that is tenacious or quasi-essential to *A*, but not to *B*. And such a modal difference, albeit not strictly an essential difference, could still be sufficient, together with Leibniz's Law, to establish the non-identity of *A* and *B*. Suppose, for the sake of argument, that it is quasi-essential to the statue, but not to the lump of clay, that it be a statue, and that it be shaped in a certain way. Such a modal difference would not, strictly speaking, be a difference in the *essential properties* of the statue and the lump. But it would nevertheless be a difference in their characteristics to which one could appeal in order to argue, via Leibniz's Law, for their numerical distinctness.[16] Similarly, the extreme haecceitist may, it is true, be debarred from saying that a particular pain *could not* have existed without being felt as pain, and thus be debarred from arguing that the pain has an essential property that is not possessed by any episode of C-fibre firing. But an extreme haecceitist may still apparently hold that it is quasi-essential to the pain, but not to the episode of C-fibre firing, that it is felt as pain, and argue on this basis that the pain and the C-fibre firing are numerically distinct.[17] Other philosophical arguments that appeal to differences in essential

[15] See Gibbard 1975; Lewis 1971 and 1986*a*, ch. 4; Noonan 1991 and 1993.

[16] On a liberal notion of 'property', *being quasi-essentially torso-shaped* (for example) may be as good a candidate for a property as is *being essentially torso-shaped*.

[17] I do not suggest that the extreme haecceitist *must* take this view, and regard the pain and the C-fibre firing as numerically distinct, differing in their quasi-essential properties. All that I want to argue is that this type of argument is *available* to an extreme haecceitist.

properties may, I surmise, be reconstrued in a similar fashion, by substituting quasi-essential properties for allegedly essential properties, and by reconstruing alleged *de re* impossibilities as possibilities that are, in the immortal words of Wodehouse's Jeeves, merely 'remote contingencies'.

Alternatively, some such arguments may be reconstrued by appeal to the contrast between 'could have been' and 'would have been' discussed above. Consider, for example, David Lewis's (1986*c*) discussion of the essences of events. Lewis points out that different verdicts about the essences of events will fit different assessments of counterfactual conditionals. However, it seems clear that, strictly speaking, it is not the *essences* of events that are relevant to Lewis's discussion. For the counterfactuals under discussion (concerning the counterfactual dependence of events on one another) concern questions about whether certain events *would* have occurred in certain circumstances, not questions about whether those events *could* have occurred in those circumstances. I see no reason why an extreme haecceitist should not arrive at judgements about what events *would* have occurred in certain circumstances that are exactly the same as the judgements of someone who is not an extreme haecceitist, even if the extreme haecceitist believes that events have no interesting essences or essential properties at all.

In addition, there are cases where essential properties figure in philosophical discussion that would retain their point if the notion of an essential property in the strict sense were replaced by the notion of a 'Weakly Aristotelian' essential property described in the previous section. This is, I think, true of the question sometimes raised in debates between psychological ('Lockean') theorists and biological ('animalist') theorists of personal identity about whether human persons are essentially persons, or essentially human animals. For example, the biological theorist appears to be committed to saying that I was once a foetus, and that I may continue to exist in the future in a persistent vegetative state; given the plausible assumption that neither a foetus nor an individual in a persistent vegetative state is a person, this implies that I once existed, and may in the future exist, without being a person. This is sometimes put as the point that, according to these animalists, human persons are not *essentially* persons. However, it is clear that the main question at issue here is not, strictly speaking, whether persons are essentially persons in the standard modern sense of 'essential'—that is, whether they *could have existed* without being persons—but rather whether *being a person* is an essential property in the 'Weakly Aristotelian' sense: in other words, whether *person* is a substance sortal.[18] What is distinctive of these animalist theorists is that they claim that, if to be a person is to have certain psychological attributes, then we should deny that *person* is a substance sortal.[19] Some of their opponents, by contrast, will claim both that *person* is a substance sortal and that to be a person is to have certain psychological attributes; hence that if I am identical with a person I cannot be an entity that once existed, or may continue to exist, without having such psychological attributes. But, as I have already noted, an extreme haecceitist can consistently hold that although I may have no non-trivial essential properties in the strict sense of 'essential', I do have non-trivial essential properties in the Weak Aristotelian sense. In denying that persons are essentially persons, extreme haecceitists need not, then, be denying that persons are essentially persons in the Weak Aristotelian sense. By the same token, the extreme haecceitist's denial that human persons are essentially animals is *not* the denial that they are essentially animals in the Weak Aristotelian sense of 'essential'; hence it is consistent with the animalist's thesis that *animal* is a substance sortal. In short, the principal issue that divides the animalist and the psychological theorist is an issue about which concepts are substance sortals, not an issue about which properties are essential properties. Hence the extreme haecceitist's denial of essential properties is in no danger of either foreclosing or trivializing this debate, a debate in which the extreme haecceitist is fully entitled to participate, on either side.

9.6. QUASI-ESSENTIAL PROPERTIES AND CHISHOLM'S PARADOX

So far, I have considered the fact that the extreme haecceitist will replace the claim that it is essential to an individual to be (an) F with the claim that it is quasi-essential to the individual that it be (an) F, where the properties envisaged as substitutes for *being (an) F* are kind

---

[18] Snowdon (1990) rightly distinguishes the question whether something that is a person is essentially a person from the question whether 'person' represents what he calls 'an abiding sort', where an 'abiding sort' is equivalent to a substance sortal kind. However, it is noteworthy that in Snowdon's discussion of the debate between the animalist and the Lockean over personal identity, the question whether persons are *essentially* persons, as distinct from the question whether 'person' refers to an abiding sort, plays virtually no role.

[19] In addition to Snowdon 1990, see, e.g., Olson 1997, ch. 2, and D. Mackie 1999.

properties (such as *being a poached egg* or *being a paper clip*). However, I take it that it would be odd (if not flatly inconsistent) for the extreme haecceitist to claim that a particular ship could have existed without being a ship at all, while also claiming that it could not have been a *ship* originally composed of parts entirely distinct from its actual original parts. If so, then it seems that the extreme haecceitist must deny the intuitively plausible principle, discussed in Sections 3.5–3.6 above, that a given ship could *not* have been (a ship) originally composed of parts entirely different from its actual original parts. However, the extreme haecceitist can, it seems, adopt the strategy of replacing this essentialist claim with the claim that although the ship *could* have existed as a ship with entirely different original parts, the possibility of its being a ship so composed is a relatively remote one: less remote, perhaps, than the possibility of its not being a ship at all, but relatively remote, none the less. We might even say that the possibility of its being a ship originally composed of entirely different parts is sufficiently remote that it counts as a quasi-essential property of the ship that it have at least some of its original parts, bearing in mind that being quasi-essential is something that can be a matter of degree.

This difference between quasi-essentialism and genuine essentialism: that a property's being quasi-essential may be a matter of degree, whereas it is not obvious that its status as essential can be a matter of degree, may be to quasi-essentialism's advantage when we consider the *sorites*-type paradoxes that threaten if we try to suppose that individuals have essences but that these essences are 'tolerant'. For example, as we saw in Section 3.6 above, the genuine essentialist who wants to say that a ship that is originally composed of three parts A1 + B1 + C1 could have been originally composed of A1 + B1 + C2 but not of A1 + B2 + C2 (where C2 ≠ C1 and B2 ≠ B1) confronts the problem that it appears to be undeniable that if the ship *had* been originally composed of A1 + B1 + C2 instead of A1 + B1 + C1, it would *then* have been possible for it to have been originally composed of A1 + B2 + C2. The quasi-essentialist, however, confronts no such problem. For the quasi-essentialist simply denies the truth of the 'restriction principle' that says that a ship originally composed of A1 + B1 + C1 could not have been originally composed of A1 + B2 + C2: of parts that include less than half of its actual original parts. Instead, the quasi-essentialist claims that although the possibility of the ship's being originally composed of A1 + B2 + C2 is more remote than the possibility of its being originally composed of A1 + B1 + C2, it is a possibility none the less. Nor need the quasi-essentialist claim that the remote possibility belongs to the realm of the merely 'possibly possible': in other words, the quasi-essentialist need not invoke a non-transitive accessibility relation between possible worlds in order to justify the claim that there is a possible world in which s1 has an original composition that is radically different from its actual original composition.

9.7. EXTREME HAECCEITISM AS MINIMALIST ESSENTIALISM

It must be admitted, as a matter of logic, that if there is *any* kind of thing such that, necessarily, everything that belongs to that kind belongs to it essentially, then, if Aristotle does *not* in fact belong to that kind, he could not have done so. For example, if we accept that every number is essentially a number, then we must conclude that Aristotle could not have been a number, since (unless we adopt some bizarre Pythagorean hypothesis about the nature of reality, which I take it is not a live option) we must admit that Aristotle is not in fact a number. (If Aristotle were a number in some possible world, and everything that is a number in some possible world is a number in all possible worlds in which it exists, then Aristotle would have to be a number in the actual world, which he clearly is not.) Now, perhaps this line of reasoning will support the conclusion that the most extreme versions of haecceitism, such as some of those cited by Adams and Kirwan and Forbes in the passages quoted in Section 9.2, can be rejected. For example, perhaps we should accept that every number is essentially a number, and that every event is essentially an event, and every abstract object essentially abstract. If so, since Aristotle is, in fact, neither a number nor an event nor an abstract object, it follows that he could not have been a thing of any of these kinds. Following the terminology I have used earlier, let us say that a kind or category is an *essential* kind or category if and only if, necessarily, anything that belongs to it belongs to it essentially. Then we can say that, although (for reasons that I have given in Chapters 7 and 8) it may be unclear which are the essential kinds or categories to which Aristotle *does* belong, it may yet be clear that there are certain essential kinds or categories to which he does *not*, and hence that there are at least some kinds of thing such that Aristotle could not have been a thing of one of those kinds. If so, it may be that any version of extreme haecceitism that is so extreme as to attempt to explain away, rather than to accept at face value, the intuition that Aristotle could not have been, say, a hurricane, a baseball game, a Platonic universal, a hypothesis, a set, or the number 17, is indefensible.

With this I agree. A sensible version of extreme haecceitism should not be so dogmatic as to deny that there may be *some* kinds or categories that are essential kinds or categories, and that, as a consequence, there are some genuinely essential properties that Aristotle has that represent limits to the ways in which he could have been different from the way that he actually is.[20] Nevertheless, this concession is evidently compatible with a fairly extreme version of haecceitism—what one might call 'minimalist essentialism'. Moreover, far from being an embarrassment to this (fairly) extreme haecceitist, the concession that there may be some essential kinds or categories, exemplified, perhaps, by such broad categories as *event* and *abstract object*, may even lend further support to the view, for reasons indicated in the opening section of this chapter. The (fairly) extreme haecceitist (minimalist essentialist) may present the following challenge. Either our intuition that Aristotle could not have been a centipede or a poached egg (like our intuition that he could not have been an event or a number) is to be explained by reference to a theory of essential kinds or categories, or it is not. If it is, what *are* the relevant essential kinds or categories that rule out Aristotle's being a poached egg or a centipede? If it is not, what is the alternative explanation? And why is it to be preferred to the explanation of the intuition that is provided by the extreme haecceitist?

9.8. IS EXTREME HAECCEITISM BELIEVABLE?

Finally, however, I must confront the incredulous stare. It may be insisted that we can make absolutely nothing of the supposition that Aristotle could have been a centipede or a poached egg. It may be insisted that to think that these suppositions (or alleged suppositions) represent genuine possibilities, however remote, is very nearly as absurd

---

[20] I do not commit myself to the claim that such categories as *event* or *abstract object* or *number are* in fact essential categories. About this I remain, at present, agnostic. All that I want to maintain is that *if* they are, this is compatible with, and has no tendency to undermine, a fairly extreme ('minimalist essentialist') version of extreme haecceitism.

as to suppose that the existence of round squares or married bachelors is not, strictly speaking, impossible, but merely extremely unlikely.

However, in the absence of a principled account of *why* Aristotle could not have belonged to these radically different kinds, I think that the insistence that these kinds represent properties that are strictly *incompatible* with his identity is unpersuasive. It is not only unpersuasive, but also gratuitous, if, as I have argued in Sections 9.3–9.5, we may explain the relevant intuitions without appeal to such an incompatibility. It may be protested that to attempt to suppose that Aristotle could have been, say, a poached egg, is to lose all significant ties with the actual Aristotle. Surely any putative candidate for being Aristotle, in any coherent counterfactual speculation, must remain 'anchored' to the actual Aristotle by retaining some significant subset of Aristotle's actual characteristics? But (surely) the required anchorage cannot be provided merely by the retention of some subset of his actual characteristics that are compatible with his being a poached egg?[21]

If this is the objection, I think that the extreme haecceitist's response should be: why not? The idea that we both can and must 'keep hold of' an individual in counterfactual situations by keeping fixed some significant subset of its actual characteristics is, I admit, extremely seductive. We have met this idea in several guises in this book: in the notion that there is some subset of a thing's properties—its individual essence—whose possession is sufficient (in all possible situations) for its being the very individual that it is, and in the notion of the 'overlap requirement', discussed in Chapters 6 and 7, according to which, for any possible situation concerning an individual, there must be some significant set of properties that it had at some time in its actual existence that it retains in that possible situation. I think that this seductive idea should be resisted. Once we fall under the spell of this conception, I think that we have no principled way of avoiding a commitment to much stronger, and far less defensible, claims about the essential properties of things than are warranted by a mere rejection of extreme haecceitism.

I admit that we do not have a clear and adequate conception of the modal natures of the ordinary individuals that we typically take as the subjects of our *de re* speculations. Indeed, I take this to be one of the lessons of this book. Moreover, our modal thinking about these

---

[21] Compare Wiggins 1980, ch. 4, 105–6 and 114–15, and Wiggins 2001, ch. 4, 109–10, 121–2, 131–3. See also Ch. 8 above.

individuals appears to involve tensions and inconsistencies that may threaten it with incoherence. However, insofar as we have any coherent conception of their modal natures, I submit that we may reasonably regard these ordinary individuals, from a modal point of view, as, if not quite bare particulars, then very thinly clad.[22]

---

[22] Cf. Lewis 1986*a*: 242 (although the phrase that I have adapted is used by Lewis in a different context).

10

Essentialism, Semantic Theory, and Natural Kinds

The preceding chapters have had, as their subject matter, essentialism about individuals. In this final chapter I turn to the discussion of some issues concerning essentialism about natural kinds.

10.1. VARIETIES OF ESSENTIALISM ABOUT NATURAL KINDS

As I pointed out in Chapter 1, essentialism about natural kinds is a view that appears in formulations of two types. One formulation, suggested by Kripke's discussion (1980) presents it as a doctrine of *de re* necessities concerning entities that are (natural) kinds: thus we get such statements as

(1) Water and H_2O are necessarily identical

or: (2) $\Box$ Water = H_2O;

(3) Gold has essentially the atomic number 79

or: (4) $\Box$ Gold has the atomic number 79;

(5) The kind *tiger* is essentially mammalian

or: (6) $\Box$ The kind *tiger* is mammalian,

where in (2), (4), and (6) 'water', 'H_2O', 'gold' and 'the kind *tiger*' function as rigid designators of kinds. On the other hand, a formulation suggested by Putnam's discussion (1973, 1975) dispenses with the designation of kinds by singular terms in favour of the postulation of necessary but a posteriori connections between predicates: thus we get such statements as:

(7) $\Box$ $\forall x$ (x is a sample of water $\leftrightarrow$ x is composed of H_2O molecules)

and   (8) $\Box\ \forall x$ (x is a piece of gold $\rightarrow$ x is composed of stuff with atomic number 79)

and   (9) $\Box\ \forall x$ (x is a tiger $\rightarrow$ x is a mammal),

where it is assumed that the quantified sentences within the necessity operator are a posteriori. If we speak loosely, we can say that (7)–(9) 'attribute essential properties to kinds'. But of course (as I pointed out in Chapter 1), strictly speaking, they do nothing of the sort. Statements like (7)–(9) do not explicitly ascribe essential properties to anything: neither to kinds nor to the things that belong to those kinds. What they do is to specify properties essential *for* kind membership. According to the sense of '*de re* essentialism' that has been employed in this book, statements like (7)–(9) do not involve a commitment to *de re* essentialism.[1] (Note that someone who endorses (7)–(9) does not appear thereby to be committed to the corresponding statements (1)–(6). It seems that one could adopt the 'natural kind essentialism' represented in (7)–(9) without being involved in any ontological commitment to kinds, and without adopting any means of reference to them, let alone reference by rigid designators. Indeed, as far as I can see, one could quite consistently accept that there are necessary a posteriori connections between predicates, as represented by statements like (7)–(9), without believing in the truth of any *de re* essentialist statement whatsoever.[2] Whether this would be a *sensible* position is, of course, another matter.)

However, although (7)–(9) are not examples of *de re* essentialism in my sense, I shall follow the policy suggested in Section 1.6 of counting (7)–(9) as essentialist on the grounds that they involve a commitment to the existence of necessary connections between predicates that are a posteriori rather than a priori. In Chapter 1 I called such essentialism 'predicate essentialism', and I shall continue to do so. I shall, however, avoid describing it as a form of '*de re* essentialism', reserving this term for those forms of essentialism that either explicitly attribute essential properties to things (such as (1), (3), and (5)) or involve rigidly designating singular terms within the scope of modal operators (such as (2), (4), and (6)). In addition, I shall follow the policy suggested in

---

[1] See Sect. 1.6, where I explain my restriction of the notion of '*de re* essentialism'. According to my terminology, (7)–(9), although in a sense essentialist, are examples of merely *de dicto* necessity.

[2] See also Sect. 10.2 below.

Chapter 1 of counting *de re* essentialist statements about kinds of the form of (1)–(6) as examples of 'essentialism about kinds' only when the 'corresponding' formulations in terms of necessary connections between predicates are a posteriori rather than a priori.[3]

It is not clear that the correspondence between the *de re* formulations and the predicate formulations is exact, even if one accepts the legitimacy of the *de re* formulations. For example, it seems that one might hold that the criteria for the identity of the kinds *water* and *H_2O* do not require that absolutely all actual and possible samples of water are samples of H_2O: perhaps it would be enough for the kind identity if in every possible world the standard, or normal, samples of water (in that world) are all samples of H_2O, and vice versa. For present purposes, however, it must be noted that unless statements like (1)–(6) are supposed to be making *some* claim about what samples of the relevant kinds in all possible worlds have to be like, we shall have left behind anything that is recognizable as the natural kind essentialism advocated by Kripke and Putnam. In particular, the identity between the kinds *water* and *H_2O* asserted in (1) had better not entail merely that in all causally possible worlds samples of water are samples of H_2O (and vice versa), otherwise (1) will not resemble the modern, controversial, essentialism about kinds. And, of course, according to Kripke (1980), (1) is stronger than this. For he takes the identity to imply that there is no possible world whatsoever in which the samples of water are all or mostly samples of some stuff other than H_2O. For the most part, then, I shall ignore the complications mentioned above (that arise if we admit the possibility of abnormal members of a kind), and shall treat the sentences (1)–(6) as if they entailed the corresponding predicate formulations (7)–(9).

The examples that I have given also exhibit a quite different distinction between forms of essentialism about kinds. If we look at the 'predicate essentialist' statements (7)–(9), we see that they fall into two classes. (7) asserts a necessarily necessary *and* sufficient condition for kind membership. On the other hand, (8) and (9) merely assert necessarily *necessary* conditions for kind membership. I shall describe both sorts of statement as involving 'essentialism about kinds' (and as 'attributing essential properties to kinds' in the loose, 'non-*de re*',

---

[3] This is in order to avoid the problem, mentioned in Sect. 1.6, that without this restriction we shall be in danger of having to treat a priori claims like '□ oculist = eye doctor' as involving 'essentialism about kinds': an unwanted result.

sense indicated above). When I want a label to distinguish the stronger essentialist claim: the one that involves sufficient (as well as necessary) conditions for kind membership, I shall refer to it as the claim that kinds have *essences*. A corresponding distinction can be made, of course, between the *de re* essentialist statements (1) and (2) on the one hand, and (3)–(6) on the other: I shall say that all of (1)–(6) involve essentialism about kinds, but only (1) and (2) posit an essence for a kind. I see no reason why someone should not be an essentialist about natural kinds without believing that natural kinds have essences. However, the resulting doctrine is less exciting than the full-blooded doctrine of essences. Perhaps for this reason, or perhaps simply because both Kripke and Putnam argued that at least some natural kinds have essences in my sense, the discussion of their versions of essentialism has tended to take it for granted that their theories involve a commitment to essences.

I do not suggest that it is uniquely appropriate to use the term 'essentialism about natural kinds' for views that, like those of Kripke and Putnam, involve claims about metaphysical necessity or what is the case in all possible worlds. One might use the term 'essence of a natural kind' to refer to some type of 'Lockean real essence': a set of properties that is basic in the explanation of the other properties of the kind, without commitment to the view that such real essences belong to the relevant kinds in all possible worlds.[4] However, to keep the terminology simple, in what follows I shall not include the belief in such 'merely Lockean' essences in the scope of the term 'essentialism about kinds'. (Kripke and Putnam chose, for their typical essences of kinds, sets of properties that could plausibly be thought of as explanatorily basic in this way, and no doubt their views would be implausible without this feature. But of course the modal implications of their views about the essences of kinds go well beyond the claim that kinds have such explanatorily basic properties.)[5]

---

[4] This is not to say that a 'merely Lockean' conception of the essence of a kind is an entirely non-modal conception: there may be a link between such Lockean essences and counterfactual conditionals. My point is simply that one could accept such Lockean real essences without holding that these real essences characterize the kinds *in all possible worlds*.

[5] The same is true of the 'scientific essentialism' defended by Brian Ellis (2001, 2002), which, unfortunately, I shall not be discussing here. Ellis's theory also involves a conception of the essences of natural kinds that gives them the status of metaphysically necessary features of those kinds: features that belong to the kinds in all possible worlds.

10.2. ESSENTIALISM ABOUT INDIVIDUALS AND ESSENTIALISM ABOUT NATURAL KINDS

In this book, I have expressed scepticism about whether ordinary persisting individuals have much in the way of interesting essential properties, either in virtue of being the particular individuals that they are, or in virtue of belonging to the kinds to which they belong. However, I think that my scepticism about the essential properties of ordinary individuals, including the 'extreme haecceitism' advocated in Chapter 9, leaves essentialism about natural kinds pretty much unscathed, with one qualification. The qualification is this. If the extreme haecceitist goes as far as to say that Aristotle could have been a *natural kind*—perhaps an element ('Aristotelium'?) or a chemical compound, for example—then the extreme haecceitist is evidently committed to the claim that not every natural kind is essentially a natural kind, since Aristotle (who is not, in fact, a natural kind) would be a counterexample to this claim.[6]

Nevertheless, this qualification is not, I think, of great significance for the question whether some version of essentialism about natural kinds is defensible. A version of extreme haecceitism could still be pretty extreme while conceding that Aristotle *does* have, as one of his essential properties, that he is not a natural kind: a view consistent with the claims that all (possible) natural kinds are essentially natural kinds, that the kind *water* is essentially the kind H_2O, and so on. In addition (and this is a quite separate point), it is important to note that it need be no part of a theory of essentialism about natural kinds to hold that the particular items that *belong* to a natural kind belong to it essentially. As I see it, one could be an essentialist about natural kinds (say, the kinds *tiger* or *water*) while holding that every actual instance or sample of a natural kind (for example, every particular tiger or sample of water) is only accidentally an instance or a sample of that kind. Thus the scepticism to which I am implicitly committed (by the arguments of the previous chapters) about whether tigers are essentially tigers, or water molecules essentially water molecules, is quite compatible with the acceptance of principles such as (7) or (9) that specify necessary

---

[6] Or rather, strictly speaking, a counterexample to the claim that anything that is a natural kind in any possible world is essentially a natural kind.

conditions for belonging to the kinds *water* or *tiger* in any possible world.[7,8]

10.3. SEMANTIC THEORY AND NATURAL KINDS

The most important question about the natural kind essentialism of Kripke, Putnam, and others is surely: is it true? Are the modern essentialists right in claiming that natural kinds have essential properties and essences?

However, a full discussion of this question would require a book to itself. Here I shall concentrate on a more limited question: what is the connection between *semantics* and natural kind essentialism?

My main question will be one discussed by both Nathan Salmon (1982) and D. H. Mellor (1977): does the acceptance of the semantic theories of natural kind terms advocated by Kripke and Putnam involve a commitment to essentialism about natural kinds? Both Salmon and Mellor give a negative answer to this question. I think that this answer is substantially correct, and part of my discussion will consist in characterizing in my own way what I take to be the salient points of their negative arguments.

I begin, though, with a slightly different semantic question. Ignoring, for the present, the differences between them, let us label the types of semantic theory of natural kind terms given by Kripke and Putnam

---

[7] Kripke says, speaking of the items in a sample of gold that is involved in a 'hypothetical . . . baptism of the substance', that 'all those items which are actually gold are, of course, essentially gold' (1980: 135, note 69). However, this claim (for which Kripke gives no explanation) is evidently not entailed by the thesis (equivalent to (8)) that in any possible world, anything that is a sample of gold in that world has (in that world) the atomic number 79. I assume that Kripke simply regards his *de re* essentialist claim about the items that are actually gold as obviously correct, quite independently of (3), (4), and (8).

[8] Ellis (2001, 2002) distinguishes between what he calls 'individual essences' and 'kind essences', where 'the individual essence of a thing is the set of its characteristics in virtue of which it is the *individual* it is' and 'the kind essence of a thing . . . is the set of its properties in virtue of which it is a thing of the *kind* it is' (2002: 12). He adds, 'when I speak about the essences, or essential properties, of things, I should always be understood as talking about their kind essences unless I specifically indicate otherwise' (ibid.). Ellis also claims that the individual essence of a thing that belongs to a natural kind need not include its kind essence (2001: 238). I take all this to imply that when Ellis speaks of the essential properties of electrons, for example, he merely means the properties that they have that are essential *to their being electrons*: in other words, a claim that I would classify as a version of 'essentialism about natural kinds', rather than a version of *de re* essentialism about the individual things that are electrons.

'the K–P semantic theory'. It has been suggested that whatever answer we give to the question whether the K–P semantic theory involves a commitment to essentialism, it is significant that semantic theories of the K–P type are *consistent* with essentialism, whereas the semantic theories that they replaced are not. For example, Stephen Schwartz (1984) has argued that there is an (admittedly diluted) sense in which the Kripke–Putnam semantic theory 'leads to' essentialism about natural kinds, as follows: the K–P semantic theory is consistent with essentialism; the semantic theories that it replaced are not; essentialism is intrinsically plausible, but there was a barrier to its acceptance as long as the old semantic theories reigned. The K–P semantic theory 'leads to' essentialism in the sense of removing this barrier and opening the way to essentialism. (It might be said that the K–P theory in fact *led* to essentialism, although it does not really *lead* to essentialism.) But is this diagnosis correct?

No one, I think, could seriously doubt that the K–P semantic theory is consistent with essentialism. The issue thus turns on whether it is true that the semantic theories it replaced are not. I take it that the problem with combining essentialism about kinds with the type of semantic theory that the K–P semantics replaced is supposed to be along the following lines (cf. Schwartz 1984: 290). These earlier theories are description theories of natural kind terms, with the following characteristics:

(a)   the relevant descriptions are associated a priori with the kind term by all or at least some (e.g., expert) competent users of the term;

(b)   the descriptions give necessary and sufficient conditions for kind membership;

(c)   the relation that holds between a sample (or member) of the kind and the relevant descriptions is simply that of *fit*. In particular, no causal relations between users and sample (or member) are involved.

Let the relevant descriptions be abbreviated to 'D', and let there be some property M—perhaps a microstructural property—which an essentialist would regard as (metaphysically) necessary for belonging to the kind, although it is not a priori that members of the kind have M. Then the following difficulty obviously arises. Suppose that there could, metaphysically speaking, be items that had D and lacked M. By (a)–(c), such items would belong to the kind. Hence the proponent of the description theory cannot accept that it is metaphysically necessary that items belonging to the kind have M, contrary to what the essentialist claims.

In addition, suppose that the essentialist also holds that the kind has some *essence* M*: some essential property that is (necessarily) not only necessary but also sufficient for kind membership, although it is not a priori that the possession of M* is sufficient for membership of the kind. Suppose that there could, metaphysically speaking, be an item that had M*, but lacked D. By (a)–(c), such an item would not belong to the kind. Hence the proponent of the description theory cannot accept that M* represents a necessarily sufficient condition for kind membership, contrary to what the essentialist claims.

The issue boils down to this. To speak of metaphysical necessity is to speak of what holds in all possible worlds. But, aside from recherché cases of contingent a priori truth, which do not seem relevant here, to speak of truth a priori is also to speak of what holds in all possible worlds. So by laying down a priori necessary and sufficient conditions for kind membership, the description theory lays down necessary and sufficient conditions for kind membership that are intended to apply in all possible worlds, and thus to be metaphysically necessary. It would then be straightforwardly inconsistent to introduce a further set of metaphysically necessary necessary or sufficient conditions that diverge from the a priori conditions.

How much force does this argument have? There may be doubts, on the grounds that the version of a description theory that I set out above may seem excessively naïve, failing to do justice to the alternatives to the Kripke and Putnam semantic theories. In spite of this worry, however, I doubt that any tinkering with the description theory that makes it more sophisticated will eradicate the basic problem. By definition, essentialism about natural kinds introduces a posteriori necessary conditions for kind membership. As long as there is the possibility that an item should fail to satisfy the essentialist's necessary conditions, while it succeeds in satisfying the description theory's conditions for kind membership, essentialism about natural kinds will be inconsistent with any description theory. In other words, to maintain that a description theory of a natural kind term is consistent with essentialism about that natural kind, it must be shown that there is no possibility of such a divergence (between the description theory's requirements and those of the essentialist).

It seems, then, that if one wants to be sure to leave room for essentialism about natural kinds, one must find some alternative to a description theory of kind terms that is more congenial to essentialism. The crucial requirement appears to be that the semantic theory allow that the descriptions known to users, even expert users, of the terms may be inadequate: by including things that do not, in fact, belong to the kind, and perhaps also by excluding things that do, in fact, belong to it. This does not mean that the descriptions known to users of the terms have no role to play. But it does mean that the relation of 'fitting' — merely satisfying — such descriptions cannot be trusted to supply necessary and sufficient conditions for kind membership.[9] What seems to be required is some further relation, and an obvious candidate is some causal relation. Even if 'fitting the descriptions' were *necessary* for kind membership, it is still plausible to suppose that a causal relation is needed to exclude certain items that fit the descriptions. It is plausible to say that the use of a natural kind term in a linguistic community is typically, if not invariably, rooted in some causal transactions between the community and certain items in their environment, in such a way that the characteristics, known or unknown, of those items, can play a part in determining what it is to be of the relevant kind.

It is, however, impossible that speakers should stand in direct causal relations to *all* members of the kind: how, then, is the opponent of description theories to determine which, of the things with which speakers have no direct causal contact, fall within the kind, and which do not? Obviously, even if the extension of the kind is partly determined by appropriate causal relations between certain items (in a simple version of the theory these would be a set of 'original samples' or 'archetypes') and users of the term, some further relation is also required: a *'same kind'* relation that links the other members of the kind to those in the favoured sample. However, the opponent of description theories is, obviously, debarred from specifying this *same kind* relation in terms of a set of properties associated a priori with the kind term. The alternative suggested by both Kripke and Putnam is that the *same kind* relation is, indeed, constituted by the sharing of certain properties, but the relevant properties are ones that are delivered by a combination of empirical investigation and scientific theory, and are not associated a priori with the kind term.

---

[9] Devitt and Sterelny (1987, ch. 5), e.g., argue for an account of natural kind terms that involves both descriptions and causal relations. Cf. the discussion of proper names in Evans 1973.

If we go as far as this, we have the result that (ignoring the complications, mentioned in Section 10.1 above, that may arise if it is conceded that a kind can have a few abnormal members) where 'K' is a natural kind term, there will be some truth of the form

(A) $\forall x(x$ is a member (sample) of K if and only if x has $\varphi)$

which specifies a necessary and sufficient condition, represented by 'φ', for membership of K, but where it is a posteriori that something is a member of K if and only if it has φ. (A) gives only a necessary and sufficient condition for being in the *actual* extension of 'K'. But Kripke and Putnam take the further step of proposing that the *same* set of properties will constitute the condition for kind membership both in the actual world and in all possible worlds. This yields the result that, where 'K' is a natural kind term, there will be truths of the form

(E) $\square \ \forall x(x$ is a member (sample) of K if and only if x has $\varphi)$

that are a posteriori. But to accept that there are such a posteriori truths is, of course, to commit oneself to essentialism about natural kinds in the sense described in Section 10.1 above. In fact, it is to commit oneself to the stronger of the two versions of natural kind essentialism: the claim that natural kinds have essences.

I have now shown how the search for an alternative to a description theory of natural kind terms might end with the postulation of essential properties, and essences, of natural kinds. But is there any necessity that this should be the destination? More particularly, do the semantic theories of natural kind terms proposed by Kripke and Putnam involve a commitment to essentialism? Thus I return to the question raised at the beginning of this section.

10.4. PUTNAM'S SEMANTIC THEORY AND ESSENTIALISM ABOUT NATURAL KINDS

The description 'the Kripke–Putnam semantic theory' may be a misnomer, since there are, as noted in Section 10.1, significant differences between the semantic accounts provided by Kripke and Putnam. To simplify the discussion, I shall consider separately whether Putnam's semantic account involves a commitment to essentialism, and whether Kripke's semantic account does so, beginning with Putnam's account.

I shall take it that, for the purposes of my discussion, the crucial features of Putnam's semantic account are as follows. A natural kind predicate has both an actual extension and an intension, which determines its extension with respect to any possible world. The intension of a natural kind predicate is determined by a combination of two factors:

(1)   A set of actual samples picked out in a way that involves causal links between speakers and those samples. (The simplest case would be where the samples are picked out by ostension in some act of 'dubbing' the kind, but much more sophisticated variants are possible.)

(2)   A *'same kind'* relation between those samples and other actual and possible members of the kind, where the *same kind* relation is not constituted by the satisfaction of predicates associated a priori with the kind term, but is a relation that it is up to scientific investigation and theorizing to reveal.[10]

Our question is whether such an account is committed to essentialism about natural kinds. Both Mellor and Salmon answer that it is not. I think that, in effect, their point is the same one, and a simple one.[11] The burden of their arguments may, I suggest, be represented as follows, using 'water' as our example. Putnam's semantic account of the term 'water' does indeed have the result that any sample of water in any possible world is (in that world) a sample of water. And it does, indeed, have the result that any sample of water in any possible world belongs (in that world) to the same kind as any sample of water in that or any other possible world. But these points are, of course, utterly trivial, and represent obvious a priori truths. The first is just the following banality:

$$\Box \; \forall x(x \text{ is a sample of water} \; \rightarrow \; x \text{ is a sample of water}),$$

and the second represents the following claim, which is no less trivial as long as quantification over possible worlds (as represented by the initial quantifiers '$\forall w1$', '$\forall w2$') is permitted:

[10]   In taking these to be the relevant features of the account, I think that I am in broad agreement with both Salmon (1982) and Mellor (1977).

[11]   Here I appear to be disagreeing with Salmon, who regards the connection between Mellor's discussion and his own as 'tenuous' (Salmon 1982: 92, note 11). However, I think that a comparison between page 186 of Salmon's book and page 306 of Mellor 1977 makes it clear that although the presentations are very different indeed, and although it is evident that Salmon developed his arguments quite independently of Mellor's discussion, the linchpin of their arguments is the same.

$\forall w1 \forall w2 \, \forall x \forall y$ (x is in $w1$ a sample of water and y is in $w2$ a sample of water $\rightarrow$ x is in $w1$ a sample of the same kind that y is in $w2$ a sample of).

Now—Mellor and Salmon in effect say—no essentialism, of any kind, can be derived from these a priori platitudes. But such platitudes are all that can be derived from the Putnam semantics alone. Hence Putnam's semantic theory is not committed to essentialism.

From where, then, does Putnam get his essentialism: for example, his claim that to be a sample of water in any possible world a thing must be composed of H_2O molecules in that world? The answer suggested by both Salmon and Mellor is: from the way in which the *same kind* relation is cashed out. Putnam supposes that the a posteriori account of the *same kind* relation, the account that empirical investigation and science will deliver, will involve the *sharing* of certain fundamental properties by all actual and possible members of the kind. But this supposition, whether warranted or not, is an optional extra, over and above the semantic account. There is a possible option—so Salmon and Mellor suggest—that remains true to Putnam's semantic account, but allows that the a posteriori cashing out of the *same kind* relation may involve *no* such sharing of properties by all actual and possible members, and thus no essentialism.[12] Hence, to suppose that Putnam's semantic theory, just by itself, generates essentialism, is mistaken. Putnam himself has made this mistake if, when he said that his account of natural kind terms 'has startling consequences for the theory of necessary truth' he meant to imply that his semantic account entails essentialism.[13]

Put like this, the verdict of Salmon and Mellor is very plausible. It is surely true that the only place for essentialism about kinds to come from in Putnam's semantic account is out of the *same kind* relation. But as long as there could be *same kind* relations that are cashed out in terms that do not involve the sharing of properties (apart from properties such as *being water*), there is a gap between the semantic

---

[12] See Mellor 1977: 306; Salmon 1982: 186.

[13] The statement comes from Putnam 1973: 708/1975: 232, quoted by Salmon (1982: 98). I am not sure that in this passage Putnam is making the claim criticized by Salmon and Mellor, although one could certainly be forgiven for thinking so. It seems possible that all that Putnam means here is that his semantic theory (like Kripke's) leaves room for a posteriori necessities about natural kinds, in contrast to description theories, which do not: the point I have endorsed in Sect. 10.3.

account and any essentialist conclusions. The semantic account may be *congenial* to essentialism about natural kinds, but it does not imply it. A fortiori, it does not imply the stronger claim that natural kinds have *essences*—properties not only necessary but also sufficient for kind membership in any possible world—as Putnam seems to suppose that *being composed of H₂O molecules* would be.

10.5. SALMON ON THE ATTEMPT TO DERIVE ESSENTIALISM FROM THE THEORY OF REFERENCE

Salmon treats the question of the relation between Putnam's semantic theory of kind terms and essentialism as part of a larger issue. He characterizes the larger issue as follows: whether non-trivial essentialism follows from, or is a consequence of, or is implied by, the semantic theory that he calls (following Kaplan) 'the theory of direct reference'.[14] What is distinctive about the theory of direct reference is that it is opposed to a description theory. Applied to a singular term, the direct reference theory says that the reference of the term is not determined by a purely qualitative or descriptive sense known to those who understand the term. Applied to a predicate (the case that concerns us here) the theory says that the *application* of the term—its extension with respect to any possible world—is not determined by a purely qualitative or descriptive sense known to those who understand the term.[15]

Salmon argues at length against the idea that there can be a derivation of non-trivial essentialism about natural kinds from the theory of direct reference applied to natural kind terms: what I shall call 'a Derivation'. (The distinction between trivial and non-trivial essentialism need not concern us at this point: suffice it to say that predicate essentialism about natural kinds, such as the view that all possible samples of water are samples of H₂O, counts as non-trivial, according to Salmon.)[16] Salmon's

---

[14] e.g., Salmon 1982: 87–92. As the authors of the 'direct reference theory' he cites Kripke, Putnam, Donnellan, and Kaplan (p. 3).

[15] See Salmon 1982: 3–4, and sects. 1.1, 1.2, and 4.1. Sometimes Salmon omits the explicit qualification that it is the existence of a descriptive sense *known to those who understand the term* that the direct reference theory denies, but I take it that this qualification is always intended.

[16] On the distinction between trivial and non-trivial essentialism, see Salmon 1982: 82–4. See also Sect. 10.10 below.

strategy is that of 'attempting to reconstruct the strongest possible case [for a Derivation] and then revealing its shortcomings' (1982: 91–2). He considers a form of argument (suggested by unpublished work of Donnellan) that might be supposed to yield essentialist conclusions from the semantic account of natural kind terms given by Putnam. Salmon shows that this form of argument fails to provide Derivations of the required kind, because the essentialist conclusions can be deduced only by employing extra premises that are themselves essentialist, and do not come from the Putnam semantic theory.

The form of argument that Salmon considers is a general one, but the example to which he gives most attention is the following, which I shall call 'Argument S1' (cf. 1982: 166–7; I have renumbered premises and conclusion).

Argument S1:

(1) It is necessarily the case that: something is a sample of water if and only if it is a sample of *dthat* (the same substance that *this* is a sample of).

(2) *This* (liquid sample) has the chemical structure H_2O.

(3) Being a sample of the same substance as something consists in having the same chemical structure.

Therefore:

(4) It is necessarily the case that: every sample of water has the chemical structure H_2O.

The first thing to note about this argument is that its initial premise, which according to Salmon purports to give an 'ostensive definition' of 'water' gives, if it gives a definition at all, a definition of the *predicate* 'x is a sample of water'. A corollary of this is the now familiar point that the conclusion, (4), does not explicitly attribute any essential property to the substance water, or to any other thing. The sense in which the conclusion is essentialist is that it asserts a necessary connection between two predicates ('x is a sample of water' and 'x has the chemical structure H_2O') that cannot be known a priori to obtain. In my terminology, the essentialism is an example of predicate essentialism, not of *de re* essentialism.

About the argument S1, Salmon has four main comments. One is that the first premise embodies an ostensive definition of 'water' that is in keeping with Putnam's version of the direct reference theory (1982: 176).[17] The main point is that the 'ostensive definition' embodies the idea that the intension of the natural kind predicate is determined by 'getting hold of' a certain actual sample, and specifying that the extension is to include all and only things of the same kind (or same substance) as the paradigm (pp. 103–4). As for the expression '*dthat*', it is a version of Kaplan's (1978) rigidifying device, which has the effect of ensuring that the expression '*dthat* (the same substance that *this* is a sample of)' is a rigid designator of the substance that the demonstrated sample is *actually* a sample of. (This allows us to treat as irrelevant the possibility—if it is a possibility—that this paradigmatic sample might not have been a sample of water.) The first premise thus obviously has the implication that the condition for some item in any possible world to be (a sample of) water is that it be a sample of the substance of which the demonstrated sample is actually a sample. (It must be emphasized that this 'direct reference theory' definition does not merely determine the actual extension of the predicate. Because of the initial necessity operator, it specifies an *intension* for the predicate: its extension with respect to any possible world.) Salmon's second remark about the argument is that premise (2) represents a straightforward empirical discovery, and carries, by itself, no essentialist commitment (p. 176). His third remark is that the argument, properly interpreted, is valid (p. 167). Salmon's fourth remark is that the validity of the argument depends on an interpretation of the third premise according to which (3) is itself essentialist (pp. 176–89). He points out that the argument is valid only if 'consists in' in premise (3) is taken to imply that all possible samples of a single substance have the same chemical structure.[18] Since (3) is not only essentialist but also, according to Salmon, not a product of the direct reference theory, he concludes that this argument does not provide a Derivation of essentialism.

Salmon shows that this result can be generalized, not only by extending it to 'ostensive definitions' of other natural kind terms (pp. 182–92), but also by extending it to a modified version of S1 that has, in place of premise (1), an alternative form of definition suggested by

---

[17] Salmon gives a detailed account of the interpretation of the 'definition' (1982: 99–116; 139–57; the formulation (1) is arrived at on p. 146.

[18] In particular, the argument is not valid if (3) is interpreted as implying only that all *actual* samples of the same substance share their chemical structure, or only that all samples *within* any possible world do so.

Putnam's account: an 'operational definition' that specifies what it is to be water in terms of being a sample of the same substance as some actual items that are identified partly by description (p. 169). Salmon's example involves the replacement, in premise (1), of '*dthat* (the same substance that *this* is a sample of)' by '*dthat* (the colorless, odorless, tasteless, thirst-quenching liquid substance that fills *that* lake and *that* ocean)'. The resulting new version of S1 obviously fares no better than the original, since the additional essentialist premise (3) is still required for the derivation of the essentialist conclusion (4).

It seems clear that Salmon's main point is, in effect, the one I attributed to him in the last section. The semantic premises that he considers do, in a sense, specify a condition that any possible sample of water must satisfy: it must be a sample of the same substance as the substance that some particular sample or samples *actually* belong to. But if this is all that is specified by the semantics of the predicate '*x* is a sample of water', then these semantics explicitly involve nothing about what properties, if any, all possible samples may have to have in common in order to be 'consubstantial'—samples of the same substance. Since Salmon holds that conditions for consubstantiality, such as (3), are not derivable from semantical premises such as (1), and, secondly, that arguments like S1 represent the best case for deriving essentialism about natural kinds from the semantic theory of direct reference, he concludes that that semantic theory does not have (non-trivial) essentialist consequences concerning natural kinds. He draws from this the moral that essentialism about natural kinds is not a product of semantics, but requires an independent justification: for example, whatever justification is required to support the essentialist premise (3).[19]

10.6. A COMPLICATION

Salmon is, I think, clearly right in holding that Argument S1 fails, and for the reasons that he gives, to provide a Derivation, as long as he is right in holding that (3) cannot be derived from (1). But there is a problem. Salmon identifies the issue as being whether non-trivial essentialism can be derived from premises that are 'consequences' or 'assertions' of the direct reference theory, together with supplementary

---

[19] Salmon also argues that (3) requires a metaphysical basis, rather than, say, a scientific one (1982, sects. 32–3).

premises that are free of non-trivial essentialist import.[20] Argument S1 enters the picture because Salmon takes it to represent one of the most promising attempts to derive essentialism about a natural kind—*water*—from a definitional premise that is a consequence or assertion of the direct reference theory. But he does not treat (1) as the only possible definition of 'water' that a direct reference theorist could adopt, as is shown by the fact that he considers, as a legitimate alternative, the so-called 'operational definition' mentioned above. And this invites the following question: just when does a premise purporting to give the semantics of the expression '*x* is a sample of water' count as a consequence or assertion of the direct reference theory? If all that is required is that the premise give an account of the semantics of the predicate that is *consistent* with the direct reference theory, it can easily be shown that essentialist conclusions about the constitution of water can be derived from semantical premises that are consequences of the direct reference theory, together with merely factual extra premises that have no essentialist import.

To see this, consider the following two purported 'Derivations', M1 and M2:

Argument M1:

(F) It is necessarily the case that: something is a sample of water if and only if it is a sample with *dthat* (the scientifically fundamental property or properties that *this* has).

(H) The scientifically fundamental property that *this* has is having the chemical structure H_2O.

Therefore:

(4) It is necessarily the case that: every sample of water has the chemical structure H_2O.

Argument M2:

(C) It is necessarily the case that: something is a sample of water if and only if it is a sample with *dthat* (the chemical structure that *this* has).

(2) *This* (liquid sample) has the chemical structure H_2O.

---

[20] Salmon 1982: 167, 169, 175, 176.

Therefore:

(4)   It is necessarily the case that: every sample of water has the chemical structure H_2O.

If S1, the argument that Salmon considers, is valid, so are M1 and M2. And M1 and M2 both derive the essentialist conclusion (4). But M1 differs from S1 in that it uses, as its initial premise, a premise that guarantees that all possible samples of water share their fundamental properties. Because of this, (H), the auxiliary premise that says what the fundamental properties of the demonstrated sample are, need be given no more than a purely factual interpretation in order to yield, in conjunction with (F), the essentialist conclusion. Similarly, M2 differs from S1 in that its initial premise (C) guarantees that all possible samples of water share their chemical structure. Obviously nothing more is then needed to derive the essentialist conclusion (4) than a specification of what the chemical structure of some relevant sample is, which is supplied by premise (2).

Both M1 and M2 derive the essentialist conclusion (4) without the need for extra essentialist premises such as (3). No one should be surprised by this. But there is nevertheless a problem. If either (F), the initial premise of M1, or (C), the initial premise of M2, can be regarded as a 'consequence' or 'assertion' of the direct reference theory, then at least one of M1 and M2 provides a counterexample to Salmon's claim that there can be no Derivation of essentialism from the direct reference theory.

Both (F) and (C) appear to satisfy Salmon's formal criteria for being legitimate 'direct reference theory' definitions of 'water'. In particular, they specify the extension (actual and possible) of the predicate 'x is a sample of water' in terms that are not purely descriptive or qualitative. They specify the extension obliquely, by reference to a paradigm: the nature of the relevant fundamental properties (Argument M1) and the relevant chemical structure (Argument M2) is not described qualitatively in (F) and (C), but awaits discovery by investigation of the properties of the paradigm. And it seems possible that a direct reference theorist might hold that it is part of the *semantics* of 'water' that all possible samples of water share the same fundamental properties, and perhaps even that it is part of the semantics of 'water' that all possible samples of water share the same chemical structure. Perhaps it should be a requirement on a direct reference theory definition of a term that it not employ concepts unfamiliar to those who understand the term. (Although such a requirement appears to have its home in more traditional semantic accounts, and I am not sure why a direct reference theorist should be committed to it.) But even if this is the case, it could be argued that those who understand the term 'water'—even laymen—*do* have to possess the concept of a fundamental property, and (although this seems less plausible) perhaps even the concept of chemical structure (even in advance of the discovery of what the chemical structure of water is).

Hence I think that our verdict should be this. For the reasons indicated above, the arguments M1 and M2 may, indeed, satisfy the letter of the requirements Salmon imposes on a successful Derivation of essentialism from the theory of direct reference. For there is essentialism in their conclusions, and it derives from their semantical, definitional, premises. But they do not satisfy the *spirit* of Salmon's requirements. Salmon would presumably not be impressed by the fact that direct reference theorists who think that, say, the sharing of fundamental properties is built into the semantics of 'water' can derive essentialist conclusions from this fact. One would expect Salmon to respond that, for such theorists, their essentialism does not come *from their semantic theory*: it is not *because* they are direct reference theorists that they believe in essentialism. The philosopher who produces 'definitions' such as (F) and (C) is someone who thinks that essentialism is implicit in the semantics of the term 'water', but not simply because of the semantic *theory* of direct reference.

10.7. ESSENTIALISM AND THE CONCEPT OF A SUBSTANCE

It would be good to pinpoint an interesting sense of the question whether essentialism can be derived from the semantic theory of direct reference that will allow us to ignore, as irrelevant, purported 'Derivations' such as M1 and M2. On the face of it, there might appear to be a simple way of doing this, while preserving the spirit of Salmon's account. We might try saying that if there is some respectable direct reference theory definition of 'water' that does not yield essentialism as a consequence (unless combined with premises that are themselves essentialist), then the direct reference theory is not committed to essentialism; but if *all* respectable direct reference theory definitions of 'water' yield essentialism as a consequence, the direct reference theorist is so committed.[21]

---

[21] The qualification 'respectable' is a gesture towards the fact that we obviously want to ignore, as irrelevant, absurd 'direct reference theory definitions of "water"' such as

However, although this may seem promising, I do not think the proposal can be right. The proposal specifies an adequate sufficient condition for the direct reference theory to be free of essentialist commitment. (If there is a respectable direct reference theory definition of 'water' that does not involve a commitment to essentialism, one can be a direct reference theorist about 'water' without being an essentialist.) However, I doubt that the proposal gives a satisfactory *necessary* condition for the direct reference theory to be free of essentialist commitment. I say this for the following reason. Consider the following modification of Argument S1:

Argument M3:

(1)   It is necessarily the case that: something is a sample of water if and only if it is a sample of *dthat* (the same substance that *this* is a sample of).

(C)   It is necessarily the case that: something is a sample of water if and only if it is a sample with *dthat* (the chemical structure that *this* has).

(2)   *This* (liquid sample) has the chemical structure H_2O.

Therefore:

(4)   It is necessarily the case that: every sample of water has the chemical structure H_2O.

This argument has, as its first premise, the 'ostensive definition' of water that was employed in Argument S1, a definitional premise that Salmon regards as a legitimate product of the direct reference theory, and from which, he argues, no Derivation of essentialism is possible. The argument M3 differs from S1 in one respect only: in place of the essentialist premise (3), specifying what 'being of the same substance' consists in, it employs (C), the statement that was the initial premise of Argument M2. In addition, since M3 consists merely in adding an additional premise ((1)) to M2, and we judged that M2 was valid, we must judge that M3 is also valid. M3, like M2, thus represents a valid way of deducing the essentialist conclusion (4).

Why, though, should the construction of M3 present any problem for Salmon: in particular, for his thesis interpreted as the claim that

---

'Necessarily, something is a sample of water if and only if it is identical with the Eiffel Tower.'

there is *some* respectable direct reference theory definition of 'water' from which no Derivation of essentialism is possible? M3 may spell trouble for Salmon for the following reason. Suppose that there is a direct reference theorist who regards (C) not as an independent premise in M3, but as merely an *amplification* of the semantical premise (1). To be more exact, suppose that the theorist holds that, because of the nature of the concept of a substance, (1) actually *entails* (C). And suppose, in addition, that the direct reference theorist is right about the entailment. If so, it is impossible to adopt the direct reference theory definition (1), and yet, consistently, not be an essentialist about water. If (1) is a legitimate consequence of the direct reference theory, and (1) entails (C), then (C) is also a consequence of the direct reference theory. It looks as if the adoption of the apparently 'austere' direct reference theory definition (1) is, after all, no guarantee that one will avoid a commitment to essentialism. But if even definition (1) involves a commitment to essentialism, perhaps *every* respectable direct reference theory definition will do so. For perhaps any such definition will involve either the notion of a substance or some other notion with essentialist commitments.

I think that the moral to be drawn is this. It might turn out that the adoption of *any* direct reference theory definition of 'water' that involves the notion of a substance involves a commitment to essentialism. This might be the case because the notion of a substance has essentialist commitments. Further, it might turn out that no respectable direct reference theory definition of 'water' can avoid employing either the notion of a substance or some other notion that has essentialist commitments. But if so, there is still a good sense in which it is not the *direct reference theory* that is doing the work of generating the essentialism. For example, if the definitional premise (1) really does entail (C), then obviously it is not possible consistently to adopt (1) while denying (C). But if the entailment holds, then it holds in virtue of a necessary connection between the concepts of *substance* and *chemical structure*. And principles about such necessary connections are not given by the semantic theory of direct reference.

The particular problem raised above arises only if it is at least plausible to suppose that the semantic premise (1) entails (C), in virtue of a necessary connection between the concepts of *substance* and *chemical structure*. It might be objected that it is not plausible to suppose that there is any such entailment.

About this response, I have two comments. The first is *ad hominem*: it is not clear that this response is available to Salmon. Recall the crucial essentialist premise (3) of Argument S1, viz.,

(3)   Being a sample of the same substance as something consists in having the same chemical structure.

We may say that an entailment holds between (1) and (C) of Argument M3 just in case (3) is a necessary truth. But Salmon appears to be sympathetic to the view that if (3) is true, it is an a priori truth, one that holds in virtue of the concepts of substance and chemical structure (1982: 257). Salmon also thinks that it is plausible to regard (3) as true. But if (3) is an a priori truth, then no one could consistently accept premise (1) while denying (C), for to do so would be to accept a statement while refusing to accept one of its a priori consequences. For this reason, I think that Salmon must be wrong in presenting the crucial issue (as he sometimes does) as an issue about whether essentialism can be derived from definitions such as (1).[22]

My second point is that there are more modest claims about conceptual connections that would allow us to extract essentialism from the definitional premise (1). The definitional premise (1) invokes the notion of 'the same substance'. But if it is part of the very concept of a substance that all actual and possible samples of a substance are consubstantial in virtue of sharing certain significant properties, then evidently it must follow, from (1), that if there are any samples of water, they share significant properties with the demonstrated sample. And as long as the relevant shared properties are ones that need to be discovered a posteriori,[23] it will follow that essentialist consequences can be derived from the definitional premise (1), without the need for any additional essentialist premises.

10.8. SEMANTIC THEORY AND ESSENTIALIST COMMITMENT

The preceding discussion shows that it is not easy to find a precise statement of what is at issue when we ask whether a semantic theory is

---

[22]   See the passages cited in note 20 above.

[23]   This qualification is required by my ruling that a necessary connection between predicates is not to count as a case of essentialism unless it is a posteriori rather than a priori. See Sect. 10.1, and Sect. 1.6.

committed to essentialism. I take the upshot to be this: the main issue is not whether there is any account of the semantics of natural kind terms that is consistent with the direct reference theory and yet fails to entail essentialism, but whether, even if there is such an entailment, it is the semantic theory that is doing the work.

A consequence of this is that the brisk treatment suggested in Section 10.4 may be oversimplified. In that section, I suggested that the core of the arguments of Salmon and Mellor could be represented as follows. 'Putnam's semantic theory involves the postulation of a "*same kind*" relation holding together all actual possible members of the kind, a relation whose constitution must be determined by scientific theory and empirical discovery. But this fact alone can have no essentialist consequences. It cannot, because the *same kind* relation might be one that does not consist in the sharing of properties by all (actual and possible) members of the kind.' However, the discussion of the last few sections suggests that even if one were to *accept* that the *same kind* relations involved in the definitions of natural kind terms provided by Putnam's semantic theory guarantee that (all actual and possible) members of the same natural kind must be so in virtue of sharing certain significant properties, one could still consistently claim that the essentialism that this entails is not a product of the semantic theory. This may seem paradoxical, but I think it is not. We can envisage the possibility that the relations *same liquid, same substance* and in general *member of the same natural kind*, may, as a matter of conceptual truth, involve a requirement of shared significant properties.[24] Perhaps they do; perhaps they don't; I have as yet taken no stand on this issue. But an important point is that *if* they do, it will be because of the concepts of *liquid, substance,* and *(natural) kind*. It will *not* be the fact that the semantic theory involves a '*same something or other*' relation whose constitution awaits a posteriori discovery that is doing the work. We may conclude that even if essentialism results from the semantic account of a natural kind term that is given by the direct reference theory, it is not the *form* of that semantic theory that is the basis of the essentialism.

---

[24] The term 'significant properties', which I use here and elsewhere, is rather vague and unsatisfactory, but I could not think of a better way of describing the type of property that is relevant. 'Fundamental properties', which I use elsewhere in this discussion, might be more appropriate, but this term may also be problematic as a description of the relevant type of property, since many of the relevant properties are obviously not *absolutely* fundamental.

Several questions remain. I have not yet discussed the fact that Kripke's work may appear to offer a different way of deriving essentialism about natural kinds, via the necessity of certain a posteriori identities between natural kind terms. I consider this in Section 10.10 below. Secondly, I should say something about whether it really is plausible to suppose that a requirement of shared significant properties (and hence a commitment to essentialism) is involved in the *same kind* relations that are invoked in the definitions of natural kind terms that are provided by Putnam's semantic theory. To this issue I now turn.

10.9. NATURAL KINDS AND SHARED PROPERTIES

It is, of course, possible to use the term 'natural kind' in a restricted sense, according to which it is true by definition that all actual and possible members of a natural kind are such in virtue of sharing certain properties: properties that would then serve as the essential properties associated with the kind.[25] However, if this restricted notion of a natural kind is adopted, although it will be trivially true that *if* 'water', say, picks out a genuine natural kind, all samples of water must share certain significant properties, obviously a crucial question will then be whether 'water', or indeed any other candidate for a natural kind term, really does succeed in picking out a natural kind (as opposed to picking out some sort or category that is not a natural kind, or failing to pick out anything at all). Another crucial question will be whether 'water', or any of the other terms that are standardly presented as examples of 'natural kind terms' in discussions of the views of Kripke and Putnam, is even *intended* to pick out a natural kind in this restricted sense.

I take it, then, that if we are considering the relation between the semantics of natural kind terms and essentialism, the important issue is not whether the best notion of a natural kind involves the sharing of significant properties by all actual and possible members of the kind, but, rather, whether it is plausible to think that this 'shared properties requirement' is built into the semantics of the terms that Kripke and Putnam classify as 'natural kind terms'. A relevant question is therefore this: would the type of account suggested by Putnam—in terms of typical or archetypal samples and a *same kind* relation to be cashed out

---

[25] Using such a restricted definition, some theorists have argued that biological kinds such as species are not natural kinds. See, e.g., the authors cited by Ellis (2001: 169–70).

a posteriori—have any point in the absence of the supposition that when the relation is cashed out, it will turn out to involve the sharing of significant properties? It seems clear that it might well have a point. First, even if the account would have no point unless the *actual* members of the kind could be supposed to share some significant properties, it does not follow that we must take the possession of those properties as required for kind membership in all possible worlds. It seems quite reasonable to suppose that, for a given kind, the *same kind* relation might not be unitary: to be an actual sample of water might involve a different, and stricter, set of requirements than to be a merely possible sample of water. As Mellor suggests, 'Suppose that all samples of water in fact share ten "important" properties, but that water could lack any one of them, so that only the disjunction of all conjunctions of nine of them is essential' (Mellor 1977: 306). This would be a pale shadow of the essentialism advocated by Kripke and Putnam: the non-transitivity of the relation 'x shares at least n properties with y' would scotch the idea that there is some set of significant properties that all samples of water must have in common.[26]

It might be objected that it is gratuitous to suppose that there are different requirements for being water in other possible worlds from those that apply to actual samples of water. But this is not obviously the case. Among the (metaphysically) possible worlds that we are considering are ones that are very different from the actual world; some of them do not even share the causal laws of the actual world. Now, one could say that in such causally impossible worlds there is no water; nor do any of the other natural kinds that we know have instances there, for the very existence of our natural kinds is bound up with the causal laws of this world. (This is suggested by David Wiggins (1980, ch. 3, *passim*, ch. 4: 118); see also Ellis 2001 and 2002.) But I do not see that the adherent of Putnam's semantic account of natural kind terms *must* say this. And if there are, in some causally impossible but metaphysically possible world, things that are of the same kind as actual instances of water, or gold, or tigers, one would expect there to be some leniency about how similar to actual instances they have to be. I suggest, then, that there is no incoherence in the idea that even if an a posteriori account of the kind may require that actual members of the kind share some

---

[26] *Being a sample of the same substance as* would itself still be an equivalence relation (cf. Mellor 1977: 306). But it would be based on relations that are not themselves equivalence relations.

fundamental properties, one may take a liberal view about how many of these properties must be possessed by something in another possible world before it is legitimate to include it in the kind.

The second point is more complicated. Some of the examples of 'natural kind terms' adduced by Kripke and Putnam are terms like 'tiger' or 'lemon', which are such that, if they pick out natural kinds at all, they must pick out biological natural kinds. Yet it is doubtful, to say the least, that a posteriori investigation will support the view that the kind *tiger* or *lemon* is demarcated by some set of 'fundamental' properties that all tigers or all lemons have in common.[27] Both Kripke and Putnam make remarks that suggest that they believe that in general there will turn out to be some 'genetic structure' or 'internal constitution' that is associated with, and distinctive of, such kinds. But it is doubtful that this is consistent with biological theory. Species, for example, are demarcated principally by the capacity of their members to interbreed, producing fertile offspring, with other members. This might be taken to represent a necessary condition for membership of the species, but this is unlikely to provide much comfort to an essentialist. For it is plausible to regard 'x is a horse (if and) only if x is capable of fertile interbreeding with other horses' as a priori rather than a posteriori. On the other hand, although there must, of course, be some scientific *explanation* to be given of why the things we call 'horses' are capable of fertile interbreeding with one another, and not with other things, there seems to be no a priori reason to think that the explanation must involve positing some set of properties, such as genetic properties, that distinguish all horses from all members of other species.

Whether there is a set of shared genetic or other fundamental properties that actually serves to distinguish one biological kind from another is a question for biologists, which I do not presume to answer. But whether there would *have* to be such a distinctive set of properties in order for it to be reasonable to adopt a semantic account of biological 'natural kind terms' like Putnam's account is another matter. I think it is gratuitous to assume that the answer must be affirmative.

---

[27] See Dupré 1981; for brief remarks see also Mellor 1977: 309–10. Dupré's paper also contains a convincing demonstration that many of the vernacular terms that we use for sorts of plants and animals do not correspond with any precision to biological categories, nor should we expect them to do so. The question of the degree of correspondence between vernacular terms and scientific categories, important though it is to any discussion of 'natural kind terms', is one that I shall not discuss here.

There is, however, a complication. The argument I have just given tells only against the suggestion that there is a conceptual connection between the notion of a 'same biological kind' relation (whose constitution must be discovered a posteriori) and the sharing of a set of properties distinctive of those things that belong to the kind. It does not tell against the weaker suggestion that all actual members of the same biological kind must share *some* fundamental properties whose nature is discoverable only a posteriori, even if those fundamental properties are also shared by members of certain other biological kinds. Yet it does seem implausible to suggest that there could be a biological kind whose members shared no such fundamental properties (such as genetic properties) whatsoever.

My conclusion is this. Assuming that Putnam is correct in holding that it is part of the semantics of terms such as 'water', 'gold', 'tiger', and so on that they involve a *'same kind'* relation that is to be cashed out in a posteriori terms, it does not appear to be an a priori truth that this *same kind* relation requires that the actual extension of the kind be demarcated by the sharing of fundamental properties distinctive of, and constitutive of, that kind. So it does not appear to be true that a definition of a kind term that is consistent with Putnam's semantic theory must guarantee that the kind (if it exists at all)[28] has what I have called (Section 10.1 above) an *essence*. It is, however, plausible to suppose that the *same kind* relation will require that all actual members of the kind have some fundamental properties in common, although these properties need not be distinctive of the kind. However, this does not mean that these shared properties must be possessed not only by all actual members of the kind but also by all possible members (in every possible world that contains instances of the kind). I am sceptical about whether this further modal requirement need be involved in the *same kind* relation. But without this further requirement, the *same kind* relation will not generate the conclusion that these properties are *essential* properties of the kind. Hence I am sceptical about whether the acceptance of definitions of natural kind terms that are in accord with Putnam's semantic theory involves a commitment to essentialism.

---

[28] If a 'distinctive shared properties requirement' really were built into the semantics of the term 'tiger' (for example), it would appear to follow that, if there are no properties that can play this role, the term 'tiger' has no application, and the kind *tiger* does not exist.

Obviously, there is much more to be said about the relation between essentialism and natural kinds. Here I can only suggest, as a tentative conclusion, that the adoption of a semantic account of natural kind terms in the style of Putnam need not involve the acceptance of definitions of those terms that guarantee that natural kinds have essences, or even essential properties. The upshot of the discussion in the previous sections of this chapter was that although Putnam's semantic theory is congenial to essentialism, the *form* of his theory does not guarantee that kinds have essences or essential properties. If the arguments of this section are correct, we may go further, and claim that, although Putnam's semantic theory is congenial to essentialism, neither the form *nor the content* of the definitions of natural kind terms that are provided by Putnam's semantic theory need involve a commitment to essences or essential properties of natural kinds.

10.10. THE NECESSITY OF IDENTITY AND ESSENTIALISM ABOUT NATURAL KINDS

Finally, what about Kripke's necessities of kind identity? Kripke may be seen as arguing thus: identity statements between rigid designators are necessary; typical a posteriori theoretical identifications such as 'water = H_2O', 'gold is the element with the atomic number 79', and 'heat is molecular motion' are identity statements between rigid designators; therefore, if they are true, they are necessarily true (Kripke 1980, especially pp. 128–40). The conclusion amounts to the claim that some true theoretical identifications are a source of what I have called '*de re* essentialism' about natural kinds. Does this provide us with a way of deriving essentialism from semantic theory?[29]

Salmon's position with regard to these *de re* essentialist conclusions of Kripke's may appear to be an awkward one. The verdict that Salmon gives (1982: 77–9, 82–4) about certain other a posteriori necessities of identity, such as 'Necessarily, Hesperus = Phosphorus', is that although such necessary identities do involve essentialism, and are also consequences of the theory of direct reference, this sort of

---

[29] I do not suggest that Kripke himself endorses the view that essentialism can be derived from his semantic account of natural kind terms without auxiliary essentialist assumptions.

essentialism is trivial, unlike the type of essentialism involved in Putnam's essentialism about natural kinds.

This verdict obviously creates a difficulty. Unless there is a significant disanalogy between Kripke's natural kind identities and identities like 'Hesperus = Phosphorus', it will follow, if we accept Salmon's reasoning, that *de re* essentialist statements about natural kinds, such as 'Necessarily, water = H_2O', *will* be consequences of the direct reference theory, although they will involve only trivial essentialism. But given that Salmon urges that Putnam's predicate essentialism about kinds is both non-trivial and not derivable from the semantic theory of direct reference, it would be very uncomfortable for him to say that a Kripkean *de re* essentialism about natural kinds is both derivable and trivial. He would be committed to the view that whether a claim of natural kind essentialism is trivial, and whether it is a consequence of semantic theory, depends on whether the claim is couched in the *de re* 'Kripkean' form or in the predicate essentialist 'Putnamian' form.

There seem to be three possible ways to solve the problem:

(i) Find a significant and relevant difference between natural kind identities and other identities that would allow us to say that although 'Necessarily, Hesperus = Phosphorus' is trivially essentialist, 'Necessarily, water = H_2O' is non-trivially essentialist.

(ii) Retract the claim about the status of 'Necessarily, Hesperus = Phosphorus', and say, instead, that it is neither trivial nor a consequence of the direct reference theory.

(iii) Say that 'Kripkean' essentialist statements such as 'Necessarily, water = H_2O' are *trivially* essentialist consequences of the direct reference theory, but make this conclusion innocuous by interpreting Kripke's essentialist statements in such a way that they neither entail, nor correspond closely to, predicate essentialist statements such as 'Necessarily, something is a sample of water if and only if it is composed of H_2O molecules.'

I think that we can adopt the first solution: that there is a significant disanalogy between natural kind identities and identities concerning particular individuals, even if natural kind identities can be stated using pairs of rigid designators.[30] Or, better, we can show that either there is a

---

[30] Salmon's response is also to adopt the first of these strategies (1982: 81, 84–5). However, since I am not sure that I understand this part of Salmon's discussion, I confine myself to presenting my own account.

significant disanalogy, or a necessary identity between natural kinds does not involve the sort of essentialism about kinds that we are interested in. In other words, we can adopt a mixed solution to the problem: if natural kind identities are interpreted as involving an interesting sort of essentialism, (i) is the correct solution; if they are not so interpreted, (iii) is the solution to adopt.

The crucial point is this.[31] Suppose that 'water = H_2O' expresses the identity of the kinds *water* and H_2O, and suppose that 'water' and 'H_2O' are rigid designators. As we have seen (Section 10.1), the necessity of 'water = H_2O' yields something recognizable as natural kind essentialism only if it entails the coextensiveness, in all possible worlds, of the predicates 'x is a sample of water' and 'x is composed of H_2O molecules'.[32] However, if the necessary kind identity is to entail the corresponding necessary coextensiveness claim, the question arises how the necessity of the identity is established. In the case of a posteriori identities between rigid designators for ordinary individuals, Kripke's model is that first the identity is established a posteriori, and the general principle of the necessity of identity delivers the result that the identity is necessary.[33] But how is the identity 'water = H_2O' to be established? If the grounds for asserting this identity must already involve the claim that the predicates 'x is a sample of water' and 'x is a sample of H_2O' coincide in all possible worlds, to establish the identity is already to presuppose essentialism about natural kinds (cf. Mellor 1977, section 5). If so, it will be misleading to represent essentialism about water as something that follows from the necessity of the identity 'water = H_2O'. Not only (a) will the necessary coextensiveness of the predicates follow directly from the identity, not just from its necessitation, but also (b) the necessary coextensiveness will follow from that identity only in the trivial sense of being presupposed by it: the argument for essentialism will be circular.

As a consequence, there will be a relevant disanalogy between 'Necessarily, water = H_2O' and 'Necessarily, Hesperus = Phosphorus'. To

---

[31] In what follows I am indebted to the discussion in Mellor 1977, sect. 5, although I do not know whether Mellor would approve of the use to which I have put his material.

[32] Subject to the proviso, mentioned in Sect. 10.1, that one might take the (necessary) identity of water and H_2O to be consistent with there being *some* samples of water that are not H_2O, as long as they are abnormal: for example, that 'water = H_2O' might be a necessary truth even if there are possible worlds in which not quite all the samples of water are composed of H_2O.

[33] For more discussion, see Sect. 1.4 above.

derive the second we need no essentialist principles except for the general necessity of identity principle. But to derive the first we shall need not only the necessity of identity principle, but the further claim, which is an explicit assertion of (predicate) essentialism, that the predicates 'x is a sample of water' and 'x is a sample of H_2O' coincide in all possible worlds.[34]

Suppose, however, that the claim that water and H_2O are identical does not *presuppose* the necessary coextensiveness of the corresponding predicates. Does this mean that we must accept that non-trivial essentialism about natural kinds can, after all, be derived from the identity of water and H_2O, together with the necessity of identity principle and nothing more? I think not. Recall that, as emphasized above, the necessity of the identity yields essentialism about natural kinds *only if it entails the necessary coextensiveness of the corresponding predicates.*[35] We can present the following challenge: if the identity of the kinds is established in a way that does not presuppose the necessary coextensiveness of the corresponding predicates, what guarantee is there that it will *entail* that necessary coextensiveness?

Someone might try to meet this challenge by saying that all that is *presupposed* by the identity claim is the coextensiveness in all causally possible worlds of the predicates; their coextensiveness in absolutely all possible worlds is a further consequence of this. However, it is unclear what would warrant the claim that if the predicates are coextensive in all causally possible worlds they are coextensive in all possible worlds, *tout court*. If there is a gap in the argument here, merely saying that the first sort of coextensiveness is sufficient for kind identity cannot close it. For the question will then arise: if so, why should we believe that the

[34] If this is correct, and the identity 'water $= H_2O$' does rest on the necessary coextensiveness claim, this may serve as a vindication of Salmon's view that while the necessity of the identity 'Hesperus $=$ Phosphorus' is a consequence of the theory of direct reference, the necessity of the identity of water and H_2O is not. Salmon evidently supposes that to make use of the necessity of identity principle in deriving essentialism from the direct reference theory is innocuous, in the sense that it does not undermine the claim that the essentialism in the conclusion is a genuine consequence of the direct reference theory (1982: 82–4). Salmon holds that the necessity of identity principle differs from other essentialist principles in this respect. Suppose that Salmon is right about this. Since the argument of the last few paragraphs suggests that, given certain assumptions, an extra essentialist principle, in addition to the necessity of identity, is required in order to establish the necessity of the identity of water and H_2O, we may conclude that the necessity of *this* identity does not count as a consequence of the direct reference theory alone.

[35] Subject to the proviso mentioned in note 32 above.

kind identity is sufficient for the coextensiveness of the corresponding predicates in all possible worlds? (cf. Mellor 1977: 308–9).

Finally, suppose that there is, in spite of my scepticism, some good argument for the claim that we can move from the coincidence in all causally possible worlds of the kind predicates 'x is a sample of water' and 'x is a sample of H_2O' to their coincidence in all possible worlds, *simpliciter*. I think it would still not be right to say that there is any straightforward connection between Kripke's claims of kind identity and essentialism about natural kinds. For it would not be the necessity of identity principle that is generating the essentialism; rather, it would be a substantial and quite separate argument about the connection between causal and metaphysical necessity.

To conclude: I suggest that Kripke's necessities of kind identity pose no more of a threat to the thesis that essentialism about kinds is an extra commitment, over and above the acceptance of a certain type of semantic theory, than does Putnam's predicate essentialism.[36]

10.11. CONCLUSION TO THIS CHAPTER

My final verdict on the central question about the connection between semantic theory and natural kind essentialism is this. There is an important sense in which Salmon and Mellor are right in saying that essentialism about natural kinds is independent of the semantic theories of Kripke and Putnam: some relevant sense of 'could' in which one could accept those semantic theories, in their application to 'natural kind terms', without being an essentialist about natural kinds. This is a significant conclusion, not least because it forces those who accept these semantic theories to confront the question whether we should be essentialists about natural kinds, and if so, why. But this is a question that I have not attempted to settle here.

---

[36] As mentioned in note 29 above, I do not suggest that this verdict conflicts with Kripke's own views about the relation between his semantic theory and essentialism.

Bibliography

Adams, R. M. 1979. 'Primitive Thisness and Primitive Identity'. *The Journal of Philosophy*, 76: 5–26.

Ayer, A. J. 1973. *The Central Questions of Philosophy*. London: Weidenfeld & Nicolson. Also published by Penguin Books (London), 1976.

Ayers, M. 1974. 'Individuals Without Sortals'. *Canadian Journal of Philosophy*, 4: 113–48.

Baker, L. R. 2000. *Persons and Bodies: a Constitution View*. Cambridge: Cambridge University Press.

Bottani, A., Carrara, M., and Giaretta, P. (eds.) 2002. *Individuals, Essence and Identity: Themes of Analytic Metaphysics*. Dordrecht: Kluwer.

Brody, B. 1980. *Identity and Essence*. Princeton, NJ: Princeton University Press.

Chandler, H. 1975. 'Rigid Designation'. *The Journal of Philosophy*, 72: 363–9.

_____ 1976. 'Plantinga and the Contingently Possible'. *Analysis*, 36: 106–9.

Chisholm, R. 1967. 'Identity Through Possible Worlds: Some Questions'. *Noûs*, 1: 1–8. Reprinted in Loux (ed.) 1979.

Coburn, R. 1986. 'Individual Essences and Possible Worlds', in French, Uehling, and Wettstein (eds.) 1986, 165–83.

Devitt, M., and Sterelny, K. 1987. *Language and Reality*. Oxford: Blackwell.

Divers, J. 2002. *Possible Worlds*. London: Routledge.

Dummett, M. 1973. *Frege: Philosophy of Language*. London: Duckworth.

Dupré, J. 1981. 'Natural Kinds and Biological Taxa'. *The Philosophical Review*, 90: 66–90.

Ellis, B. 2001. *Scientific Essentialism*. Cambridge: Cambridge University Press.

_____ 2002. *The Philosophy of Nature: A Guide to the New Essentialism*. Chesham: Acumen.

Evans, G. 1973. 'The Causal Theory of Names'. *Proceedings of the Aristotelian Society*, suppl. vol. 47: 187–208. Reprinted in Evans 1985.

_____ 1979. 'Reference and Contingency'. *The Monist*, 62: 161–89. Reprinted in Evans 1985.

_____ 1985. *Collected Papers*. Oxford: Clarendon Press.

Fine, K. 1978. 'Model Theory for Modal Logic Part I: the *De Re/De Dicto* Distinction'. *The Journal of Philosophical Logic*, 7: 125–56.

Forbes, G. 1980. 'Origin and Identity'. *Philosophical Studies*, 37: 353–62.

_____ 1985. *The Metaphysics of Modality*. Oxford: Oxford University Press.

_____ 1986. 'In Defense of Absolute Essentialism', in French, Uehling, and Wettstein (eds.) 1986, 3–31.

_____ 1994. 'A New Riddle of Existence', in J. Tomberlin (ed.), *Philosophical Perspectives 8: Logic and Language*. Atascadero, Calif.: Ridgeview, 415–30.

Forbes, G. 1997. 'Essentialism'. In Hale and Wright (eds.) 1997, 515–33.

——— 2002. 'Origins and Identities', in Bottani, Carrara, and Giaretta (eds.) 2002, 319–40.

French, P., Uehling, T., and Wettstein, H. (eds.) 1986. *Midwest Studies in Philosophy XI: Studies in Essentialism*. Minneapolis: University of Minnesota Press.

Gale, R. M. 1984. 'Wiggins's Thesis D(x)'. *Philosophical Studies*, 45: 239–45.

Garrett, B. J. 1988. 'Identity and Extrinsicness'. *Mind*, 97: 105–9.

Geach, P. T. 1967. 'Identity'. *Review of Metaphysics*, 21: 3–12. Reprinted in Geach, *Logic Matters* (Oxford: Blackwell, 1972).

Gibbard, A. 1975. 'Contingent Identity'. *The Journal of Philosophical Logic*, 4: 187–221. Reprinted in M. Rea (ed.), *Material Constitution: a Reader* (Lanham, MD: Rowman & Littlefield, 1997).

Hale, B. 1997. 'Modality', in Hale and Wright (eds.) 1997, 487–514.

——— and Wright, C. (eds.) 1997. *A Companion to the Philosophy of Language*. Oxford: Blackwell.

Hawthorne, J., and Gendler, T. S. 2000. 'Origin Essentialism: the Arguments Revisited'. *Mind*, 109: 285–98.

Kant, I. 1929. *Critique of Pure Reason*, trans. by N. Kemp Smith. London: Macmillan.

Kaplan, D. 1978. 'Dthat', in P. Cole (ed.), *Syntax and Semantics, 9: Pragmatics*. New York: Academic Press, 221–43. Reprinted in P. Yourgrau (ed.), *Demonstratives* (Oxford: Oxford University Press, 1990).

Kirwan, C. 1970. 'How Strong are the Objections to Essence?' *Proceedings of the Aristotelian Society*, 71: 43–59.

Kripke, S. 1972a. 'Identity and Necessity', in M. K. Munitz (ed.), *Identity and Individuation*. New York: New York University Press, 135–64.

——— 1972b. 'Naming and Necessity', in D. Davidson and G. Harman (eds.), *Semantics of Natural Language*. Dordrecht: Reidel, 252–355. (Reprinted in revised form as a monograph by Blackwell, Oxford, 1980.)

——— 1980. *Naming and Necessity*. Oxford: Blackwell. (Expanded monograph version of Kripke 1972b.)

Leibniz, G. W. 1973. Selections from Leibniz, *Philosophical Writings*, ed. Parkinson. London: Dent.

Lewis, D. 1968. 'Counterpart Theory and Quantified Modal Logic'. *The Journal of Philosophy*, 65: 113–26. Reprinted in Loux (ed.) 1979, and (with additional 'Postscripts') in Lewis 1983.

——— 1971. 'Counterparts of Persons and Their Bodies'. *The Journal of Philosophy*, 68: 203–11. Reprinted in Lewis 1983.

——— 1973. *Counterfactuals*. Oxford: Blackwell.

——— 1983. *Philosophical Papers, vol. 1*. Oxford: Oxford University Press.

——— 1986a. *On the Plurality of Worlds*. Oxford: Blackwell.

——— 1986b. *Philosophical Papers, vol. 2*. Oxford: Oxford University Press.

_____ 1986c. 'Events', in Lewis 1986b, 241–69.

Linsky, L. (ed.) 1971. *Reference and Modality*. Oxford: Oxford University Press.

Locke, J. 1975. *An Essay Concerning Human Understanding*, ed. P. Nidditch. Oxford: Oxford University Press. Originally published in 1690.

Loux, M. (ed.) 1979. *The Possible and the Actual*. Ithaca, NY: Cornell University Press.

Lowe, E. J. 1995. *Locke on Human Understanding*. London: Routledge.

_____ 2002. *A Survey of Metaphysics*. Oxford: Oxford University Press.

McGinn, C. 1975–6. '*A Priori* and *A Posteriori* Knowledge'. *Proceedings of the Aristotelian Society*, 76: 195–208.

_____ 1976. 'On the Necessity of Origin'. *The Journal of Philosophy*, 73: 127–35.

McKay, T. J. 1986. 'Against Constitutional Sufficiency Principles', in French, Uehling, and Wettstein (eds.) 1986, 295–304.

Mackie, D. 1999. 'Personal Identity and Dead People'. *Philosophical Studies*, 95: 219–42.

Mackie, J. L. 1974. '*De* What *Re* is *De Re* Modality?' *The Journal of Philosophy*, 71: 551–61.

Mackie, P. 1987. 'Essence, Origin, and Bare Identity'. *Mind*, 96: 173–201.

_____ 1989. 'Identity and Extrinsicness: Reply to Garrett'. *Mind*, 98: 105–17.

_____ 1994. 'Sortal Concepts and Essential Properties'. *The Philosophical Quarterly*, 44: 311–33.

_____ 1998. 'Identity, Time, and Necessity'. *Proceedings of the Aristotelian Society*, 98: 59–78.

_____ 2002. 'Forbes on Origins and Identities', in Bottani, Carrara, and Giaretta (eds.) 2002, 341–52.

Mellor, D. H. 1977. 'Natural Kinds'. *British Journal for the Philosophy of Science*, 28: 299–312. Reprinted in Mellor, *Matters of Metaphysics* (Cambridge: Cambridge University Press, 1991).

Mills, E. 1991. 'Forbes's Branching Conception of Possible Worlds'. *Analysis*, 51: 48–50.

Moore, A. (ed.) 1993. *Meaning and Reference*. Oxford: Oxford University Press.

Noonan, H. 1983. 'The Necessity of Origin'. *Mind*, 92: 1–20.

_____ 1985a. 'Wiggins, Artefact Identity, and "Best Candidate" Theories'. *Analysis*, 45: 4–8.

_____ 1985b. 'The Only x and y Principle'. *Analysis*, 45: 79–83.

_____ 1989. *Personal Identity*. London: Routledge.

_____ 1991. 'Indeterminate Identity, Contingent Identity, and Abelardian Predicates'. *The Philosophical Quarterly*, 41: 183–93.

_____ 1993. 'Constitution is Identity'. *Mind*, 102: 133–46.

Nozick, R. 1981. *Philosophical Explanations*. Cambridge, Mass.: Harvard University Press.

Olson, E. 1997. *The Human Animal*. Oxford: Oxford University Press.

Parfit, D. 1984. *Reasons and Persons*. Oxford: Oxford University Press.

Plantinga, A. 1974. *The Nature of Necessity*. Oxford: Clarendon Press.

Prior, A. N. 1960. 'Identifiable Individuals'. *Review of Metaphysics*, 13: 684–96. Reprinted in Prior 1968.

――― 1968. *Papers on Time and Tense*. Oxford: Clarendon Press.

Putnam, H. 1973. 'Meaning and Reference'. *The Journal of Philosophy*, 70: 699–711. Reprinted in Schwartz (ed.) 1977, and in Moore (ed.) 1993.

――― 1975. 'The Meaning of "Meaning"', in Putnam, *Mind, Language, and Reality: Philosophical Papers, vol. 2*. Cambridge: Cambridge University Press, 215–71.

Quine, W. V. 1961. 'Reference and Modality', in Quine, *From a Logical Point of View*. New York: Harper & Row, 139–59. Reprinted in Linsky (ed.) 1971.

Robertson, T. 1998. 'Possibilities and the Arguments for Origin Essentialism'. *Mind*, 107: 729–49.

Robinson, D. 1985. 'Can Amoebae Divide Without Multiplying?' *Australasian Journal of Philosophy*, 63: 299–319.

Rosen, G. 1990. 'Modal Fictionalism'. *Mind*, 99: 327–54.

Salmon, N. 1979. 'How *Not* to Derive Essentialism from the Theory of Reference'. *The Journal of Philosophy*, 76: 703–25.

――― 1982. *Reference and Essence*. Princeton, NJ: Princeton University Press.

Schwartz, S. (ed.) 1977. *Naming, Necessity, and Natural Kinds*. Ithaca, NY & London: Cornell University Press.

――― 1984. 'Salmon on Reference and Essentialism'. *Pacific Philosophical Quarterly*, 65: 288–91.

Shoemaker, S. 1984. 'Personal Identity: A Materialist's Account', in S. Shoemaker and R. Swinburne, *Personal Identity*. Oxford: Blackwell.

Snowdon, P. 1990. 'Persons, Animals, and Ourselves', in C. Gill (ed.), *The Person and the Human Mind*. Oxford: Clarendon Press, 83–107.

Stalnaker, R. 1986. 'Counterparts and Identity', in French, Uehling, and Wettstein (eds.) 1986, 121–40.

Strawson, P. F. 1959. *Individuals*. London: Methuen.

――― 1976. 'Entity and Identity', in H. D. Lewis (ed.), *Contemporary British Philosophy, Fourth Series*. London: Allen & Unwin, 193–220. Reprinted in Strawson 1997.

――― 1979. 'May Bes and Might Have Beens', in A. Margalit (ed.), *Meaning and Use*. Dordrecht: Reidel, 229–38. Reprinted in Strawson 1997.

――― 1981. 'Critical Notice of Wiggins, *Sameness and Substance*'. *Mind*, 90: 603–7.

――― 1997. *Entity and Identity*. Oxford: Clarendon Press.

van Inwagen, P. 1985. 'Plantinga on Trans-world Identity', in J. E. Tomberlin and P. van Inwagen (eds.), *Alvin Plantinga*. Dordrecht: Reidel, 101–20. Reprinted in van Inwagen, *Ontology, Identity, and Modality: Essays in Metaphysics* (Cambridge: Cambridge University Press, 2001).

Wiggins, D. 1967. *Identity and Spatio-temporal Continuity*. Oxford: Blackwell.

_____ 1976. 'The *De Re* "Must": a Note on the Logical Form of Essentialist Claims', in G. Evans and J. McDowell (eds.), *Truth and Meaning*. Oxford: Clarendon Press, 285–312.

_____ 1980. *Sameness and Substance*. Oxford: Blackwell.

_____ 2001. *Sameness and Substance Renewed*. Cambridge: Cambridge University Press.

Yablo, S. 1988. Review of Forbes, *The Metaphysics of Modality*. *The Journal of Philosophy*, 85: 329–37.

Index